The changing nature of Asian-Latin American economic relations

German King
José Carlos Mattos
Nanno Mulder
Osvaldo Rosales

Editors

UNITED NATIONS

ECLAC

Economic Commission for Latin America and the Caribbean (ECLAC)
Santiago, December 2012

Libros de la CEPAL

115

The preparation of this document was supervised by Osvaldo Rosales, Chief of the Division of International Trade and Integration. Nanno Mulder, Economic Affairs Officer of the Division of International Trade and Integration, was responsible for its technical coordination. In addition to Osvaldo Rosales and Nanno Mulder, Alicia Frohmann, José Carlos Mattos and Germán King participated in the preparation of the chapters and drafting of the summary and overview. Statistical assistance was provided by Gaston Rigollet.

ECLAC gratefully acknowledges the financial support provided by the Republic of Korea and the logistical support of that country's Ministry of Foreign Affairs.

Cover design: José Manuel Vélez

United Nations publication
ISBN: 978-92-1-121829-9 • E-ISBN: 978-92-1-055983-6
LC/G.2551-P
Sales No. E.12.II.G.17

Printed at United Nations, Santiago, Chile • 2012-329

Contents

Tables

Diagrams

Figures

Maps

Foreword

The swift expansion of developing Asia is probably the most significant structural change in the world economy of the twenty-first century. Some economies in this region —including Japan, Hong Kong Special Administrative Region of China, the Republic of Korea, Singapore, and Taiwan Province of China— had already undergone a rapid growth process in the second half of the twentieth century. Over the past decade, the economies of China and other developing nations of Asia have also expanded rapidly and turned this region into the main growth pole of the world economy. Even amid the global financial and economic crisis of 2008 and 2009, China and most other developing Asian economies continued to post positive growth, whereas the rest of the world economy was in recession. For the remainder of this second decade of the twenty-first century, developing Asia will probably continue to be the growth engine of the world, in a context of weak growth prospects for the developed countries.

Latin America, and in particular South America, have strongly benefited from developing Asia's surge. A decade ago, the region's trade and investment ties with Japan were already well developed, but links with China and other developing countries in Asia were still incipient. This changed rapidly afterwards, as Latin America's exports to, and imports from, China and the rest of developing Asia grew at double digit rates until the outbreak of the financial crisis and resumed their vigorous growth in 2010. As a consequence, China has become one of the region's main trade partners. In particular, it is now the largest export market for Brazil, Chile and Peru, and the second largest for Argentina, the Bolivarian Republic of Venezuela, Cuba and Uruguay. China is also the main origin of imports for Panama and Paraguay, and the second for nine other Latin American countries. The fast rebound of Asian imports after 2009 has supported Latin America's own economic recovery from the recent global economic crisis.

Foreign direct investment (FDI) flows between the two regions, while smaller than trade flows, are growing rapidly. FDI from Asia to Latin America has risen significantly over the past decade, while flows in the opposite direction are smaller but also increasing. Latin America has become an increasingly important destination for Asian multinationals, as traditional investments from Japan have been followed more recently by those from the Republic of Korea, China and India. In the particular case of China, the bulk of the country's FDI in the region is still directed towards off-shore financial centres such as the British Virgin Islands and the Cayman Islands. However, in recent years Chinese FDI elsewhere in the region has gathered momentum.

The growing trade and FDI relations between the two regions reflect the ongoing shifts in the world economy, in which developing countries increasingly trade and invest with each other. Thus it is expected that South-South trade will overtake trade among industrialized countries (North-North trade) by 2020.

Despite their benefits, strengthened trans-Pacific economic relations have also become a cause for concern in Latin America, due to major imbalances of different kinds. First, bilateral trade flows have expanded much faster than bilateral FDI flows, suggesting a possible lack of complementarity and synergies between the two types of links. Second, China and the rest of Asia are running a growing surplus in trans-Pacific trade flows. Third, biregional trade is of an inter-industry nature, meaning that Latin America (especially South America) exports a limited range of commodities, whereas China and other developing Asian countries export mainly manufactures. The commodity export boom which started during the last decade contributed to currency appreciation in South America, reducing the competitiveness of non-commodity exports. Simultaneously, the surge in manufactured imports from developing Asia has intensified competition with Latin American manufactures in both domestic markets and abroad. Fourth, Asian FDI flows to Latin America have been far larger than Latin American FDI flows to Asia, which may be related to Asia's more competitive environment as compared to Latin America and to the fact that Asian multinationals outnumber Latin American ones. Fifth, some analysts consider that most Asian investments in Latin America are of the enclave type, characterized by limited links with the local economy in host countries. Lastly, Latin American countries have not yet agreed upon a regional institution or forum that may represent the region in discussions and negotiations with Asia-Pacific on trade, investment and economic cooperation.

To shed more light on the aforementioned issues, the Ministry of Foreign Affairs and Trade (MOFAT) of the Republic of Korea and the Economic Commission for Latin America and the Caribbean (ECLAC) organized the joint research project "Changing nature of Asia-Latin America economic relations". This project consisted of four studies by international experts in the field of trade and investment relations between the two regions. Draft versions of these studies were discussed in two seminars. The first of these was hosted by ECLAC in Santiago on 28 July 2011. The second was hosted in Seoul by the Korean Ministry of Foreign Affairs and Trade (MOFAT), the Korea Institute for International Economic Policy (KIEP), the Korea Brazil Society and Kyung Hee University on 4 October 2011.

This book captures the outcome of the research project. Its purpose is twofold. On the one hand, it aims to document the growing investment and trade relations between Latin America and Asia, as well as some of their imbalances. On the other hand, it provides several examples on how to upgrade trans-Pacific economic relations. First, the book provides an in-depth analysis of the participation of Asian multinationals in Latin American and global value chains in agriculture, manufacturing and services, and how these firms have contributed to the transfer of knowledge and technology to domestic producers. Second, it looks into the experience of selected Latin American multinationals in Asian markets, and provides some lessons for other firms in the region considering following suit.

It is concluded that increasing biregional trade and FDI flows can play a crucial role in upgrading the performance of Latin American producers and increasing their participation in Asian and global value chains. The promotion of bilateral investment and intra-industrial trade between Asia and Latin America will deepen trade integration and contribute to more balanced economic relations.

This book is offered to the Asian and Latin American policymaking, academic and business communities, as a contribution to bridging the gaps in our knowledge of economic relations between the two regions. It is also hoped that the recommendations contained in this volume may contribute to the upgrading of biregional trade and investment flows in terms of value added, technology and knowledge content.

Alicia Bárcena
Executive Secretary
Economic Commission for
Latin America and the Caribbean (ECLAC)

Introduction

Over the past decade, Asia and Latin America have become the new drivers of world growth. As a indication of their dynamism, their participation in the world economy, global trade and investment has increased markedly over the past ten years. Together, Asia and Latin America were responsible for roughly one third of global economic activity in 2011, which is more than the European Union or the United States, which contributed 25% and around 8%, respectively. Their cumulative share in world trade is about 30%, with Latin America contributing 5% and Asia the remainder. However, their participation in global FDI flows is much smaller: Asia accounts for 11% and Latin America for around 7%. Nevertheless, all these shares were substantially lower one decade ago.

The financial and economic crisis of 2008 and 2009 hit the growth potential of industrialized economies hard, yet the emerging economies have continued to perform well. They showed remarkable resilience and emerged stronger than developed economies from the crisis. Growth in the latter group will remain subdued for several years to come, owing to stringent fiscal policies to rein in public debt and persistently high unemployment, meaning that the economies of the South will continue to be the engine of the world economy in the near future. The South's growth prospects depend in part on its internal dynamics, in other words, the links forged between developing and emerging economies through South-South trade, investment and cooperation. Within the South, developing Asia accounts for four fifths of total trade. The centre of gravity of world trade has, in short, shifted from North to South and from the Atlantic to the Pacific over the past decade.

This book reviews how economic relations between Latin America and Asia have changed over time. For many years the two regions had little contact: geographical distance, cultural barriers and information gaps created a lack of mutual understanding and hindered political and economic cooperation between the two continents. Asia lacked expertise on Latin America, as did Latin America on Asia. However, this has changed beyond recognition over the last decade, and economic ties between Latin America and Asia-Pacific have recently undergone rapid expansion and diversification. Biregional trade and, to a lesser extent, investment flows have grown at double-digit rates over the past decade. Complementary demand may explain many of these strengthened trans-Pacific links. Asia is important to Latin America as a source of manufacturing products, forming the basis of the latter's rapid export growth. Latin America, meanwhile, is a strategic partner for Asia, in particular for China, Japan, Korea and India, providing the commodities needed to sustain its economic expansion. Bilateral investment relations have also expanded, although most investment has come from Asian multinationals in Latin America, with little investment by Latin American multinationals (trans-Latins) in Asia.

This introductory chapter documents general trends in bilateral trade and foreign direct investment (FDI) and presents the main messages of the book. It is followed by three chapters presenting detailed analyses of Asian investment in Latin American agriculture, manufacturing and services, respectively. The final chapter deals with the activities of selected trans-Latins in Asia.

A. Trans-Pacific trade

During the past decade, the region's trade with the Asia-Pacific region showed much stronger growth than its trade with other major partners. For example, between 2006 and 2010, Latin American and Caribbean exports to Asia-Pacific countries expanded at more than three times the rate of the region's exports to the rest of the world. To a large extent, this was the result of a steep rise in exports to China, which grew at five times the rate of total exports to the rest of the world (see figure 1). The region's imports from the Asia-Pacific countries, in particular from China, have also grown more rapidly than total imports. Imports outweigh exports in the region's trade relationship with the Asia-Pacific region, which has generated a widening trade deficit with that region. Only a decade ago Asia represented just over 10% of all external trade with the region; now Asia's share is over 20%. This increasing relevance coincides with Asia Pacific's rising influence in world trade.[1]

[1] While in 1985 Asia-Pacific was responsible for 23% of global exports and 19% of imports, by 2010 it accounted for 34% and 31% of world exports and imports, respectively (United Nations Commodity Trade Statistics Database (COMTRADE)).

Figure 1
LATIN AMERICA AND THE CARIBBEAN: GROWTH OF TRADE WITH MAIN PARTNERS, MARCH 2006-DECEMBER 2011
(Index: March 2006=100)

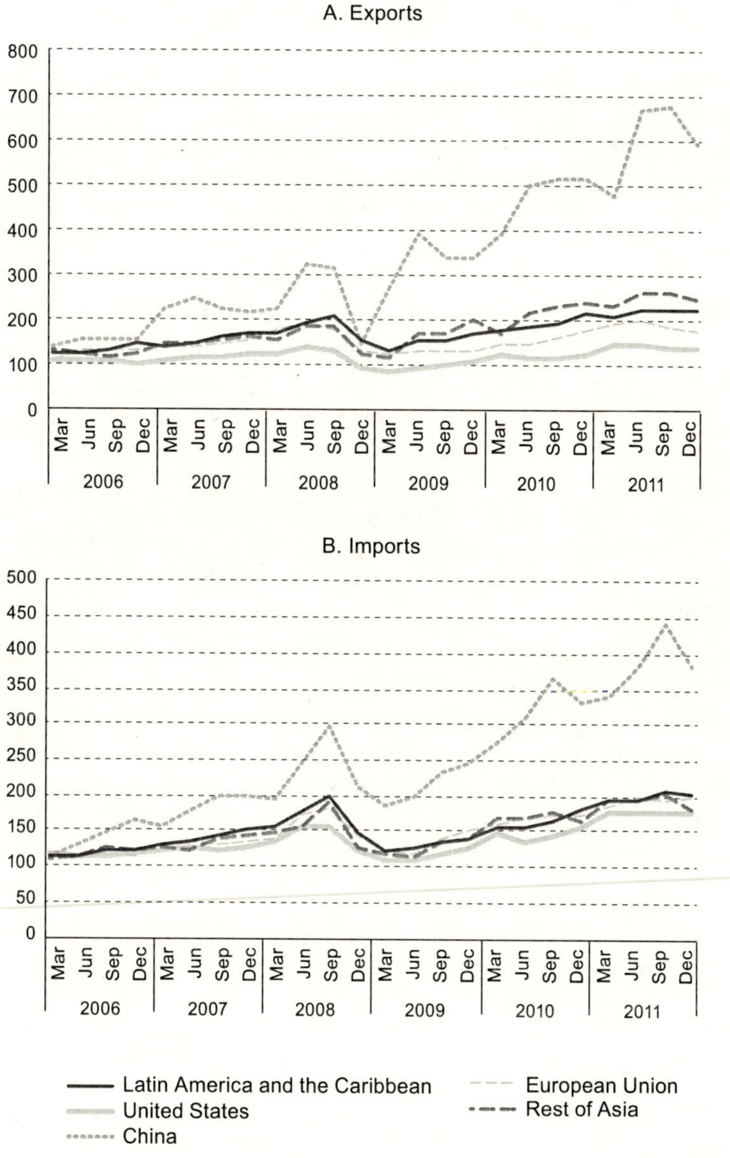

Source: Economic Commission for Latin America and the Caribbean (ECLAC), on the basis of national statistics.

The overall expansion of bilateral trade over the past quarter-century hides major shifts in the relative importance of each trading partner in the Asia-Pacific region. While in 1985 Japan was the destination for 50% of Latin American and Caribbean exports to the Asia-Pacific region and the source of 70% of the region's imports, its share in both has fallen steadily. By contrast, China's share of Latin American and Caribbean exports to the Asia-Pacific region has risen steadily (from the mid-1990s), as have its exports to the region (from the early 1990s). Consequently, between 2000 and 2005, China overtook Japan as the region's leading Asia-Pacific trading partner (see figure 2). India, meanwhile, in spite of strong growth over the past two decades, receives only 6.4% of Latin American and Caribbean exports to the Asia-Pacific region and supplies 3.4% of its imports. This places it behind the Republic of Korea as a trading partner for the region.

China is likely to overtake the European Union as the region's second trading partner around 2014-2015. Assuming that demand for the region's products in the United States, the European Union and the rest of the world continues to grow at the current pace, and demand from China grows at just half the rate recorded during the past decade, China may overtake the European Union in 2014 and become the second-largest market for the region's exports. A similar outcome is projected for imports, and China is expected to surpass the European Union in 2015.

The relative importance of Asia as a market for Latin American and Caribbean exports varies significantly from country to country. While on average Asia accounted for slightly over 16.5% of the region's exports on average between 2007 and 2010, it receives almost 40% of Chilean and Peruvian exports and over 24% of Brazilian exports. At the other extreme, Asia receives 10% or less of total exports from Mexico, Central America (except for Costa Rica) and most Caribbean countries (see table 1).

Asia is even more important to the region as a source of imports than as a destination for exports, with strong differences among countries. Asia's share of total imports is equal to or greater than 20% for the South American countries (except for the Bolivarian Republic of Venezuela) and Mexico, but is generally smaller for the Central American and Caribbean countries.

Figure 2
ASIA-PACIFIC (SELECTED COUNTRIES AND GROUPS): SHARE OF TRADE WITH LATIN AMERICA AND THE CARIBBEAN, 1985-2011[a]
(Percentages)

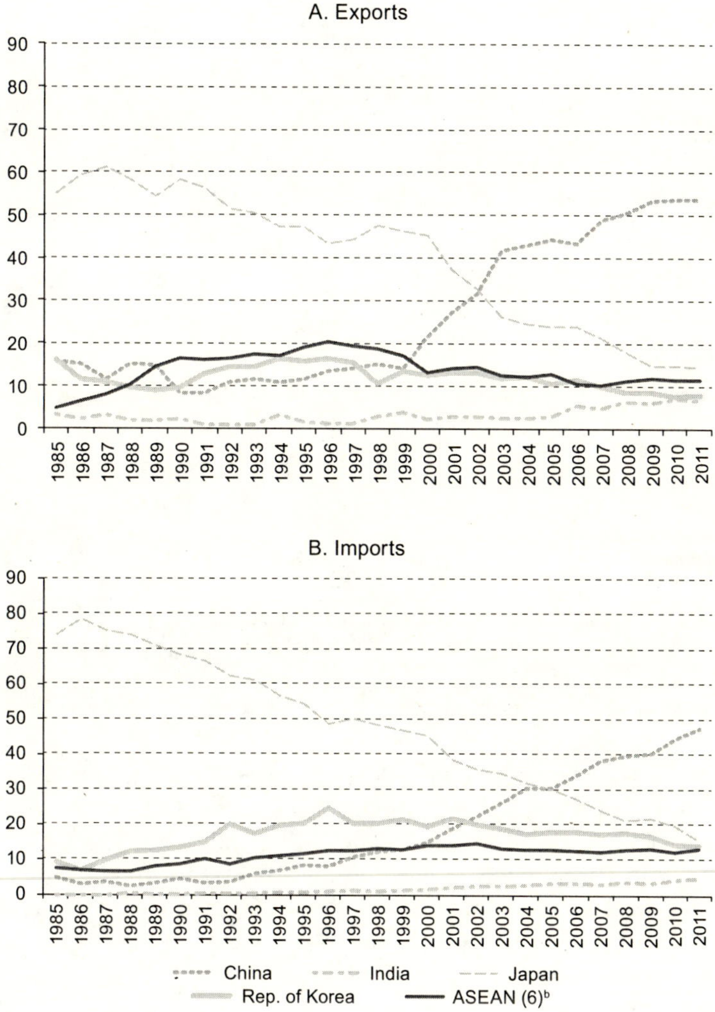

Source: Economic Commission for Latin America and the Caribbean (ECLAC), on the basis of United Nations Commodity Database (COMTRADE) and Monetary Fund (IMF), Direction of Trade Statistics (DOTS) database for Viet Nam (1985-1996 and 2011) and Philippines, Singapore and Viet Nam (2010).

[a] These statistics were obtained from Asian countries and may not coincide with national data reported by Latin American and Caribbean countries.

[b] Includes Indonesia, Malaysia, Philippines, Singapore, Thailand and Viet Nam.

Table 1

LATIN AMERICA: SHARE OF MAIN TRADING PARTNERS IN EXPORTS, 2007-2010

(Percentages of total)

	Region / country	United States	European Union	Asia	Latin America and the Caribbean
	Latin America	40.1	14.0	16.5	19.3
MERCOSUR[a]	Argentina	7.7	17.6	17.5	40.8
	Brazil	12.9	22.7	24.1	22.4
	Paraguay	2.6	7.2	17.1	61.1
	Uruguay	5.7	15.9	10.7	45.4
CAN[b]	Bolivia (Plurinational State of)	9.1	8.4	17.1	61.0
	Colombia	36.0	13.5	7.9	25.4
	Ecuador	35.3	11.9	8.4	40.2
	Peru	25.3	22.0	37.8	33.9
MCCA[c]	Costa Rica	33.1	13.6	15.8	27.1
	El Salvador	44.3	5.4	5.0	42.9
	Guatemala	39.2	6.0	6.1	40.0
	Honduras	39.4	15.8	6.2	35.0
	Nicaragua	26.6	11.0	8.6	43.5
	Chile	12.8	19.4	39.3	21.6
	Mexico	72.7	7.0	10.3	6.1
	Venezuela (Bolivarian Republic of)	47.4	10.1	11.9	18.6
		>30		>10<30	

Source: Economic Commission for Latin America and the Caribbean (ECLAC), on the basis of United Nations Commodity Trade Statistics Database (COMTRADE) data.

[a] Southern Common Market.

[b] Andean Community.

[c] Central American Common Market.

The situation with China is analogous. China has become a key export market for Cuba, Chile, Brazil, Peru, Argentina and the Bolivarian Republic of Venezuela, in decreasing order. In contrast, less than 3% of exports from Paraguay, Ecuador, the Central American countries (except for Costa Rica) and most Caribbean countries go to China. When ranked against other export markets, China was fairly insignificant in 2000, but by 2011 it had become the main market for Brazil, Chile, Perú and the Bolivarian Republic of Venezuela, the second market for Argentina and Uruguay and the third for Mexico. China's rise as a source of imports has been even more dramatic, as it was one of the top three sources of imports for all Latin American countries in 2011 except for El Salvador, Honduras and the Bolivarian Republic of Venezuela (see table 2). China is the main source of their imports. China is the main source of imports for Panama and Paraguay, and the second source for Argentina, the Bolivarian Republic of Venezuela, Brazil, Chile, Colombia, Costa Rica, Ecuador, Mexico and Peru.

Table 2
LATIN AMERICA AND THE CARIBBEAN: CHINA'S RANKING AMONG IMPORT AND EXPORT PARTNERS, 2000 AND 2010

	Exports			Imports		
	2000	2010	2011	2000	2010	2011
Argentina	6	2	2	4	2	2
Bolivia (Plurinational State of)	18	10	8	7	4	3
Brazil	12	1	1	11	2	2
Chile	5	1	1	4	2	2
Colombia	36	2	4	9	2	2
Costa Rica	30	10	13	15	2	2
Ecuador	18	12	17	10	3	2
El Salvador	49	34	38	23	4	4
Guatemala	43	27	28	19	3	3
Honduras	54	10	12	21	7	5
Mexico	19	3	3	7	2	2
Nicaragua	35	24	19	20	3	3
Panama	31	30	32	25	1	1
Paraguay	15	25	23	3	1	1
Peru	4	2	1	9	2	2
Uruguay	4	3	2	7	3	3
Venezuela (Bolivarian Republic of)	35	3	1	18	2	2

Source: Economic Commission for Latin America and the Caribbean (ECLAC), on the basis of official figures provided by the central banks and national statistical institutes of the respective countries.

The Latin American and Caribbean region was China's most dynamic trading partner during the second half of the last decade, and Japan's second most dynamic partner. Between 2005 and 2010, China's exports to Latin America and the Caribbean and its imports from the region grew at almost double the rate of total imports and exports. The region's share of trade with China has increased gradually, rising from a very low starting point to a 6% share of total Chinese exports and imports in 2010. Japan's exports to Latin America and the Caribbean grew faster than its exports to any other destination, while Japanese imports from the region were surpassed only by those from the Commonwealth of Independent States.

All in all, Latin America posted a burgeoning deficit in its trade with Asia during the last decade, mostly due to the growing trade deficit of Mexico and Central America. As mentioned earlier, only a small proportion of those countries' exports go to Asia, while an increasing percentage of their imports come from that region. The result is a widening trade deficit with China and the rest of Asia. Meanwhile, the South American economies, many of which send a high proportion of their exports to Asia, registered a more even trade balance with China and the rest of Asia during the last decade. That outcome is largely attributable to higher prices for the commodities exported to Asia by South American countries during much of the decade.

The composition of trade flows is another relevant factor when analysing trade between the two regions. Latin America and the Caribbean's trade with Asia-Pacific is mostly inter-industry, consisting primarily of commodity exports and high and medium-tech imports. Except in the cases of Costa Rica and Mexico, the export mix of the countries of the region to Asian countries remains concentrated in a few commodities. In almost every country except for Mexico, the three main export products represent over 80% of the value of total exports to the main destinations in Asia. It is worth noting that high-tech products figure among the main products exported by Costa Rica, El Salvador and Mexico.

More recently, Asia has begun to import new products from Latin America, although these do not generally feature among the top three export products. They include poultry, vegetable oils, fresh fruit, frozen fish, crustaceans and molluscs, fruit and vegetable juices, wine and processed woods. Some fall into the category of primary products, but are not considered commodities because there may be some qualitative differentiation among them.

B. Trans-Pacific investment

Inward foreign direct investment in Latin America and the Caribbean has not increased by the same margin as that in Asia. While the share of the former in global FDI inflows almost doubled from 7% to 14% during the first decade of this century, the share of the latter almost tripled from 11% to 28% (see figure 3). In both regions, the share in global FDI outflows was smaller than the share in global FDI inflows. However, the contrast between Asia and Latin America and the Caribbean in FDI outflows is even more marked than in FDI inflows: Latin America's share has stayed roughly constant over time, whereas the Asian share reached over 23% in 2011.

Figure 3
ASIA AND LATIN AMERICA: SHARE IN GLOBAL FDI INFLOWS AND OUTFLOWS, 2000-2011

A. Global FDI inflows
(percentages and billions of dollars)

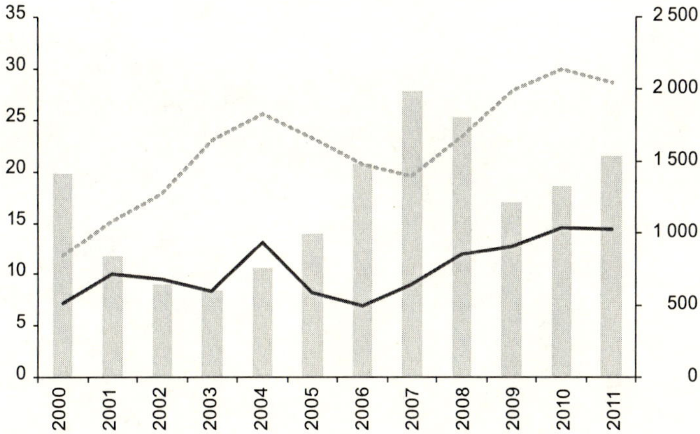

B. Global FDI outflows
(percentages and billions of dollars)

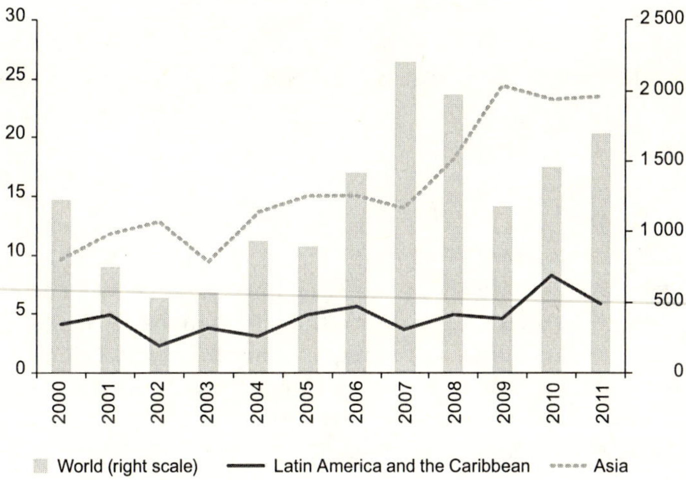

Source: Economic Commission for Latin America and the Caribbean (ECLAC), on the basis of UNCTADSTAT, Foreign direct investment statistics.

The main investors in Latin America are developed countries. According to ECLAC data, during the period 2006-2010 the United States' investment amounted to around 23% of total inward FDI, the Netherlands' share was 7%, Spain's was 9% and Canadian investment represented 5%. Intraregional investment constituted only 9% of total inward FDI (see figure 4).

Figure 4
LATIN AMERICA: FDI INFLOWS BY GEOGRAPHICAL ORIGIN, 2006-2010 AND 2011
(Period average)

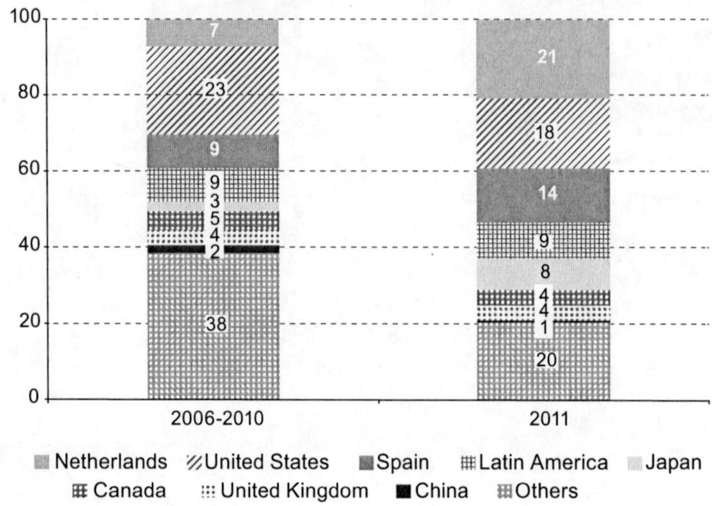

Source: Economic Commission for Latin America and the Caribbean (ECLAC), 2012.

Asian FDI was very limited during this period, representing only 3% of FDI inflows from 2006 to 2010, but its share has increased recently.[2] In 2011 Japan's FDI share jumped to 8%, following some major acquisitions. China's share likewise surged in 2010, but fell back in 2011. Korean companies are also active in the region, particularly in vehicle assembly operations and the iron and steel sector. Brazil and Mexico remain the largest recipients of Asian FDI in Latin America, although both countries experienced a decrease in Asian FDI flows from 2008 to 2009, which then recovered in 2010 and 2011.

---

2 In Argentina, for instance, it represented only 1.7% of the total FDI received in 2008. In Brazil, Asian countries invested an amount corresponding to 4.6% of the total inflow of 2008 —although 4.4% came from Japan alone, with the rest of the countries contributing in negligible numbers. In several Latin American countries, Asian investments are so small that they are included in the "other countries" category.

Most FDI in Latin America has traditionally gone to the services sector (telecommunications, finance and public utilities), although natural resources have been capturing a larger share in recent years. In fact, according to ECLAC (2010), while in 2000 about 60% of total inward FDI went to the services sector and 10% to the exploitation of natural resources, these percentages were 45% and 18%, respectively in 2011. The manufacturing share increased from 20% to 38% over the whole period.

Latin America became a destination of some importance for Asian multinationals around a decade ago, starting with investments from Japan, followed later by those of Korea and China. For China, Korea and Japan, the region accounted for approximately 38%, 7% and 13%, respectively, of their overseas FDI stock in 2009-2010. In the case of China, the bulk of its investment was directed towards financial off-shore centres in the region (British Virgin Islands and Cayman Islands), but in 2010 the confirmed investments outside these off-shore centres jumped from a cumulative amount of US$ 7.3 billion during the period 1990-2009 to US$ 15.2 billion in 2010, while investments in 2011 were somewhat smaller.

Figure 5
CHINA, JAPAN AND REPUBLIC OF KOREA: GEOGRAPHICAL BREAKDOWN OF OUTWARD FDI STOCK
(Percentages)

	China		Rep. of Korea		Japan	
	2003 (US$ 33 billion)	2010 (US$ 317 billion)	2003 (US$ 34 billion)	2010 (US$ 255 billion)	2003 (US$ 336 billion)	2010 (US$ 831 billion)
Africa	1.5	4.1	0.7	2.3	0.3	0.3
Middle East	1.4	0.7	0.1	1.9	0.0	0.5
Europe	1.5	5.0	16.9	18.0	22.8	21.3
Oceania	1.4	2.7	1.6	2.5	3.7	5.1
North America	1.7	2.5	28.0	22.7	42.6	31.6
Asia (excluding Middle East)	79.2	71.2	36.1	46.0	18.8	24.9
Latin America	14.0	13.8	2.2	5.4	2.3	11.1

Source: Japan External Trade Organization (JETRO), 2011 *JETRO Global Trade and Investment Report,* Tokyo, 2010, Figure III-32, p. 91, on the basis of official figures from the respective countries.

Asian FDI in Latin America is motivated mainly by three factors: (1) access to natural resources in order to meet domestic demand, such as Japanese industrial conglomerate Mitsui's investment in Brazil's ethanol production operations, and investments by the Chinese energy company CNPC in the exploration and development of the oil capabilities of the Bolivarian Republic of Venezuela; (2) increased efficiency for exporting to the United States market, including investments in Mexico's manufacturing sector by firms such as Toyota (Japan), Samsung and LG (Republic of Korea), and textile companies investing in Central America and the Caribbean; and (3) access to large local markets, mostly taking the form of investments by multinational corporations in Brazil.

Asian firms have clear preferences when it comes to the investment destination, depending on the host economy's advantages. Mexico's strong points are electronics, steel, automobiles and textile retailing. Central American countries attract textile manufacturers and Costa Rica, high-tech firms. Firms interested in mining and/or petroleum are drawn to Chile and Peru. Brazil is the destination for electronics, automobile, mining, petroleum and steel activities (see table 3).

Table 3
PATTERNS OF ASIAN INVESTMENT IN LATIN AMERICA

	Sectors	Motivation
Brazil	Electronics	Market-seeking
	Automobile	Market-seeking
	Mining	Natural-resource-seeking
	Petroleum	Natural-resource-seeking
	Steel	Efficiency-seeking
Mexico	Electronics	Efficiency-seeking / Market-seeking
	Automobile	Efficiency-seeking / Market-seeking
	Steel	Market-seeking
Central America	Textile	Efficiency-seeking
Chile and Peru	Mining	Natural-resource-seeking
The Caribbean	Tourism	Market-seeking

Source: Prepared by the authors.

Aside from in Brazil and Mexico, Asian investment in Latin American countries does not demonstrate a wide sectoral diversity. Smaller economies focus on attracting Asian investments in areas where they have a comparative advantage, such as textiles in Central America or mining in Chile. Asian FDI in Latin America also reflects some home-specific characteristics. Japanese firms are withdrawing their strong presence in the region. The number of operations of electronic companies is shrinking in terms of direct involvement. Most Chinese FDI is State-driven, and tends to centre on the natural-resource sector. However, actual investments were very small until 2010. There are also some examples of market-seeking and efficiency-seeking investments by Chinese firms in Latin America's manufacturing sector, including those by Huawei, Lenovo and Chery Automobile.

C. Summary of chapters

The four chapters in this volume deal with investment and trade relations between Latin America and Asia. Chapters one to three analyse the activities of Asian multinationals in the Latin American agribusiness, manufacturing and services industries, respectively. Chapter four looks at the activities of the few Latin American firms operating in Asia.

The first chapter by Ruth Rama and John Wilkinson examines trends and determinants of Asian investment in Latin American agribusiness. First, the authors survey global inward flows of foreign direct investment (FDI) in agriculture, forestry and fishing. These expanded rapidly after 1990, but continue to account for a tiny share of global FDI inflows. Within these global flows, developing countries and transition countries increased their share from 56.5% to 62.5% between 1990 and 2010, taking advantage of the availability of land and the importance of agriculture. Within Latin America, Brazil is by far the largest recipient of FDI, followed by Chile, Ecuador, Costa Rica, Honduras and Peru. Inward FDI in the food and beverages industry also expanded rapidly over the past two decades. Accordingly, the share of developing economies increased from 13% of total in 1989-1991 to 16% in 2010, owing to the decrease of inward FDI from developed economies. World leaders in this industry, mostly from Western Europe and the United States, operate in Latin American markets and often consider the region as important. The largest Japanese transnational companies which are active in this sector are highly concentrated in Asia and in the home country.

There have been three waves of Asian investment in Latin American agribusiness. During the first wave, starting in the 1970s, Japan contributed to the opening up of the Brazilian savannah region to soy and later to horticulture production, as part of the Programme for the Development of the Brazilian Savannah (PRODECER). In particular, the Japanese government and firms aimed to develop competitive farms for the export of key crops to satisfy their country's surging demand. Bilateral cooperation took the form of a public-private partnership executed by a bi-national firm —CAMPO— created for this purpose, while the

Japanese International Cooperation Agency (JICA) provided financing and supervised the programme. Bilateral cooperation was also facilitated by the role of Japanese immigrants in the modernization of Brazilian agriculture and their direct involvement in the different phases of the programme. Despite its success in terms of grain and soy exports, the large farms developed under PRODECER gave rise to serious environmental problems and suffered from huge debts, which were in part responsible for the Programme's discontinuation in 2001.

The second wave occurred in the 1990s, when Asian logging firms began to explore the Amazon in response to the substitution of the humid tropical forests of Asia by palm oil plantations. These investments were led by Indonesia, Malaysia, Thailand and China through joint ventures with local firms or direct acquisitions. As these undertakings grew rapidly in the early 1990s, they were held responsible for the Amazon's deforestation, and a number of powerful NGOs pressured the Brazilian government to take measures. Some years later, attention on these firms subsided as their activities expanded less rapidly than foreseen, and because it turned out they were more likely to abide by existing regulations on logging and forestry management than domestic firms. In the Peruvian Amazon, a Dipteryx timber supply chain was developed for the Chinese market. Initially, ethnic Chinese timber firms in Peru started to export to China. By the end of the decade, however, multinationals from China had assumed control over this trade, in part because they were better able to comply with the complex international and domestic logging regulations.

The third period concerns recent investments in biofuels and food by Asian countries with few natural resources. Although other Asian actors have also entered the field, in particular China, Japan has developed the most systematic investment programme. As Japan largely depends on imports for its energy needs, it has formed a strategic cooperation with the Brazilian Agroenergy Programme. The Japan Development Bank (JBIC) has provided financing for various initiatives within this Programme. Moreover, several Japanese firms have established joint ventures with Brazilian enterprises to develop and produce biofuels. However, Japan has held back from large direct investments and has become a leading voice opposing large-scale land purchases, a common practice among other cash-rich and resource-poor countries. It has promoted the Principles for Responsible Agricultural Investment (RAI), which aim to curb the global movement towards large-scale land acquisitions.

The chapter by Jae Sung Kwak assesses the changing nature of Asian FDI in Latin American manufacturing, with a focus on the position of Latin America within Asian global value chains. Most Asian investments in Latin American manufacturing are concentrated in four sectors: steel, automobiles, electronics, and textiles. In the case of steel, Japanese firms' involvement in the production of steel products in Latin America started in the mid-1950s, Korean firms have also recently invested in this regional industry. The steel industry's value chain includes the transformation of natural resources into steel by-products for the production of automobiles, home appliances, industrial machinery and other devices. Latin America's participation is concentrated in natural resources and markets for steel by-products. Three major Asian producers have entered the Latin American steel industry, but only two have survived: POSCO (Republic of Korea) and NIPPON (Japan). Both operate in Brazil and Mexico. More recently, Chinese and Indian companies have started exploiting iron ore mines in Bolivia and Peru.

With regard to automobiles, rising demand and the strengthened global competiveness of Chinese, Korean and Japanese firms have led to large-scale investment projects in Latin America. Japanese companies such as Toyota, Honda and Nissan paved the way for their Korean and Chinese peers to follow. The automobile sector's value chain comprises four sections: transformation of raw materials (including steel and rubber by-products); the production of parts and components; research and development (R&D) and assembly; and marketing, sales and after-sales activities. Latin America is an attractive location not only for companies seeking to export outside the region, but also for firms selling within the region, given its growing market.

Asian brands are leading the global market as principal innovators in the field of electronics. Asian firms have made efficiency-seeking investments in Mexico for the United States market and market-seeking investments in Brazil. The electronics value chain includes several layers of parts and components producers, selling not only among themselves, but also directly to the brand or company in charge of final assembly. Another vital part of the chain is R&D and design, which is closely related to the manufacturing of components and final assembly lines. Brand marketing is also important in a highly competitive market and given the rapid pace of technological change. Most Asian investors in Latin America have integrated their operations throughout the entire value chain, except for the production of raw materials and the creation of R&D centres. One exception is LG Brazil, which underwent a complete internationalization of its operations and relies heavily on local human resources for the development of its regional business. Another exception is the Chinese group Huawei, which has a production plant for telecommunication products in Brazil, together with a manufacturing management support centre, a training centre for its employees, a spare parts centre and a logistics centre.

Central America has become an export platform of the textile and garment industry for the United States market, and some of the main investors are Korean firms. Over the past two decades, Korean companies have focused on the mass production of pre-ordered designs for their customers. However, large producers such as Sae-A, Hansoll and Hansae have recently started to enter the original design manufacturing (ODM) business, whereby companies participate in the entire production process, including fabric development, fashion design and creation of their own collection.

The author concludes that the most successful examples of Asian subsidiaries and domestic suppliers in Latin America that have upgraded in the four industries analysed were not the result of microeconomic incentives and regulations (such as local content requirements), but rather related to broader efforts to improve macroeconomic stability and promote competitive markets.

The chapter by Joaquín Piña deals with the off-shore services industry, which may play a key role in strengthening economic integration between Asia and Latin America. Off-shoring (offshore sourcing) is an international business strategy that enables companies to shift manufacturing or service activities overseas, sourcing highly skilled human resources with cost advantages. Services off-shoring is a by-product of software off-shoring in the early 1990s and has evolved since then to include a wider range of services. One of its key drivers has been the spread of information and communication technologies (ICTs). New communication platforms and automation tools have allowed vertically integrated companies to break up value chains through process outsourcing and remote operation (off-shoring). The off-shoring industry is a by-product of economic globalization, and has experienced unprecedented growth in terms of specific segments, market size, and corporate country strategies of multinational companies.[3]

Latin America entered the global services arena only recently through a follow-the-sun model, which allows services providers to leverage geographically distant (off-shore) operations with closer (near-shore) ones. Companies can thus access language skills and cultural affinities, while reducing operational risk and benefiting from time-zone differences to accelerate project-cycle development. Operations in medium to high-cost countries (such as Canada, the United States and Western Europe) can be combined with others in low-cost regions such as Asia-

---

[3] India, Ireland and Eastern European countries are the main off-shoring services providers today. Recent data and estimates lend support to the notion of a new stage of slower growth rates and consolidation within the industry.

Pacific, Eastern Europe and Latin America. Following in the footsteps of the first two regions, Latin America has a unique opportunity to become a major player in a context of industry and business model reconfiguration by international providers.

Available data show significant asymmetries in the development of the off-shoring industry between Asia and Latin America, as well as weak integration between the two regions. According to WTO estimates, Asian countries accounted for almost one quarter of global services exports in 2008, while Latin America as a whole accounted for only 3%. Six Asian countries are among the top 10 services exporters in the world (Japan, India, China, Hong Kong Special Administrative Region (SAR) of China, Singapore and the Republic of Korea). Only one Latin American country figures in the top 20 (Brazil, at number 14).

Export of services is a relatively new area for Latin American commodity-based, export-oriented economies. In trade negotiations Latin American governments still consider merchandise exports as a priority issue, and are extending this pattern to their negotiations with Asian countries. Only a handful of public institutions responsible for trade promotion and negotiation have realized the importance of global services industries. Trade agreements that facilitate services trade between the two regions are scarce; only 12 agreements between Latin America and Asia cover this area. Chile has the largest number of agreements that include services chapters, followed by Mexico, Panama and Peru.

Global services centres in Latin America are mainly subsidiaries of European and United States companies. Around 60 projects in few countries concern off-shore centres of Asian companies from India, Japan and the Republic of Korea. Limited in number as they are, these centres are examples of possible services integration between Asia and Latin America.

Latin America has a newly-gained role as a near-shore services provider for the United States market and an increasing one as a support-centre hub for Japanese and Korean hardware manufacturers. Competitive advantages have been built up to offset historical prejudices and perceptions of Latin America as a politically and economically high-risk region. Some global services firms see Latin America not as a competitor to Asia, but rather as a complementary provider.

To take advantage of the current scenario, Latin American countries need to consolidate a set of advantages and skills. Current off-shoring providers are not necessarily forced to choose between Asia, Europe or Latin America; instead, they seek a well-balanced mix of operations on the three continents, allowing them to develop a truly global services supply in at least three time-zones. In the case of R&D, this combination of different teams working simultaneously shortens access-to-market for knowledge-based goods and services, from Internet search engines to chip-design software and biotech applications.

The final chapter by Andrés López, Daniela Ramos and Iván Torre analyses the experiences of four Latin American multinational companies that have invested in Asia. The first is the Techint Group, an Argentine multinational which in 2011 employed more than 57,000 people worldwide and had revenues of over US$ 24 billion. One of this company's core activities is the seamless tube business of its subsidiary Tenaris, which now has 10% to 15% of its total production capacity in Asia. Tenaris' deployment in Asia has been slow, as it took almost three decades for the company to go from remote exporting to its first greenfield project. The second case study is that of Industrias Metalúrgicas Pescarmona S.A. (IMPSA), which is the flagship of the Pescarmona Group from Argentina, with assets of US$ 700 million and 5,000 employees. The first activities undertaken by IMPSA in Asia were the manufacturing and installation of port cranes and the execution of hydroelectric projects in Indonesia, Thailand, India, China, Philippines and Taiwan Province of China. By 2004, Asia accounted for about 30% of the company's revenues. During the years that followed, the firm's focus shifted to the renewable energy business, with major ongoing investments in Malaysia and Viet Nam.

The third case study is that of Bimbo, a Mexican multinational selling bakery products. In 2010 it had more than 96,000 employees and 103 facilities distributed in 17 countries throughout Latin America and Asia, plus the United States. The company is highly product-diversified and vertically integrated —including transport, packaging, raw materials production and machinery manufacturing. It began to expand internationally in the 1990s, with the North American Free Trade Agreement (NAFTA) providing an opportunity for joint ventures to penetrate the United States market. To enter the Asian market, it purchased a subsidiary of its main competitor in Spain, Panrico. Bimbo Asia has 800 workers and a production plant in Beijing. The final case study concerns Embraer, a Brazilian company, which is the third-largest aircraft maker in the world and employs around 17,000 workers (excluding its subsidiaries OGMA and HEAI). It has produced more than 5,000 aircraft that operate in 92 countries on five continents. It is the market leader for commercial jets with up to 120 seats. Embraer is strongly internationalized, with sales offices and distributions centres located worldwide, and production facilities in the United States and China. The company first opened sales and spare parts distribution centres in Asia in 2000, in Beijing and Singapore. In December 2002, Embraer signed an agreement to build a production unit in China as part of a joint venture with two subsidiaries of AVIC II (China Aviation

Industry Corporation II). By 2010, the Asia-Pacific region represented 22% of the company's revenue.

The experiences of these four Latin American companies in Asia over the past 20 years are similar in a number of ways. All were leaders in their business sector back home. Investing in Asia requires the expertise and financial backing that only a solid position in home markets can offer. Investment in Asia comes only after the companies have successfully expanded in neighbouring countries. Tenaris, for instance, did not open its first manufacturing plant in Asia until 2008, more than 20 years after the company's holding group (Techint) had set up its first plants outside Argentina. IMPSA opened its Lumut plant after it had well-established subsidiaries in Brazil. Investing in Brazil is an almost indispensable step for a firm seeking to expand its operations outside its borders. Brazilian companies have the advantage of being the incumbents in such a large market. Deployment in Asia was a lengthy process. Tenaris and IMPSA started their first commercial operations in Asia in the 1980s, but it was not until the 1990s that they went beyond that stage, and manufacturing plants were only built in the last decade.

In order to successfully adapt to the Asian market, these firms had to adapt their micro-business practices. Strong interpersonal relationships are vital for a successful blending into Asian markets. The presence of local executives in top managerial positions at foreign subsidiaries is another condition for any kind of operation in Asia. Moreover, even when there are no restrictions, local authorities particularly welcome export-oriented investments and those that seek the development of linkages with domestic suppliers. Latin American companies need to understand these informal practices that are so different from Western-style business practices.

From the analysis of these cases, it is clear that investment in Asia cannot be handled in a simple and conventional manner. In general, local governments are keen to attract foreign investors. The difficulties lie mainly in establishing successful links with local agents, such as suppliers, workers and universities. To overcome this, companies should support their operations with policies oriented to building solid ties with the local environment both inside the firm (by hiring local executives and involving them in key decision-making) and outside the firm (by investing time and resources in cultivating interpersonal relationships). It is clear that companies that enjoy a good position in their home market are best suited to carry out investments in Asia, not only because they may have more expertise in their business but also because the deployment strategy may take several years, something that requires a continuous flow of resources towards a project that will take a long time to produce healthy profits.

Chapter I

Asian agribusiness investment in Latin America, with case studies from Brazil

Ruth Rama

John Wilkinson

Introduction

Over the past two decades, there has been a boom in natural-resource-based exports from Latin America to Asia and, in particular, to China. The demand for commodities in these markets has increased on an unprecedented scale. This trend is part of a geographic shift in global economic interdependencies. Latin America's agro-industrial sector, is not simply returning to a traditional tropical-commodities export pattern (although the demand for these products is certainly booming), but is experiencing a fundamental paradigm shift which began in the 1970s under the influence of the first Asian giant: Japan.[1]

1 In 1973, the Nixon Administration imposed an embargo on soy exports to protect domestic demand. In response, Japan, which at that time depended entirely on supplies from the United States, developed a long-term cooperation plan for the promotion of an alternative supply base in Brazil in order to meet the demand generated by its population's increasingly soy-dependent diet.

At the same time, the main corridor of trade, investment and global agro-industrial value chains is shifting from a North-South to a South-South orientation (UNCTAD, 2006). In the global agrifood and agro-industrial sectors, Asian multinationals are playing an increasingly important role, in part thanks to the support they receive from their respective governments. The global agro-industrial strategy and policy first launched by Japan, then by the Republic of Korea and, more recently, by China has been motivated primarily by concerns about food and natural-resource security. The State's strategic role in this effort goes beyond the protection of domestic markets and the promotion of domestic actors to encompass long-term policies on access and supply. At the same time, access to Asian markets has been constrained by the emergence and consolidation of Asian traders, while current supply strategies are also driven by the desire to counter the economic power of global Northern traders. These factors, together with the rapid growth of the Asian economies, have contributed to the expansion of Asian agrifood transnationals both in trading (Wilmar, Noble) and in product chains (Charoen Pokphand (CP) Group of Thailand and Salim Group of Indonesia). Asian firms have also attained global competitiveness in fermentation-based activities and associated biotechnologies (Ajinomoto, Yokult, Kirin, Snow Brand).

This chapter looks into the determinants of foreign direct investment (FDI) in the Asian agrifood industry based on a literature review and an analysis of data on leading agrifood firms. It highlights the distinctive features of Asian FDI, especially in terms of the role of government and cultural variables. The part played by vertical integration strategies and natural-resource-seeking FDI strategies will also be discussed. The analysis then turns to general trends affecting Asian FDI in Latin America before focusing on the specific importance of FDI in agriculture, forestry and fishing and in the food and beverage industry. It concludes with a country review of Asian FDI in Latin America that takes a particularly close look at Japan and China, but that also includes other Asian investors.

Large-scale Asian involvement in Latin America can be divided into three different periods. The first started in the 1970s when Japan began to open up the Brazilian savannah region to soy production and later to horticulture. This drive included large-scale infrastructure projects and the development of key mineral resources. As part of this process, private firms moved in alongside and in synergy with broader cooperation programmes (e.g., Mitsui and Mitsubishi in trading, Campo in the promotion of agricultural production and Cenibra in the forestry sector). The second period was the 1990s, when Latin America received a wave of investment, particularly from Asian logging firms in the Amazon as palm oil plantations encroached on the humid tropical forests of Asia. These investments were led by Indonesia, Malaysia and Thailand, but China was also involved. In contrast to what occurred with the State-level cooperative effort to open up the savannah region, these investments gave rise to negotiations and conflict with civil society actors and to a parliamentary inquiry. A case study of Chinese investment in this sector in the Peruvian Amazon will be included in the discussion in order to shed light on the more recent dynamic of Asian investment in this sector. The hallmark of the third period is recent investment in biofuels and the food industry by capital-rich, resource-poor countries. While other Asian actors are certainly involved and China, in particular, has begun to play a strategic role in this period, the discussion will focus on Japan's involvement, since it is the country that has developed the most systematic investment programme to date and has, in addition, positioned itself in relation to the controversial issue of the role of land acquisitions in such investments.

Many of the studies that have been done on the internationalization of agrifood markets have focused on the interrelated dynamics of trade and FDI and, in particular, on the conditions under which one or the other strategy has tended to prevail and the complementarities between the two. These studies have drawn heavily upon Dunning's eclectic model, with its mix of ownership, location advantages and internalization variables (Rama and Wilkinson, 2008). This type of analysis has proved to be useful when considering the strategies used by individual firms, but current globalization trends involving complex interdependencies across different activities and geographic locations have shifted the unit of analysis from individual firms to value chains, clusters and global production networks. In this context, key questions revolve around opportunities for dynamic re-positioning within the value chain and the challenges that this poses, as well as around the dangers of a negative lock-in, especially for those actors and countries whose initial entry into these activities was based on natural-resource advantages.

These questions have been widely studied in Latin America in the wake of the move away from import-substitution growth strategies (Pietrobello and Rabelotti, 2003). Initially, hopes were pinned on the East Asia model based on light manufacturing and subsequent upgrading. After a decade of structural reforms, however, it became apparent that few Latin American countries had succeeded in shifting away from natural-resource-based activities. The focus then turned to the potential of development strategies that build upon natural-resource competitiveness. The examples of resource-rich countries in widely differing contexts —Australia, Canada and the Nordic countries— suggest that effective development strategies based on diversification across activities involving natural-resource advantages are possible (Lederman and Maloney, 2007). In agriculture, the discussion has focused on the opportunities opened up by the shift from traditional tropical commodities to "non-traditional exports" that fit in with emerging demand patterns in the Northern countries, in which fresh products, particularly horticulture and seafood, play a prominent role.

Asia's involvement in Latin America's agro-industrial value chains raises the issue of the role of State policy.[2] A number of Asian countries are concerned with food security, renewable energy and broader access to natural resources. In Japan, this has led to the development of a long-term cooperation programme that has helped private-sector investment to step in as public programmes reach maturity. Cooperation was initially directed towards traditional commodity exports, but now also involves technology transfers focusing on upstream value-added activities. Examples include Japan's role in opening up Brazil's savannah region to soy production and its recent entry into biofuels in Brazil, as well as the cooperation programme launched by Japan, Brazil and Mozambique for the development of the latter's large savannah regions.

A. Asian transnational agrifood corporations

This section reviews the literature dealing with Asian transnational corporations (TNCs) in the agrifood sector in order to shed light on the motivating forces and the modus operandi of these firms, as well as their potential role as sources of FDI in Latin American agro-industries.[3]

1. Investment, trade and trade agreements between Asia and Latin America

The first major event to have an impact on trade and investment relations between Latin America and Asia was probably the pilfering of rubber plants from the Brazilian Amazon so that rubber production could be relocated to Indonesia and Malaysia. Within a few decades, Brazilian rubber production went into decline, and Asian plantations became the main sources of global supply. A few decades later, the recruitment of

---

2 So far, most of the literature on value chains has focused on private forms of governance or coordination, on the shift in global value chains from a producer- to a buyer-driven dynamic and on the different modalities for coordination, which open up different development opportunities (Gereffi, Sturgeon and Humphrey, 2005).

3 For the purposes of this discussion, agro-industries are defined as including agriculture, fisheries, forestry, aquaculture, silviculture, bioenergy industries and food-processing and food and beverage industries.

Japanese workers to work on the São Paulo coffee plantations opened the way for the establishment of a Japanese presence in Brazil's agricultural sector. Japanese farmers played a decisive role in the development of horticulture and the promotion of cooperative forms of organization, and they proved to be key players in the Japanese cooperation programmes that helped to open up the Brazilian savannah region.

While Japan and the Republic of Korea are highly dependent on food and fibre imports, this is not the case for other parts of Asia. Thailand, for example, now competes with the Southern Cone as a white meats exporter, is a major rice exporter and has been a key supplier of feedstock to Europe. Malaysia and Indonesia have huge forestlands and are world leaders in the palm oil market. India and China, for their part, have vibrant agricultural sectors which have allowed them to achieve high levels of self-sufficiency and, particularly in the case of China, to become large-scale exporters as well. Nevertheless, these two countries have become major importers of specific crops, with India buying up large volumes of sugar for circumstantial reasons and China importing, as a result of structural conditions, large quantities of soy, pulp and other items whose production requires large inputs of land and water. Import-dependent countries have largely sourced their demand from within Asia, which also includes the agro-industrial powerhouses of Australia and New Zealand. The main source of extraregional trade has been the United States.

Until the rise of China, the main Asian food importers were Japan and the Republic of Korea. In 2000, Japan's total food imports amounted to US$ 50 billion, as against a mere US$ 2.3 billion of food exports. These imports were mostly supplied by subsidiaries of Japanese multinationals. Unlike European and United States subsidiaries, for which the home market has often been the principal attraction, Japanese FDI has largely focused on the development of offshore production for the Japanese market. Only 22% of the total sales of Japanese food subsidiaries overseas were in the host market. In 1970, Australia was the leading exporter to Japan, followed by the United States, Taiwan Province of China, China and Thailand. By the turn of the millennium, the United States was first, followed by China, Taiwan Province of China, Australia and Thailand (Wilkinson, 2004).

The Republic of Korea's levels of food self-sufficiency (30%) and dependence on imports are similar to Japan's, although its population is much smaller. Like Japan, the Republic of Korea has traditionally been heavily dependent on the United States for a range of products (maize, meat, wheat, soybean meal and cotton), while its remaining imports have been supplied regionally. In recent years, two developments have led to changes in this import profile. On the one hand, like Japan, the Republic of Korea has boosted its imports of soy from the MERCOSUR countries, and its imports from the European Union have shifted to increasingly processed products. By the turn of the millennium, both Japan and the Republic of Korea were converging with the developed countries in terms of their food consumption patterns. This has heightened their trade dependence on the European Union and the United States, whose share in those countries' total trade in processed foods has been climbing since the 1980s and now stands at 75% of total trade in that category.

At the same time, the share of developing countries' total agricultural commodity exports that were sold to other developing countries rose from 31% to 44% between 1985-1990 and 1996-2000 (FAO, 2004). Most of this increase, however, was accounted for by the upswing in intraregional trade triggered by the establishment of regional trade agreements as part of these countries' adoption of structural reforms (UNCTAD, 2006).

2. Emerging-market transnational corporations

Are TNCs based in emerging Asian markets different from Triad-based TNCs? As noted by Sim (2007): "theories and explanations on the internationalization (or expansion across national boundaries) of firms were largely based on Western MNEs." Burch and Goss (2005) endorse this point of view. They argue that most of the current literature characterizes globalization as a process driven by large corporations based in the Triad,[4] a view which fails to consider TNCs based in developing countries. Even less research has been done on the role of agrifood TNCs based in such countries, in spite of their significant regional and even international operations. Ranked by foreign assets in millions of United States dollars as of 2007, data compiled by the United Nations Conference on Trade and Development (UNCTAD, 2009) show that 10 of the world's 25 largest TNCs based on agriculture and plantations were from developing Asia in 2007, with the Malaysian Sime Darby Berhad company ranking first (total assets amounting to US$ 10.9 billion, of which US$ 4.7 billion were foreign assets). By the same token, 8 of the world's 50 largest food and beverage TNCs were based in developing Asia.

Banalieva and Sarathy (2006) characterize TNCs based in emerging markets as follows: (i) they are latecomers to internationalization; (ii) they suffer from significant competitive disadvantages as compared

[4] The "Triad" refers to Europe, Japan and the United States.

to Triad-based TNCs; (iii) they may face institutional constraints (e.g., inefficient justice systems) in their home countries that may increase the risks and costs of doing business; and (iv) they may suffer from a home-region disadvantage, since their neighbours are often very poor nations (Banalieva and Sarathy). On the other hand, however, emerging-market TNCs often enjoy advantages such as access to low-cost natural resources and labour in their home country and government support for their internationalization strategies.

The three main factors which may account for the behaviour of Asian agrifood TNCs are the role of government, the role of cultural linkages and the role of vertical integration.

3. The role of government

The so-called "Western theories" regarding TNCs have neglected the role played by government support, which, in some Asian economies (Malaysia, Singapore, Taiwan Province of China and Thailand), has made a major contribution to the success of companies based in those countries (Sim, 2007). Emerging in an influential institutional context, in the 1980s and 1990s Chinese outward FDI was largely driven by the government's attempts to ensure a stable supply of domestically scarce natural resources (Buckley and others, 2007). In their case studies of two large agrifood TNCs (the Charoen Pokphand (CP) Group of Thailand and the Salim Group of Indonesia), Burch and Gross (2005) emphasize these companies' close ties to the State and the political system as a major reason for their successful international expansion. Luo and Tung (2007) also consider that home-government support for companies' internationalization campaigns is characteristic of TNCs based in emerging economies such as Indonesia and Thailand. Moreover, a hefty share of China's outward investment is accounted for by State-owned enterprises, since private firms were not allowed to go global prior to 2003.[5] The Chinese government may also influence the amount and location of FDI, especially when the project involves the supply of domestically scarce natural resources (Buckley and others, 2007). As noted by these authors, China has "built" some of its TNCs, as have Singapore, the Republic of Korea and Malaysia. State-owned or State-associated firms, they argue, may obtain capital at below-market rates. Capital-market imperfections "may account for the ease with which both natural-resource FDI (typically in energy and raw materials) and strategic

---

5 In 2005, 81% of Chinese outward FDI stock was still in the hands of State-owned companies. See Nicolas and Thomsen, 2008, "The rise of Chinese firms in Europe: Motives, strategies and implications." in Asia Pacific Economics Association Conference, Beijing.

asset-seeking FDI might be undertaken by Chinese MNEs" (Buckley and others, 2007, p. 502). Based on previous research, these authors point to some key sectors, such as timber, fisheries and agriculture, where this may occur.

Though the State continues to play a substantial role, things may be changing in China. Since October 2004, under the policy espoused by the National Development and Reform Commission, Chinese firms that are going global are empowered to make their own investment decisions (Nicolas and Thomsen, 2008). Local governments have been given more authority than in the past, while the central government is seen to be simply a guide and a service provider. According to these authors, the ownership structure of Chinese State-owned firms is also changing as new types of shareholders, such as township firms, private firms and even foreign TNCs, play an increasingly important role.

4. The role of cultural linkages

As predicted by theories of international corporate expansion such as those put forward by the Uppsala school of thought, cultural aspects have been an essential factor in the spread of Asian TNCs (Sim, 2007). Chinese social and ethnic networks, for example, play a key role in this sort of expansion, especially in the case of small and medium-sized enterprises (SMEs). Augustin-Jean (2006) emphasizes the role of common values, trust, networks, social capital, and ethnic and cultural ties in the expansion of Japanese agrifood firms in China. The Japanese companies build strategic alliances with "overseas Chinese" in order to better understand the dietary preferences of Chinese consumers. The internationalization strategies of South-East Asian and Taiwanese firms have also often been founded on cost-based competencies and other location-based advantages, all of which are brought together within an extensive web of ethnic networks. As will be seen below, cultural linkages and ethnic networks have also played some role in the spread of Chinese and Korean companies in Latin America, especially in the case of SMEs.

5. The role of vertical integration

The capacity to integrate vertically along the entire commodity chain "in a way that no Western agrifood multinational has been able to do" is key to an understanding of the regional and global expansion of large South-East Asian agrifood TNCs (Burch and Goss, 2005, p. 277). In these authors' opinion, vertical integration has enabled these companies to avoid the types of conflicts that have marked the relationship between the food processing industry and retailers in Western countries. The use of conglomerates as a tool for penetrating foreign markets also seems to have been of crucial importance for some Japanese agrifood companies (Agustin-Jean, 2006). Other studies seem to confirm the idea that vertical integration plays some role in the successful growth of Asian agrifood companies. Analysing four Asian TNCs, Sim (2007) notices that they have mainly relied on cost advantages and have moved vertically along the food chain towards food processing, packaging and retailing. At the same time, they have also attempted to create their own brand names. These studies seem to suggest that the internalization of markets (i.e., the use of internalization or "I" advantages, in Dunning's (2000; 1980) eclectic paradigm) is a salient feature of Asian TNCs which may help to account for their successful international expansion.[6]

Another I advantage of Asian agrifood conglomerates could be the internalization of financial markets (Buckley and others, 2007).[7] Asian conglomerates, these authors argue, may operate an inefficient internal capital market which can subsidize FDI. Market imperfections may become ownership advantages for firms based in emerging markets. This strategy may also be adopted by smaller Asian firms; for instance, family-owned companies are able to gain access to cheap capital from family members. As will be seen below, SMEs have played a role in FDI in Latin American agrifood industries. While in early versions of the theory of international production, vertical integration was viewed as a monopoly device for providing extra profits, in more recent works this strategy is regarded as a competitive weapon used by integrated firms against non-integrated ones (Dunning and Rugman, 1985). In short, support from home-country governments, cultural linkages and internalization strategies may have contributed to the successful internationalization of some Asian agrifood companies.

As institutional, cultural and corporate embeddedness may have greatly contributed to the international expansion of Asian agrifood TNCs, it stands to reason that Latin American governments should adopt two types of policies to attract those companies. First, they need to adopt a proactive role vis-à-vis such investments (much more so than

---

6 In Dunning's eclectic OLI paradigm, the likelihood that an enterprise will engage in international production depends on its O (ownership) advantages, such as brand names, the L (location) advantages of different countries and the I (internalization) advantages which enable a company to internalize imperfect (e.g., technology) markets.

7 Vertical integration with agricultural or retailing activities is a strategy in decline among large Western food and beverage TNCs (Rama, 1992; 1998). Integration with agricultural activities and foreign trade was an important strategy for British and United States agrifood firms in the early stages of their internationalization, however (Stopford and Dunning, 1983).

in the case of Triad-based investments, which, generally speaking, are not especially encouraged or guided by home-country governments). Second, they need to improve the domestic institutional environment. TNCs based in developing Asian economies will be more attracted to those Latin American countries which can offer stable rules of the game with regard to FDI and an institutional environment that is conducive to doing business (e.g., independent and rapid court settlements). These firms may be faced with institutional constraints in their home countries (Banalieva and Sarathy, 2006).

6. Is outward Asian FDI resource-seeking?

It has often been claimed that outward Asian FDI is resource-seeking, as Japan is one of the world's largest food importers. However, current Japanese food-security policy is less based on self-sufficiency than on the control of imports by Japanese companies and the diversification of suppliers (Agustin-Jean, 2006). Nowadays, self-sufficiency is the objective only in the case of certain staples, such as rice.

The nature of Asian FDI has been examined in several empirical studies. Fung and others (2009) use data for four Asian countries to test the hypothesis that outward Asian FDI is resource-seeking. One variable in their econometric model refers to the host country's agricultural resources, proxied by the share of its food exports in its total exports. Their hypothesis that Asian FDI is driven by the availability of food resources in host countries holds for Japan and the Republic of Korea but does not hold up for Taiwan Province of China, which mainly invests in economies that do not have particularly large endowments of food resources.[8] Finally, they found that firms based in China tend to invest in countries that are rich in agricultural resources, although great geographic distances seem to be a deterrent for them. Even within the same national group, Asian agrifood TNCs may use widely differing market strategies, and not all of them target the home market (Augustin-Jean, 2006).

Asian investors' motivations may have changed over time. Securing natural resources and acquiring raw materials may have become less important reasons to internationalize than they once were (Fung and others, 2009). According to this study, developing local markets and utilizing local labour have become much more powerful reasons for the internationalization of Korean companies.

---

8 Other variables in their model include the GDP of the home and host economies and the physical distance between the home country and the host country.

Finally, the business cycle may have some influence on the types of FDI undertaken by Asian agrifood investors. According to UNCTAD (2009, p. 88), "the global financial crisis could to some extent promote more natural-resource-seeking investments by Asian firms", a circumstance which may be making Latin America more attractive to such companies. Second, according to this same source, Chinese and Indian companies may be drawn to acquire devalued assets, brand names and distribution networks that may be currently available. This strategy may stimulate FDI in the food and beverage industry and in retailing. However, according to the report, such investors are more likely to target developed economies. This would seem to support the view that companies based in emerging markets, such as China and India, are seeking to acquire foreign technology and brands through internationalization as a means of compensating for their insufficient resource endowments. Luo and Tung (2007) argue that there is a key difference between TNCs based in newly industrializing economies (NIEs) and TNCs based in emerging markets: while the former have been driven by "push" factors, such as appreciating currencies and escalating costs at home, the latter are driven by "pull" factors, such as the need to secure critical resources and new technology.

A final target for resource-seeking Asian FDI is often the home market. The fact that Japanese consumers expect food supplies to meet very high quality and safety standards (Rama, 1992) could pose a challenge to Latin American countries that aim to attract Japanese investment in agrifood industries as a means of expanding their agrifood exports. However, some Asian resource-seeking companies have broadened the geographic scope of their objectives, as illustrated by some of the Japanese agrifood companies which operate in China (Agustin-Jean, 2006). The Charoen Pokphand (CP) Group of Thailand has invested in China not only to serve the local market for value-added agrifood products, but also to take advantage of low costs there to produce agrifood products for export to Japan and other international markets (Burch and Goss, 2005). One typology of TNCs from emerging markets classifies CP as a "world stage aspirant" which has not yet acquired the size and scope of the largest TNCs in this sector but which, nevertheless, has a great potential for global competition in areas where cost advantages are critical (Luo and Tung, 2007).

As noted earlier, some Asian agrifood TNCs also target the host-country market. Japanese agrifood investors located in the Shanghai region and in southern China target both the urban markets of the host country and their home market (Agustin-Jean, 2006). The methods of governance adopted by these Japanese TNCs for these two markets differ, however. According to this study, Japanese investors remain in control of food supplies to their home country, but often need to collaborate with Western firms and with regional investors (e.g., Taiwanese firms) in their food and beverage processing and distribution activities in the host-country market. Alliances with "overseas Chinese", who are more aware of local dietary preferences, and with local institutions and State-run enterprises are also important parts of the strategy used by Japanese investors in Chinese agrifood industries. These examples suggest that there may be a potential for domestic companies to partner with Asian agrifood investors in order to meet local demand in Latin American countries. The possibility of setting up joint ventures with local partners is already being explored by the Japanese International Cooperation Agency (JICA) as an additional attraction for Japanese investors willing to invest in Latin America (Girado, 1999).

B. FDI trends worldwide and in Latin America

1. FDI in agriculture, forestry and fishing

Global inward FDI flows in agriculture, forestry and fishing have expanded rapidly, jumping from US$ 721 million in 1990-1992 to US$ 6.3 billion in 2008-2010, with more than US$ 5 billion of that amount being directed towards developing economies. The inward flows for this sector continue to account for no more than a tiny share of total global FDI inflows, however (0.4% in 2008-2010) (UNCTAD, 2012).

From 1990 to 2010, inward FDI stock in this sector increased from US$ 8.5 billion to US$ 55.7 billion (see table I.1). In spite of this recent growth trend, however, it accounted for only 0.3% of total inward stock in 2010. During this period, there was a switchover in the relative levels of inward FDI stock in developed and developing economies since, for the first time, developing nations received more investment (US$ 34.8 billion) than developed nations did (US$ 17.5 billion).[9] UNCTAD attributes this situation to the availability of land and the importance of agriculture in developing nations. According to this source, FDI in agriculture, forestry and fishing represents a fairly large proportion of total inward FDI in several developing countries of Asia and Africa; however, the only Latin American country reported to be in this position is Ecuador, although Paraguay's food and beverage industry has also received a relatively large share of agricultural FDI.

9 The remaining US$ 3.4 billion were invested in south-eastern European and other transition economies.

Table I.1
ESTIMATED INWARD FDI STOCK WORLDWIDE, BY SECTOR AND INDUSTRY, 1990 AND 2010
(Millions of dollars and percentages)

	1990			2010			
	Developed countries	Developing countries	World	Developed countries	Developing countries	South-East Europe and Commonwealth of Independent States	World
Primary	160 915 (83.3%)	32 183 (16.7%)	193 098	953 007 (67.2%)	403 017 (28.4%)	61 332 (4.3%)	1 417 355
Agriculture, hunting, forestry and fishing	3 730 (43.5%)	4850 (56.5%)	8 580	17 468 (31.4%)	34 789 (62.5%)	3 431 (6.2%)	55 688
Manufacturing	687 360 (80.4%)	167 540 (19.6%)	854 899	3 499 677 (71.4%)	1 306 004 (26.7%)	93 606 (1.9%)	4 899 288
Food, beverages and tobacco	76049 (87.3%)	11 028 (12.7%)	87 077	462 134 (81.7%)	90263 (16%)	13 321 (2.4%)	565 717
Services	834 618 (82.3%)	179 459 (17.7%)	1 014 077	9 011 434 (70.3%)	3 575 046 (27.9%)	238 246 (1.9%)	12 824 726

Source: UNCTAD, author's calculations on data from Web table 24. Estimated world inward FDI stock, by sector and industry, 1990 and 2010.
Note: Data should be interpreted with caution. The world total was extrapolated on the basis of data covering 57 countries in 1990 and 97 countries in 2010, or latest year available. They account for over four-fifths of world inward FDI stock in 1990 and 2010. Only countries for which data for the three main sectors were available were included. The distribution share of each industry of these countries was applied to estimate the world total in each sector and industry. As a result, the sum of the sectors for each group of economies is different from the totals shown in annex table 3. In the case of some countries where only approval data were available, the actual data was estimated by applying the implementation ratio of realized FDI to approved FDI to the latter (19% in 2007 for China, 15% in 1997 for Indonesia, 56% in 1994 for Japan, 10% in 1990 and 8% in 1999 for Lao People's Democratic Republic, 91% in 2010 for Mongolia, 9% in 1990 and 34% in 2005 for Myanmar, 41% in 1990 and 35% in 1999 for Nepal, 62% in 1995 for Sri Lanka, 73% in 1990 and 58% in 2010 for Taiwan Province of China). The world total in 1990 includes the transition economies, although data by sector and industry are not available for that region.

Most outward FDI stock in this sector came from developed countries both in 1990 and 2010, though their share sharply decreased during the period (see table I.2). The increasingly important role played by investors based in developing countries is attributable to the presence of investors from China, the Republic of Korea and the Gulf States in Africa, Pakistan and some transition countries. Data on outward FDI flows in agriculture (see below) confirm the existence of this new trend.

Table I.2
ESTIMATED OUTWARD FDI STOCK WORLDWIDE, BY SECTOR AND INDUSTRY, 1990 AND 2010
(Millions of dollars and percentages)

	1990			2010			
	Developed countries	Developing countries	World	Developed countries	Developing countries	South-East Europe and Commonwealth of Independent States	World
Primary	180 406 (98.4%)	2 926 (1.6%)	183 332	1 314 830 (90.0%)	146 306 (10.0%)	321 (0.0%)	1 461 458
Agriculture, hunting, forestry and fishing	4 012 (91.8%)	360 (8.2%)	4 372	7 294 (30.3%)	16 653 (69.2%)	101 (0.4%)	24 049
Manufacturing	897 918 (99.1%)	8 410 (0.9%)	906 328	4 064 188 (93.5%)	277 528 (6.4%)	5 720 (0.1%)	4 347 436
Food, beverages and tobacco	85 238 (99.6%)	342 (0.4%)	85 580	484 980 (98.7%)	5 791 (1.2%)	670 (0.1%)	491 441
Services	985 659 (98.8%)	11 708 (1.2%)	997 367	2 146 454 (85.4%)	2 043 835 (14.4%)	27 602 (0.2%)	14 217 891

Source: UNCTAD. Author's calculations on data from Web table 24. Estimated world outward FDI stock, by sector and industry, 1990 and 2010.
Note: Data should be interpreted with caution. The world total was extrapolated on the basis of data covering 29 countries in 1990 and 55 countries in 2010, or latest year available. They account for 82% and 92% of world outward FDI stock, respectively, in 1990 and in 2010. Only countries for which data for the three main sectors were available were included. The distribution share of each industry of these countries was applied to estimate the world total in each sector and industry. Approval data were used for India (2005 instead of 2010) and Taiwan Province of China. For 1990, the world total includes the transition economies although data by sector and industry are not available for that region. Moreover, as major home developing economies were not covered due to lack of data, the respective shares for developing economies were underestimated in that year.

Table I.3 displays data on inward FDI flows and stock in agriculture, forestry and fishing by income group. The share of FDI infows for developed economies fell from 6.9% to 1.2%, in 2002-2007, then increased to 8.4% in 2008-2010. At the same time, the share of transition economies fluctuated between 3.9% at the beginning of the period (2002-2004) to 9.3% by 2005-2007 and 8.8% in 2008-2010. During 2002-2007 the share of developing economies in inward FDI flows was stable at about 89% of global flows. However, at the end of the period, these economies' share rose strongly to 8.4% at the expense of the developing economies, which saw their share in total FDI inflows in agriculture fall to 82.8%. Within Latin America, Brazil is by far the largest recipient of FDI, with inflows climbing from US$ 153 million in 2002-2004 to US$ 421 million in 2005-2007. Chile, Ecuador, Costa Rica, Honduras and Peru also receive substantial FDI inflows. Foreign investors have been attracted by the business potential in Latin America of products such as cereals, soybeans, sugar cane, fruits, cut flowers, meat and poultry. Some projects in the sugar-cane industry are oriented towards the production of biofuels (UNCTAD, 2009).

Table I.3
INWARD FDI IN AGRICULTURE, FORESTRY AND FISHING, VARIOUS YEARS [a]
(Millions of dollars and percentages)

Host region/ economy	Millions of dollars						Percentage share in total					
	Flows			Stock			Flows			Stock		
	2002-2004	2005-2007	2008-2010	2002[b]	2007[c]	2010	2002-2004	2005-2007	2008-2010	2002[b]	2007[c]	2010
World	2 287	3 328	6 290	18 970	32 010	55 688	100	100	100	100	100	100
Developed economies	157	39	529	6 695	11 830	17 468	7	1	8	35	37	31
Transition economies	89	309	552	297	2 183	3 431	4	9	9	2	7	6
Developing economies	2 041	2 980	5 208	11 978	17 997	34 789	89	90	83	63	56	62
Latin America:												
Brazil	153	421	-	392	384	-	7	13	-	2	1	-
Chile	5	50	-	790	950	-	0	2	-	4	3	-
Ecuador	46	32	-	-	-	-	2	1	-	-	-	-
Honduras	49	36	-	-	-	-	2	1	-	-	-	-
Mexico	42	31	-	-	-	-	2	1	-	-	-	-

Source: UNCTAD. Authors'calculations based on data from World Investment Report, 2009, 2012; "Web table 24. Estimated world inward FDI stock, by sector and industry, 1990 and 2010", and "Web table 26. Estimated world inward FDI flows, by sector and industry, 1990-1992 and 2008-2010".

[a] Including the hunting industry.

[b] Or closest year available.

[c] Or latest year available.

Note: The world totals, as well as totals for developed economies, developing economies and south-eastern Europe and the Commonwealth of Independent States, were extrapolated from data for countries for which detailed statistics on FDI in agriculture were available. The coverage of the available data was as follows: about 100 countries for inward flows, accounting for over 90% of inward FDI flows worldwide, and around 90 countries for inward stock, accounting for over 85% of FDI inward stock worldwide. Data should be interpreted with caution. The world total was extrapolated on the basis of data covering 57 countries in 1990 and 97 countries in 2010, or latest year available. They account for over four-fifths of world inward FDI stock in 1990 and 2010. Only countries for which data for the three main sectors were available were included. The distribution share of each industry of these countries was applied to estimate the world total in each sector and industry. As a result, the sum of the sectors for each group of economies is different from the totals shown in annex table 3. In the case of some countries where only approval data were available, the actual data was estimated by applying the implementation ratio of realized FDI to approved FDI to the latter (19% in 2007 for China, 15% in 1997 for Indonesia, 56% in 1994 for Japan, 10% in 1990 and 8% in 1999 for Lao People's Democratic Republic, 91% in 2010 for Mongolia, 9% in 1990 and 34% in 2005 for Myanmar, 41% in 1990 and 35% in 1999 for Nepal, 62% in 1995 for Sri Lanka, 73% in 1990 and 58% in 2010 for Taiwan Province of China). The world total in 1990 includes the transition economies, although data by sector and industry are not available for that region. Data should be interpreted with caution. The world total was extrapolated on the basis of data covering 79 countries in 1990-1992 and 113 countries in 2008-2010, or the latest three-year period average available. They account for 83 and 90 per cent of world inward FDI flows respectively in the periods 1990-1992 and 2008-2010. Only countries for which data for the three main sectors were available were included. The distribution share of each industry of these countries was applied to estimate the world total in each sector and industry. As a result, the sum of the sectors for each group of economies is different from the totals shown in annex table 1. Approval data were used for the Islamic Republic of Iran (1994-1996 instead of 1990-1992 and 2002-2003 instead of 2008-2010), Jordan (2001-2003 instead of 2008-2010) and Mongolia (1991-1993 instead of 1990-1992). In the case of some countries, the actual data was estimated by applying the implementation ratio of realized FDI to approved FDI to the latter : Bulgaria (54% in 1992-1994), China (25% in 1990-1992), Indonesia (16% in 1990-1992), Islamic Republic of Iran (8% in 1994-1996), Japan (51% in 1990-1992), Kenya (7% in 1992-1994), Lao People's Democratic Republic (1% in 1990-1992),

The relative position of developing countries as source countries for investment in agriculture and related primary industries has also changed, and outward FDI flows have therefore also undergone considerable changes in recent years. Outward FDI flows from developing countries, which had amounted to only US$ 45 million in 1989-1991, reached US$ 495 million in 2005-2007: an amount comparable, for the first time ever, to the FDI originating in developed nations (US$ 599 million).

The UNCTAD report (2009) lists a group of Asian companies among the top 25 TNCs in agribusiness industries in 2007. These firms include, in decreasing order of the level of parent-company assets: Sime Darbi Bhd (Malaysia), which has invested in Asia and, to a lesser extent, in Africa and the Middle East; Charoen Popkhand Foods Public Company Ltd. (Thailand), which has chiefly invested in China and other Asian countries; Kuala Lumpur Kapong Bhd (Malaysia), which has expanded its operations into other Asian countries and Europe; Kulim (Malaysia) Bhd, which has mainly invested in Singapore, Brunei and the Salomon Islands; PPB Group (Malaysia), which has businesses in China, India and Indonesia, in addition to its home country; Carsons and Cumberbatch PLC (Sri Lanka), which owns plantations in Malaysia and Indonesia, in addition to a joint venture with Carlsberg, a Danish brewer, in India; THS resources (Malaysia), which is involved in the production of vegetable oil and cocoa and owns plantations in Indonesia, as well as exporting to several other countries (e.g., a number of European countries, the Russian Federation, Egypt); Multi Vest Resources Bhd (Malaysia), which owns plantations and is involved in the production of palm oil both in its home-country market and in Indonesia; and Karuturi Global Ltd. (India), which owns greenhouses (for floriculture) in several African countries. As far as is known, none of these firms has yet invested in Latin America.[10] By contrast, a number of Indian agrochemical TNCs have invested in Argentina, Brazil and Peru (Nazareth, 2011).

2. FDI in the food and beverage processing industry

Between 1990 and 2007, the geographic patterns of FDI in the food and beverage industry also changed substantially. Inward FDI flows in this industry increased from US$ 7 billion in 1989-1991 to US$ 41 billion in 2005-2007. Surprisingly, the share of developing economies fell from 33% of the total in 1989-1991 to only 12% in 2005-2007 owing to the steeper rise of inward FDI flows in developed economies; FDI trends in south-eastern Europe and other transition economies (Chobanova, 2007) may also have played some role. The inward FDI stock grew, in this industry, from US$ 87 billion to US$ 565 billion, while the share of developing economies increased from 12% of the total in 1990 to 16% in 2010 (see table I.1).

---

[10] Information on the companies was obtained from their web pages and from secondary sources.

Outward FDI flows rose from US$ 13 billion in 1989-1991 to US$ 48 billion in 2005-2007. Evidencing the expansion of food and beverage TNCs based in such countries, outward FDI flows from developing economies increased tenfold during the period. However, the share of these countries in total outward FDI flows fell from 2% to 0.4% owing to the even sharper growth of outward FDI flows from developed nations. Regional integration in the European Union and the accession of new member countries in 2004 and 2007 have led European food and beverage companies to generally confine their expansion plans to their own region.

As comprehensive country data for FDI stocks or flows in the food and beverage industry are not available, a scope measure, i.e., the location of the affiliates owned by major food and beverage TNCs, will be used to analyse the geographic patterns prevailing in this international industry. Unpublished information for 2002 is the most recent data available. In 2002, the world's 100 largest food and beverage companies controlled around 8,000 affiliates worldwide, of which 830 were located in Latin America. Map I.1 shows the geographical distribution of these affiliates, by home country of the parent company. A variety of European food and beverage investors operate in Latin America, especially in the dairy industry. Companies operating in this subsector include, for instance, Arla, a Danish TNC, and Friesland, a Dutch TNC. Danone, a French dairy producer, which has diversified into bottled water and other foodstuffs, has located its affiliates mainly in the MERCOSUR area, Mexico and Colombia. In the Latin American and Caribbean region, other European TNCs operate in lines of business such as alcoholic drinks, mineral water and sugar. Nestlé (Switzerland) and Unilever (the United Kingdom and the Netherlands) are two of the big European conglomerates which control a large number of affiliates in a variety of Latin American markets.

In the Latin American and Caribbean region, United States food and beverage TNCs mainly operate in non-alcoholic beverages, animal feed, pet food, grain milling, breakfast cereals, biscuits, snacks and aviculture. Examples include Coca-Cola and PepsiCo, two global producers of non-alcoholic beverages which have sometimes forged alliances with Latin American TNCs (ECLAC, 2005). Two large United States conglomerates, Procter & Gamble and Sara Lee, are active in a variety of Latin American industrial markets, such as those for food, toiletry and household care products, and textiles. Regional TNCs include Latin American companies such as Grupo Modelo and Grupo Bimbo; both of these Mexican companies have expanded into South American countries. Finally, the "other countries" group shown in map I.1 includes companies based in other source nations for FDI in the food and beverage industry (e.g., South Africa and New Zealand).

Map I.1
MAJOR INTERNATIONAL PLAYERS IN LATIN AMERICAN AND CARIBBEAN FOOD AND BEVERAGE INDUSTRIES, 2002
(Number of foreign affiliates)

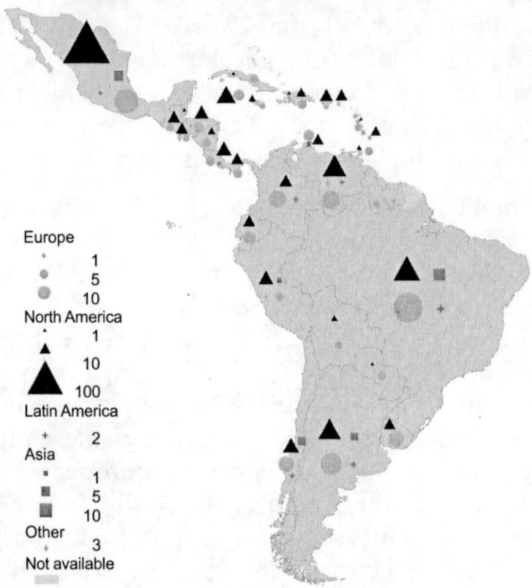

Source: Authors' calculations based on the AGRODATA database.

The location of affiliates can also be used to gauge differences between the spatial behaviour and strategies adopted by foreign investors based in Asia and foreign investors based elsewhere. From 1974 to 2000, the increased presence of Japanese TNCs in the top 100 firms in this sector signalled a major change in this industry (Tozanli, 2005). According to Tozanli, the emergence of very large Japanese TNCs in this sector may be attributable to the changes made in international trade rules in the 1970s and 1980s, since the new international norms prompted Japanese companies to go global for the first time. As one example of how this new strategy worked, she cites the investments made by Japanese fishing companies in Latin America to bypass the provision in the 1974 International Law of the Sea which had changed the limits of national territorial waters, thereby making it necessary for these companies to establish affiliates in the region if they wished to continue to fish there.

Map I.2 illustrates the geographical distribution of the affiliates of major Asian TNCs in the food and beverage industry. In the top 100, the only Asian investors which operate in Latin America are Japanese companies; most of the foreign affiliates of these companies are positioned in China and the United States, however.

Map I.2
MAJOR ASIAN TNCs IN THE FOOD AND BEVERAGE INDUSTRY: DISTRIBUTION OF FOREIGN AND DOMESTIC AFFILIATES, 2002
(Number of foreign affiliates)

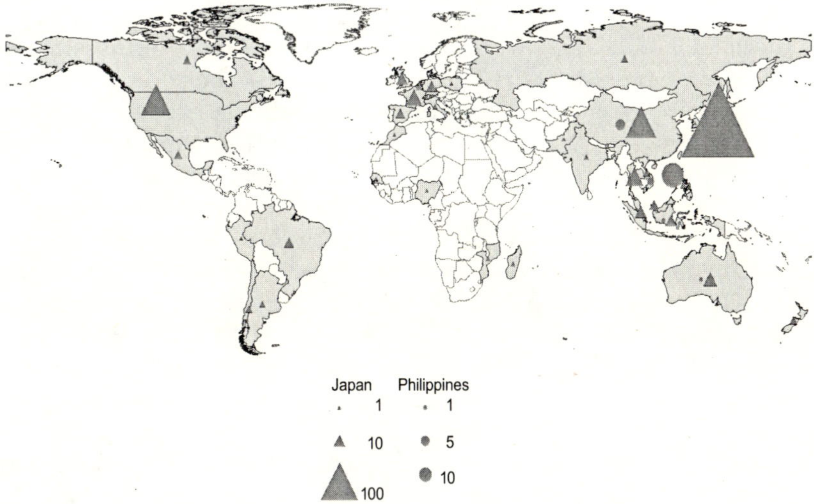

Source: Authors' calculations based on the AGRODATA database.

C. Country analysis

1. Japan

Japanese FDI in electronics and motor vehicles has been analysed extensively, but the subject of Japanese FDI in agrifood industries has been somewhat neglected (Agustin-Jean, 2006). Nevertheless, these investments are far from negligible. The Japanese Ministry of Finance reports that, in 1989-1994, 1,229 Japanese investments totalling ¥528.1 billion were made worldwide in agriculture, fisheries, lumber and pulp, and food processing. As shown in table I.3, the value of investment projects, especially those in the food sector, rose quickly between 1989-1994 and 1995-1999. However, in 2000-2004, the number of investments fell to 282, with a total value of ¥535.9 billion. The reduction in the number of projects and the relative stability of the value of foreign investments over such a long period of time confirm the occurrence of an atypical retreat on the part of Japanese agrifood companies (as compared with their Western counterparts) from international markets. For Japanese investors operating in this group of industries, the most active ones, in descending order of the value of their foreign investments, are food, lumber and pulp.

Confirming the information supplied by the affiliate data used to construct map I.2, statistics on investment values show that, although Latin American nations are not among the main host countries, they have been receiving substantially larger volumes of Japanese investment. The share of these investments entering the region rose from just 13% of the total in 1989-1994 to nearly 28% of total Japanese investment in agrifood industries in 2000-2004. As mentioned above, in terms of the value of investment projects, the food industry generally receives the most investment funds. Most of these Japanese food-industry investment projects are undertaken in Asia, however, and, in the case of Latin America, the largest recipient industry, both in 1989-1994 and in 2000-2004, was lumber and pulp. In Latin America, Japanese investments in farming and forestry, which were the second-highest in 1989-2004, had declined somewhat by the second half of this period. The average value of projects, by year, fell from ¥3.92 billion in 1980-1994, to ¥ 940 million in 1995-1999 and to only ¥ 340 million in 2000-2004. On the whole, these trends may reflect the favourable effect of the new laws adopted in the region concerning investment in the forestry sector (Girado, 1999). Japanese investors seem to be quite interested in the high-value-added segment of the lumber/wood chain and, to a lesser extent, in its low-value-added segment (forestry). At the level of host countries, these Japanese investments may be of considerable significance. For instance, in the 1990s, the sectors receiving the most Japanese investment in Argentina were, after motor vehicles, pulp and wood, while, in Chile, after mining, they were fishing and forestry (Girado, 1999).

Japanese investment in the Latin American and Caribbean region's food industry grew rapidly, rising, from just ¥8.2 billion in 1989-1994 to ¥56.1billion in 2000-2004. The size of the enlarged supranational MERCOSUR market and increased demand for processed food in some Latin American nations, such as Brazil, may have helped to boost the level of these Japanese investments in the region (Farina and Viegas, 2005; Girado, 1999). Finally, investment in fisheries, which had declined in relative terms in 1995-1999, had recovered somewhat by the end of the period. Girado (1999) reports, for instance, that Japanese investments in salmon production in Chile and in other fisheries in Argentina are resource-seeking investments because they are aimed at supplying the home market. In this respect, the relative position of Latin America needs to be examined in the light of the changes taking place in the geography of specific Japanese industries. (For instance, Oceania has now become the most important site for Japanese fishery projects (see table I.4)).

According to data from the Japanese Ministry of Finance, Brazil's food manufacturing industry, followed by Chile's farming and forestry sector, were the two Latin American markets that received the largest amounts of Japanese outward investment in agrifood industries in 2004.

entered into by such companies).[12] On the other hand, no closures of Japanese facilities were reported in this industry during that period in Latin America (or elsewhere), which contrasts with the high volatility of other food and beverage investments in the region (Tozanli, 2005). During the period in question, the author notes that major food and beverage TNCs sold off subsidiaries or divisions that were operating in non-core businesses or that were producing insufficient value. The large Japanese firms included in the top 100 did not, however, participate in major sell-offs, divestitures or spin-offs in Latin America (though Japanese companies did undertake such operations in North America and Oceania after 1992).

These trends are confirmed by a study on foreign TNCs in the Brazilian food and beverage industry which suggests that Japanese (or other Asian investors) did not play a central role in major M&A operations. From 1988 to August 2001, out of 48 purchasers, only one company was based in the Middle East, while the rest were based in the region (Brazil included), the United States and Western Europe (Farina and Viegas, 2005). In sum, Asian investors did not play a part in the turmoil that overtook the Latin American food and beverage industry during that period, or, at the very least, do not seem to have played a leading role.

According to another study, at least part of the changes in Latin America's export package of resource-based products may be attributable to China's and India's imports from the region. The gains obtained from the increase in resource-based Latin American exports have not been very widely distributed, however (Lederman and others, 2009).

In Latin America, there has also been some concern about competition between Asia (especially China) and Latin America for export shares in the United States market (Lederman and others, 2009); this may be of particular concern in the case of Mexican exports of manufactures (Santiso, 2006). On the other hand, however, Mexican exporters enjoy competitive advantages owing to their proximity to the United States. According to another study, the deterioration of the position of Latin America and the Caribbean in third markets relative to China and India is attributable to domestic supply conditions rather than to any reduction in demand for the region's products as a result of China's and India's increasing market shares (Lederman and others, 2009). The study's authors admit, however, that some specific subsectors and some countries (e.g., Mexico, Central America) have probably been negatively affected by the expanding share of Asian exports. None of

---

12 It should be noted that, for these Japanese companies, the share of North American operations accounted for 13.4% of total operations and Western European operations amounted to 28.4%. In other words, very large Japanese TNCs active in food and beverage processing seem to have used this mode of entry to penetrate or expand in developed-country markets, but not in Latin American markets.

the more vulnerable Latin American manufacturing sectors is analysed in that study, however, apart from the furniture (timber-based) industry.

Finally, unlike the case of other Asian agrifood investors, the presence of Japanese agrifood firms in the region seems, on the whole, to be unrelated to the presence of a Japanese immigrant population. Cultural embeddedness has not been the foundation for any of the main strategies used by Japanese companies to enter Latin American markets. An important exception here would be the cooperation programme launched for the development of soybean production in Brazil's savannah region, which will be analysed below.

2. China

According to data from the Chinese Ministry of Commerce, that country's outward (non-financial) FDI stock amounted to US$ 262 billion as of the end of 2010. Non-financial outward flows stood at US$ 60.1 billion, or 26% more than the previous year. The share of agriculture in outward flows and stock fell, respectively, from 5.2% and 1.9% in 2004 to just 0.7% and 0.8% in 2010. Though these investments increased during the period, investment in other sectors climbed more rapidly. According to the same source, there is only one agrifood company among China's top 50 non-financial TNCs. China National Cereals, Oils and Foodstuffs ranks sixth in terms of outward FDI stock, thirteenth in terms of foreign assets and tenth in terms of foreign revenue.

According to official Chinese statistics, China's FDI in Latin America and the Caribbean averaged around US$ 4 billion per year between 2003 and 2009. Around 97% of that sum was channelled into tax havens in the Caribbean. If these countries are excluded, then, in 2009, the largest recipients in terms of outward FDI stock were the Bolivarian Republic of Venezuela, Peru and Mexico.[13] In Latin America, China has mainly invested in minerals, petroleum fields and coal-tar fuels (Saavedra-Rivano, 1999), although a recent study suggests that Chinese FDI in the region is currently turning towards manufacturing (Nicolas and Thomsen, 2008). Confirming other observers' views (see the previous section), Malamud (2007) suggests that, in the case of China, economic decisions are largely based on political and diplomatic action rather than on economics forces alone. According to this author, China's main interest in Latin America focuses on energy, some minerals (such as copper) and soybeans.

According to Santiso (2006), Chinese investors are now following a similar pattern to the one followed in the 19th century by Western companies, since their major objectives are to obtain strategic inputs and to access the transport networks and port facilities they need in order to export products from Latin America to China. However, Santiso is

---

13 Includes financial FDI stock.

sceptical about the potential of Chinese FDI in the region and believes that Chinese investors, unlike their Western counterparts, will prefer formulas involving contracts between their State-owned enterprises and Latin American governments (for infrastructure projects, for example) over FDI.

In Gutierrez's (1998) view, China's interest in Latin American agrifood production is closely related to the following home-country factors: a very large population; a growing demand for food; new patterns of consumption that include goods produced by Latin America (e.g. beef, coffee); rapid urbanization; and the low productivity of Chinese agriculture. For China, he argues, it is cheaper to purchase Latin American foodstuffs than to modernize the domestic agricultural sector. By the end of the 1990s, Daila Hua Feng Enterprises, probably the largest Chinese agrifood company, had invested through its affiliate Lanco Pacific Argentina in slaughterhouses and meat processing plants in Argentina in order to supply the home market. This was a joint venture with San Justo Corporation S.A., ThyssenKrupp (a German firm which was supposed to build up the meat processing facility) and a French investor. However, owing to very serious difficulties with the Argentine partner, which was sued by the Chinese TNC, the deal fell through. After this frustrated FDI experience, China authorized imports of Argentine beef and poultry to meet the growing demand generated both by its domestic market and by tourism. Since 2005, some 11 domestic and foreign meat processing plants have been authorized to operate in Argentina following inspections by Chinese authorities. Although the above joint venture never started up operations, these subsequent commercial transactions confirm that the Chinese investor's motivation was clearly to export to China. As shown by UNCTAD (2009), many large Chinese agrifood TNCs also undertake FDI because they need to secure brands, distribution networks and technology.

As stated earlier, cross-border M&A operations have been an important entry strategy for food and beverage TNCs wishing to penetrate foreign markets; hence the need to analyse the distribution of Chinese outbound M&As and the relative scale of their Latin American operations. In 1995-2007, Chinese investors participated in 196 of such operations valued at US$ 64.8 billion (Nicolas and Thomsen, 2008). During this period, the sectors which attracted the most Chinese outward investments were oil and gas (US$ 21.3 billion) and financial services (US$ 19.6 billion). As noted earlier, the level of Chinese investment in tax havens in the Caribbean is substantial. The food and beverage industry attracted only US$ 1.1 billion distributed over 11 operations, with Latin America accounting for only US$ 100 million and the rest being distributed between Asia and Western Europe. Another study, which covers a more recent period (2000-2007) and analyses information from the Thomson One Banker database, concludes that Chinese investors participated in seven international deals relating to agriculture and food production but that none of these operations concerned the acquisition of companies located in Latin America (Sethi, 2009). In 2008-2010, Chongqin Food Group acquired an agricultural company in Brazil but the rest of Chinese international agrifood M&As targeted Africa and a few developed countries.[14] The studies confirm that, as stated above, the presence of Asian investors in this type of operation in Latin America has been limited.

On the other hand, the so-called "China effect" (i.e., China's potential negative effect on inward FDI in Latin America) has also caused concern in the region. The available empirical evidence is still inconclusive, though authors seem to agree that the effects, if any, are mild. According to some authors, there is evidence to suggest that inflows of manufacturing FDI into Latin America and the Caribbean, and particularly South America, have been substituted by inflows into China and India (Lederman and others, 2009). However, these authors admit that their results are not statistically robust —even in the case of Mexico and Central America, which seem to be the most heavily affected economies. Another study concludes that the China effect is negligible in the case of Latin American inward FDI and sometimes even mildly positive (Chantasasawat and others, 2008). Finally, other authors find that inward FDI in China has had little effect in terms of reducing inward FDI in Latin America, with the exception of investments received by Mexico and Colombia in some specific years.

Some TNCs based in other Asian countries have also expanded into Latin American agrifood industries. Examples include a number of Indian TNCs operating in edible oil businesses and Shree Renuka Sugars, which has invested in leading Brazilian sugar and ethanol companies (Nazareth Satyanand 2011). Korean investments in Latin America have been led mainly by large conglomerates (*chaebol*). Korean *chaebol* have large investments in fisheries in Uruguay and especially in Argentina, although the level of local processing is very low (Girado 1999). Some Korean food SMEs that cater to Korean immigrants in countries such as Argentina, Brazil, Chile, Peru and Paraguay may also be maintaining a presence of some importance.

D. Case studies

1. Japan and the Cerrados Region Development Programme (PRODECER) in Brazil

Japan's model of cooperation and associated investments in the Latin American agribusiness sector is illustrated by the Cerrados Region Development Programme (PRODECER). The main objective was to develop medium-sized farms that would be competitive in the production of key

[14] http://www.heritage.org/research/reports/2012/01/china-global-investment-tracker-2012.

export crops. The programme, which was in operation between the 1970s and 2001, helped to open up Brazil's vast central savannah region to grain production. It is an interesting example of a public-private partnership for which the executing agency was a bi-national firm —CAMPO— that had been created specifically for that purpose. JICA provided financing and supervised the programme.

Both Brazil and Japan pursued strategic interests through PRODECER. For Brazil, this programme served as a direct continuation of two other programmes for the development of the central region.[15] For Japan, it contributed to the diversification of the supply of major agricultural commodities on the world market at a time when its demand for commodities was rising rapidly. In the 1970s, the implications of Japan's dependence on external supplies were highlighted when a temporary embargo on soy exports was imposed by the United States.

The large second-generation (Nisei) population of Japanese descent in Brazil, which by the 1970s was dominating major sectors of agricultural production in the southern central region, played a key role in the programme's introduction. Japanese immigrants have figured prominently in the development of Brazilian agriculture since the beginning of the twentieth century: after substituting for slave labour on São Paulo's coffee plantations, they built a horticulture sector from which two cooperatives emerged. Both were leaders in the modernization of Brazilian agriculture in the southern central region and helped to provide farmers settling in the Cerrados region with assistance through PRODECER. The crucial role of second-generation Japanese immigrants was certainly an important factor in cementing Japan's commitment to the programme.[16]

There were three different phases of PRODECER, and its coverage of the Cerrados region increased as the programme moved from one phase to the next. The first (1979-1982) was a pilot project in the State of Minas Gerais that covered 70,000 hectares, while the second (1985-1994) extended the model to other areas of that state and to the states of Goiás, Bahia, Mato Grosso and Mato Grosso do Sul, incorporating another 200,000 hectares. The third phase (1994-2001) added 80,000 hectares in northern Brazil (Maranhão and Tocantins). In the course of these three phases, over 700 farmers were settled in 21 projects in 8 states. A range of products were promoted, including corn, rice, cotton, coffee and soy. By the third

---

[15] The first was the Programme for the Development of the Alto Parnaiba region in the State of Minas Gerais (PADAP) and the second was POLO-CENTRO. Both programmes involved investment in infrastructure and the extension of credit to medium-sized commercial farmers (with tracts of between 200 and 300 hectares). The government also created the Cerrados Centre for Agricultural Research (CPAC) to promote the large-scale development of the Cerrados region, which later received technical support from JICA.

[16] Nevertheless, the programme had strict rules for the selection of farmers, with the criteria used including age, educational level, management capacity and financial track record.

phase, the average farm size had increased to 1,000 hectares, and soy was accounting for some 80% of overall output.

PRODECER was discontinued in 2001, although the CAMPO firm continued its operations. It was terminated because farmers participating in the programme found themselves saddled with heavy debts at a time of high inflation and abrupt macroeconomic shifts, while the leading cooperatives went bankrupt. Moreover, the commercial transformation of the Cerrados region was well under way by then, and targeted support was no longer needed. Nevertheless, CAMPO continued its activities even while its shareholding structure was being modified.[17] CAMPO has four subsidiaries and a farm where genetic material is developed and farming practices are tested.[18]

A bi-national evaluation of PRODECER found that its outcome had generally been positive in terms of its contribution to the transformation of the Cerrados region into an export platform for grains and particularly soy products on the basis of medium- to large-scale commercial farming operations integrated into cooperatives. During the two decades that it was in operation, some US$ 550 million were invested in the incorporation of 350,000 hectares in seven states. Annual income was calculated at US$ 165 million, with US$ 30 million being collected in the form of taxes. Twenty-one individual projects involving 758 farmers organized into 16 cooperatives created 20,000 direct and 40,000 indirect jobs. Some 620,000 tons of grain were produced annually, with an additional 1 million tons being produced as the result of multiplier effects.

The Cerrados frontier thus became an alternative source of soy for Japan, even though most of that country's needs continued to be met by United States production. However, United States soy producers no longer enjoy a monopoly, and Japan has undoubtedly benefitted from the contribution made by the Cerrados region to the reduction of world soy prices. In this sense, the PRODECER cooperation programme can offer important lessons to countries that now have concerns similar to those of Japan with regard to ensuring commodity supplies in the context of rapid economic growth.

---

17 JALECO, the Japanese holding company, sold its 49% equity share to employees of CAMPO and to a number of Japanese firms in Brazil. BASAGRO, a Brazilian holding company, held on to its 51% share, some 65% of which was controlled by the Federal Union and the Brazilian Cooperative Organization (OCB), respectively. The development banks of Minas Gerais, Bahia and the federal government accounted for a further 16% of that stock, and some 15 private banks and Brazilian firms held the rest.

18 The first of those subsidiaries provides consultancy services to Brazil, Japan and other countries. The second is a plant micropropagation firm that works with bananas, pineapples and soybeans. A third specializes in soil analysis, with key support from the Japanese, while the fourth supplies plants to the Amazon.

Nevertheless, there have been several downsides. First, the farming systems in use gave rise to serious environmental problems, which later became a focus of joint research programmes. The destruction of biodiversity was partly due to the adoption of a predominantly monoculture farming system.[19] Second, the state governments underinvested in the construction of roads and related infrastructure. The third and greatest problem, however, was the high level of indebtedness of the farmers involved in the programme, which became evident in its second phase. This was due not only to high inflation and macroeconomic instability, but also to specific features of the programme itself, including the high level of investment required in order for farmers to establish themselves on the Cerrados frontier and the high interest rates which were applied, particularly in the third phase. Finally, NGOs and academics have criticized the programme model, which was based on the use of medium-sized and large farms, because this led to the expulsion of small farmers, with the end result being a net exodus from the rural regions where the programme was implemented and a deterioration in income distribution in those areas.

2. Asian logging investments in the Brazilian and Peruvian Amazon

Over the last two decades, planted forests have expanded rapidly in the Southern cone and are competing with crops and livestock production as agriculture and forestry rapidly converge. In Brazil, tree plantations now cover over 6 million hectares. Coffee and fruit producers (apples, orange juice) have received funding in the form of reforestation credits. The opening up of the central-western and northern regions has typically involved a three-phase cycle that combines logging, livestock and grain production. The production of palm oil for use in biofuels is being used as a reforestation strategy for the degraded lands of the Amazon. This convergence is perhaps most marked in the biofuels sector, where second-generation raw materials are likely to be based on advances in cellulosic enzyme technology, which will tend to make forestry and agricultural crops interchangeable as raw material inputs. Thus, forestry and paper and pulp firms have become increasingly involved in the biofuels sector. Investment decisions have shifted from specific crops and products to the issue of gaining access to the increasingly scarce resources needed to produce them, in particular water.

Except for one Japanese firm (Eidai), which started up its logging investments in 1973, other Asian logging investments in the Brazilian Amazon did not begin to take off until the 1990s (Harago, 1993). Several

---

19 In response, the Brazilian Agricultural Research Corporation (EMBRAPA) developed a mixed livestock- cropping system which is currently being proposed as a solution for degraded lands.

firms from Malaysia, Indonesia, Thailand and China invested in Brazil. Their interest in Brazil stemmed from the decline of tropical forests in Asia and increasingly strict regulations, together with the difficulty of entering the African market due to the dominance of European firms (Greenpeace, 1997; 1999).[20] Asian investments generally took the form of joint ventures or acquisitions of local firms that had been hard-hit by the decline in exports sparked by the revaluation of the Brazilian currency after 1994.[21] It should be noted, however, that while Greenpeace drew attention to the presence of Asian firms, in particular, its data attest to the predominance of United States and European investments during the period in question.

In the 1990s, Asian firms were held responsible for the Amazon's deforestation. Greenpeace and other NGOs directed public attention to the growing deforestation of the Amazon and what they characterized as the key role of Asian investments in that connection. Greenpeace acknowledged that Asian investments accounted for only 3% of production in 1997, but it also highlighted the sharp differences in installed capacity, which it contended could lead to their increasing domination of the sector.[22] As this was seen as a possible threat to the future of the Amazon, a parliamentary commission of inquiry was created to investigate Asian logging firms' operations in the Amazon (Vianna, 1998). In parallel with this, Greenpeace launched a campaign against the export of mahogany that focused on Amaplac (the firm bought by WTK), Eidai and the French firm Lapeyre, which led the government to impose a moratorium on new mahogany exports (Greenpeace, 2003/2005). The government also beefed up its policing capacity and set up a satellite monitoring system.

As time went by, however, the focus on Asian investments in the Amazon diminished, as the conclusion began to be reached that the "the Asian invasion had not materialized" (Macqueen, 2003). Asian investments were increasing less than had been foreseen, and Asian investors adhered more closely to existing regulations on logging and forestry management than domestic firms did. Moreover, it turned out that domestic firms were causing much more deforestation than exporters were (Borregaard,

---

20 In a context of large-scale illegal logging and weak monitoring that hindered data collection, Greenpeace (1999) was one of the few organizations that succeeded in collecting information on a group of 17 multinational logging companies in the Amazon, which was a subset of Asian investment in the 1990s.

21 In the 1990s, the first Asian companies that were active in the Amazon were Rimbunan Hijau and WTK, both from Malaysia. In 1995, WTK took control of Amaplac, a Brazilian firm in Manaus, and a forest property in Carauari (Amazônas State). In 1996, Tianjin Fortune Timber from China bought into Compensa. In 1997, Rimbuna Hijau took over two firms in Belém (Pará State) and Carolina (Amazonas State).

22 Local firms had a capacity of 4,000 to 6,000 cubic metres per year, compared to 120,000-170,000 cubic metres in the case of Eidai and over 600,000 cubic metres in the case of Rimbunan Hijau.

Dufy and Winchester, 2008). Exports accounted for only 15% of timber production, while the rest was sold on the domestic market.[23] Furthermore, exports were dominated by United States and European firms, while the Asian firms had a minority share.

Asian investors' expansion in Brazil was also limited because of their geographic diversification (in other South American countries, as well as other locations) and their industrial diversification into other agribusiness-related technologies or even wood substitutes.[24] Another factor that may have held back Asian companies' expansion is tighter regulation and the increased attention that was focused on the Amazon.

The mobilization that occurred around the issue of "Asian investments" in the Brazilian Amazon underscores the risks involved in FDI when it is identified with sensitive resources. In the case of PRODECER, it became clear how a strategic concern with food security and, more generally, commodity supplies led Japan to develop a very high-profile government cooperation programme. In the case of these more recent Asian investments, however, what is at issue is the alternative sourcing strategies being used by individual firms to reposition themselves within global markets. Without the support of a broader cooperation programme and in a situation where the major players are from a country which has had very little prior investment in Brazil, unmediated FDI became very vulnerable and quickly became the focus of opposition.

Another example of Asian investments in the Latin American forest industry is the increasing presence of Chinese firms in the Peruvian Amazon. In 2000, the Fujimori Administration enacted a new forestry law which expedited the granting of logging concessions. The aim was to promote sustainable logging systems, and the World Wildlife Fund (WWF) office in Peru was influential both in the formulation and subsequent implementation of the new forestry regulations. China has become an increasingly important destination for Peru's timber exports, and in 2009 became the leading importer. Peru has a very large ethnic Chinese population which is very active in the timber industry.

[23] It should be mentioned, however, that the steep devaluation of the real in 1998 boosted exports, which represented 36% of output in 2004 (Lentini, Verissimo & Pereira, 2005).

[24] Japanese firms invested in China and Viet Nam, which were closer to their home market. Samling (Malaysia) entered other South American markets and expanded into Australia, New Zealand and China in businesses related to forest resources and wood products. Rimbunan Hijau has become one of the largest Malaysian conglomerates, with a worldwide presence in the production of fertilizers, plantation technology, agro-chemistry, aquaculture and biotechnology. WTK (Malaysia) has expanded into other Asian countries, Oceania and the United States and has diversified into land development, edible oil milling, packaging and hospitality. Finally, the Chinese government is promoting the development of a domestic wood pulp industry, which may erode Chinese investors' interest in South American forests.

The organization of the timber supply chain between Peru and China illustrates how new forms of public and private governance have led to new forms of coordination. This is demonstrated by a study on 10 firms that export the Dipteryx wood species to China. Using the global value chain (GVC) framework of Gereffi and others (2003), Putzel and others (2008) show that the Peru-China Dipteryx timber supply chain is shifting from a producer-driven to a buyer-driven dynamic. In the early 1990s, timber firms owned by members of the ethnic Chinese population in Peru began to explore the Chinese market. By the end of the decade, however, that trade flow was increasingly being organized by multinationals from China, with a focus on the importation of raw materials for subsequent processing and re-exportation by firms in China. In other words, there has been a shift in the governance of the timber trade away from firms that specialize in exports and buy timber on the market and towards multinationals headquartered in China, which have logging teams and sawmills in Peru but do the final processing in China.

This shift of control into the hands of Chinese multinationals is partly the result of the advent of new forms of global governance in which forest management and chain-of-custody certification have become essential. Chinese firms successfully adapted to Peru's new forestry law (which was heavily influenced by the Peruvian branch of the World Wildlife Fund) and to global demands for certification, as illustrated by the 776 certificates for forest management and timber processing issued by the Forestry Stewardship Council (FSC) by 2009. Another factor was China's obligation to adapt its legislation to the United States Lacey Act on illegal logging under United States-China bilateral free trade agreements and the European Forest Law Enforcement, Governance and Trade (FLEGT) requirements. These new regulations favour large-scale operations and benefit those enterprises that are able to provide the necessary evidence of compliance.[25]

3. Japanese investments in Brazilian biofuels

Japan has defined a strategic policy with regard to the biofuels sector in Brazil. Its first biofuels plan, in 2002, was amended after the entry into force of the Kyoto Protocol in 2005 to include incentives for the adoption of biofuels for the transport sector, which depends entirely on imported fuel. Its 74 million motor vehicles consume some 60 billion litres of gasoline and 36 billion litres of diesel fuel per year. While Japan's long-term goal is to promote domestic biofuels production using cellulosic technology, over the medium term its

[25] The documents necessary for the provision of such evidence have themselves become a market. In the meanwhile, illegal logging still predominates, in part as a response to what is perceived as being an inequitable situation in which the current regulations benefit large-scale players.

commitment to the reduction of CO2 emissions has involved the promotion of trade and investment with supplier countries such as Brazil.

In 2006, Japan launched a cooperative effort with Brazil to ensure a stable, long-term supply of biofuels. The Japanese Bank for International Cooperation (JBIC) offered the Brazilian Agricultural Research Corporation (EMBRAPA) support for the implementation of the National Agroenergy Programme (Seedlings, 2007). In a departure from earlier cooperation programmes, however, the objective was to ensure direct, long-term contractual supply arrangements for the Japanese market (Mongabay, 2010). In this first agreement, Japan proposed to finance research, agricultural development and the construction of industrial plants for ethanol and biodiesel for R$ 1.286 billion. These soft loans were executed by the Brazilian Development Bank (BNDES) and were provided on an individual project basis (Zanatta, 2006).

At the same time, several Japanese firms entered into agreements with Brazilian firms. In 2007-2008, Japanese firms committed some US$ 600 million to the biofuels sector in Brazil (Equipe Ecoviagem, 2005). Examples include:

- From 2007 onward, Japanese imports of bio-ETBE have been conducted by Japan Biofuels Supply LLP (JBSL). In 2008, JBSL signed a long-term supply contract with Copersucar. The Mitsui Oil Co. initiated the sale of E3 gasoline, supplied by a Japanese affiliate of Petrobras. In 2008, Mitsui and Petrobras announced the launch of a joint investment programme for the construction of ethanol plants in the Brazilian Cerrados region (Soares, 2007).
- In 2007, the Japanese trading company Sojitz, together with the Brazilian company Odebrecht, created ETH Bioenergia for the production and marketing of sugar and alcohol (D´Ercole, 2007). Sojitz acquired a 33% interest in ETH. ETH took over the Alcidia plant in São Paulo State in 2007 and planned to invest R$ 5 billion for the construction of 10 new units in São Paulo, Mato Grosso and Goiás. In 2010, ETH, along with Sojitz, acquired a majority share (65%) in the ailing Brenco enterprise, out of which emerged ETH Bioenergia (Scaramuzzo, 2009). These two firms have already invested R$ 3.8 billion in the sector and by 2012 will be producing 3 billion litres of ethanol, will be generating 2,700 GWh of electrical energy and will be milling 40 million tons of sugar cane in 9 plants. ETH Bioenergia is striving to be the leading firm in the sector and has attracted the interest of Petrobras, which has plans to become a minority shareholder (Bronzatto, 2010). ETH Bioenergia already has a sugar-cane venture in Angola and is looking to expand its investments into other Latin American countries and into Africa.

- Petrobras, for its part, formed a joint venture (Brazil-Japan Ethanol (BJE)) with Japan Alcohol Trading Company. It set up a plant in Japan for the production of E3 with a capacity of 3 million litres per month. The gasoline is supplied by the Nansei Sekiyu refinery in Okinawa, in which Petrobras has an 87% share. With this investment, Petrobras is aiming to convince the Japanese business community of the economic and technical viability of this new fuel (Rosas, 2009).

Despite these individual initiatives by Japanese and Brazilian firms, the Japanese government was not confident that long-term biofuels supplies would be secure. To address this concern, in 2007 Petrobras and Mitsui announced their intention to invest US$ 8 billion in the construction of some 40 plants for the export of ethanol to Japan. The Japan Development Bank (JBIC) would help finance these distilleries provided that their output was destined exclusively for the Japanese market (Soares, 2007). In addition, Petrobras, once again along with Mitsui and in collaboration with the Brazilian firm Camargo Correia, announced that studies were being conducted on the possibility of constructing a pipeline for the export of ethanol to Japan. The Petrobras – Mitsui initiative is one of three plans for proposed pipelines. A second involves a leading Brazilian firm, Cosan, with which China is negotiating long-term supply contracts, and Brenco (now ETH Bioenergia – Odebrecht & Sojitz), which has been developing plans with a Dutch holding company aimed primarily at the United States market (Latin American Herald Tribune, 2010).

Japanese policy also promotes the development of biodiesel. Government policy provides for a blending ratio of under 5%, but tax exemptions have sparked many initiatives aimed at attaining a 100% biodiesel (B100) fuel. Local governments and NGOs have promoted the production of rapeseed oil for cooking and its subsequent collection for recycling as a biofuel. Another policy option in the case of diesel fuel has been the introduction of tax incentives for the adoption of clean (sulphur-free) diesel, which is now available nationally. The principal strategy, however, would seem to be the extraction of oil from algae, which is thought to be capable of meeting from 10% to 20% of domestic demand for diesel (GAIN, 2010). The JICA cooperation programme also supports a biodiesel programme being run by the government of the State of Rio Grande do Norte (2009-2013), which involves the planting of a range of oil crops by 2,000 small farmers with the assistance of the Brazilian government and with crop-purchase guarantees from Petrobras (ABC, 2009).

JICA, Mozambique and Brazil signed a tripartite agreement in 2009 that was aimed at reproducing the success of the cooperation initiative that opened up the Brazilian Cerrados region to food crop production. The Cerrados development model is an alternative to the large-scale land purchases now being undertaken by resource-poor countries, which could weaken regional food security. The proposed new model is geared to enhancing the productivity of small farmers and promoting wider regional development through the establishment of agricultural processing systems (JICA, 2010).

The Japanese government has played a proactive role in the definition of responsible agricultural investment (RAI). It co-organized two round tables on the subject in 2009 and 2010 that were attended by representatives of many countries and multilateral and civil society organizations. The round tables dealt with growing international concerns about the recent surge in large-scale vertical investments in developing-country agriculture, in particular those involving land acquisitions by foreign investors. Poorly conceived or executed investments can have unintended negative impacts in terms of political stability, social cohesion, household food security and environmental protection for the receiving country, especially at the local level (government of Japan, 2010). In view of this state of affairs, the Japanese government and four international organizations formulated a number of RAI principles.[26] Attendees discussed the utility of an agreed set of voluntary RAI principles, while acknowledging the complex challenges associated with their implementation (government of the Unites States, 2010).

E. Final considerations

The potential for Asian investment in Latin American agribusiness needs to be evaluated in the context of the major changes which have taken place in this sector in the past two decades. In developing countries, the agricultural sector has become relatively more attractive to foreign investors, while the manufacturing segment (food and beverage processing) has become less attractive than it is in developed economies. The availability of land seems to have become a priority for foreign investors (especially those from resource-poor countries) and, as a consequence, in recent years developing nations have received more inward FDI stock in agriculture, forestry and fishing than developed nations have. In Latin America, more specifically, foreign investors have been attracted by activities related to food production,

[26] In particular, RAIs should respect rights to land and associated natural resources; improve food security; be transparent; be monitored and ensure accountability on the part of all stakeholders; respect the rule of law; reflect the industry's best practices; be economically viable; result in durable, shared value; generate desirable social and distributional impacts; encourage sustainable resource use; minimize the risk/magnitude of negative impacts; and mitigate those impacts.

(cereals, soybeans, poultry and meat), but also by the relatively new business of biofuels production. At the same time, developing countries have become relatively less attractive to FDI in the food and beverage processing industry, and more investment in that industry has been channelled to developed economies. This situation may now be changing due to the high growth rates of emerging markets.

Developing Asia has emerged as an important source of FDI in agriculture, forestry and fishing in Latin America. Asian investors are already active in various Latin American industries. Examples include Korean investments in fisheries (Argentina and Uruguay); Taiwanese business alliances with local entrepreneurs of Chinese descent in other agrifood businesses; and Malaysian investments in logging (Brazil), beef production (Argentina) and fisheries (Chile). Chinese companies have also showed an interest in soybean production in Latin America. Many Asian investors are from countries which are poor in natural resources. Because of this, Asian governments often support Asian companies' efforts to invest in foreign agricultural sectors by providing them with cheap credit or by supporting the investors' negotiations with host countries. As a consequence, Latin American governments will probably need to adapt their FDI policies and strategies, since, in this respect, Asian investors differ from the "traditional" Western investors in this Latin American sector.

Asian FDI in the food and beverage manufacturing industry has exhibited a different dynamic. Unlike Western TNCs in this industry, Japanese TNCs have preferred to concentrate on their home region, including their own domestic market. There has been some Japanese investment in a few nations in the region, such as Brazil, however. This trend in Japanese investment is likely to grow stronger in the future, especially in those Latin American countries where the demand for processed foods and beverages is increasing owing to high rates of economic growth.

The case studies show that Asian FDI differs from Western FDI. The Japan-Brazil Cerrados cooperation programme, seen by Japan as its most significant initiative in this connection in the 1980s and 1990s, was not matched by comparable investments from its leading TNCs. These firms were more focused on Asia and/or developed-country markets and benefitted little from the opportunities opened up through the consolidation of the Brazilian soybean complex. Asian and particularly Malaysian investments in logging in the 1990s, on the other hand, were unrelated to broader bilateral cooperation programmes or agreements. They were instead part of the global strategies of leading Asian TNCs whose concern was to access new sources of raw materials.

China, for its part, operates quite differently in some sectors. In the case of logging investments in Peru, China's involvement differed from that of the United States in that this sector was not subject to specific regulations with regard to the negotiation of bilateral agreements. On the one hand, the adoption of a forestry certification strategy by China in its domestic market certainly provides a different framework for private investment decisions. In the food and biofuels sector, on the other hand, the Chinese government and State firms are more directly involved.

Japan's recent focus on FDI in Brazil, in addition to its triangular cooperation arrangement with Brazil and Mozambique for the development of the latter country's savannah region, has been combined with long-term contractual agreements for the provision of supplies to Japan's domestic market and with strong incentives for Japanese firms to invest in these sectors. Both objectives differ considerably from those that underlay the strategy adopted under the earlier cooperation programme aimed at opening up Brazil's central-western agricultural frontier.

Nevertheless, one feature that is common to both phases of Japan's cooperation activities has been their alignment with the priorities of the host country. In the case of the central-western frontier, cooperative efforts built upon the Brazilian government's PRODECER programme while, more recently, Japan's cooperation and investment proposals have been aligned with the host country's ethanol and the biodiesel programmes. Although, as discussed, the cooperation programme was the object of criticism from both an environmental and a social perspective, it was not the subject of an ongoing controversy within civil society. The same cannot be said of Asian logging investments in Brazil in the mid- and late 1990s. In this case, private firms from a number of Asian countries made a range of individual investments which failed to take into account the direction of government policy in the region or the sensitivity of civil society organizations and movements regarding the question of deforestation. The result was a parliamentary committee of inquiry which denounced the "Asian invasion".

Successful investment strategies adapt to the host country's and global concerns. Earlier fears at the local level about an "Asian invasion" of Latin American natural resources (including land, forests and mining) have been succeeded by a global concern with investment strategies that are seen as involving "land-grabbing", together with the spread of minimum social and environmental standards from niche markets to large-scale traditional agricultural commodities. Indeed, the justification given for the new biofuels markets is that they respond to social and environmental concerns. If they are to be successful, investment strategies must be in keeping with emerging global governance concerns. Japan has taken a lead here with the promotion of the Principles for Responsible Investment Initiative, which may become a minimum requirement of international credit institutions for future investments or part of the access conditions for major markets. The increasing attractiveness of Latin American countries to foreign investors suggests that RAI-style standards may become a key component of the future investment climate.

During the last decade, Latin American countries have increasingly directed their agriculture-based exports to emerging Asian markets. While this has been an important driver for Latin America's rapid growth during this period, there is concern that this trade pattern is associated with a trading-down strategy whereby the region is limiting its global competitiveness to primary production. This pattern has therefore posed the challenge of devising sustainable value-added investment strategies. Asian agribusiness, which has traditionally sited its investments in its own region, or in the markets of the developed world, has begun to increase its investments in Latin America. As demonstrated here, this is by no means a homogeneous process, and it is difficult to discern the accompanying patterns, given how very recent the trends under scrutiny are. This analysis does suggest, however, that virtuous-circle investment strategies are, above all, aligned with host-country priorities and with the emerging patterns of global governance.

Bibliography

ABC (2009), "Brasil e Japão firmam Projeto de Cooperação Técnica para Incentivo de produção de Biodiesel", 29 January [online] www.abc.gov.br/lerNoticia.

Agustin-Jean, L. (2006), "Les investissements directs étrangers agro-alimentaires japonais en Chine et la recomposition des territories: du global au local", *Géographie, Économie, Société*, No. 8.

Anastassopoulos, G. and R. Rama (2005), "The performance of multinational agribusinesses: effects of product and geographical diversification", *Multinational Agribusinesses* , R. Rama (ed.), New York and London, Haworth Press Inc.

Banalieva, E.R. and R. Sarathy (2006), "The impact of international trade agreements on the global orientation of emerging market multinationals", *Management International Review.*

Bronzatto, T. (2010), "Petrobras avalia entrar na ETH-Brenco", Portal Exame, 18 February [online] http://portalexame.abril.com.br.

Borregaard, N., A. Duffy and L. Winchester, (2008), "Effects of Foreign Investment versus Domestic Investment on the Forestry Sector in Latin America (Chile and Brazil)", Working Group on Development and Environment in the Americas, Discussion Paper, No. 15 [online] http://ase.tufts.edu/gdae/WGOverview.htm.

Buckley, P.J. and others (2007), "The determinants of Chinese outward foreign direct investment", *Journal of International Business Studies*, No. 38.

Burch, D. and J. Goss (2005), "Regionalization, globalization, and multinational agribusiness: a comparative perspective from Southeast Asia" *Multinational Agribusinesses*, R. Rama (ed.), New York, Haworth Press Inc.

Chantasasawat, B., K.C. Fung, H. Izaka, and A. Siu (2008), "Multinational enterprises in China, East Asia, Latin America and Eastern Europe. Moving out or moving in?", *Journal of Chinese Economic and Foreign Trade Studies*, No. 1.

Chobanova, Y. (2007), "Global strategies of Nestle, Unilever and InBev and their impact in the CEE region", Social and Political Science Department, Firenze (Italy), European University Institute.

D´Ercole, R (2007), "Odebrecht se associa à Japonesa Sojitz para a Produção de Álcool e Açúcar", *O Globo*, 30 October.

Dunning, J. H. (2000), "The eclectic paradigm of international production: a personal perspective", *The Nature Of The Transnational Firm*, C.N. Pitelis and R. Sugden (eds.), London, Routledge.

Dunning, J.H. (1980), "Toward an eclectic theory of international production: some empirical test", *Journal of International Business Studies*, No. 11.

Dunning, J. H. and A. Rugman (1985), "The influence of Hymer's dissertation on the theory of FDI", *American Economic Review*, No. 75.

ECLAC (Economic Commission for Latin America and the Caribbean) (2005), "Trans-latins in the food and beverages industry", *Foreign Investment in Latin America and the Caribbean, 2005*, Santiago Chile.

Equipe EcoViagem (2005), "Japoneses estão interessados em investir no Biocombustível Brasileiro", AG Comunicação Ambiental.

FAO (Food and Agriculture Organization of the United Nations) (2004), *The State of Agricultural Commodity Markets*, Rome.

Farina, E. and A. Viegas (2005), "Multinational firms in the Brazilian food industry", *Multinational Agribusinesses*, R. Rama (ed.), New York, Haworth Press.

Filippaios, F. and R. Rama (2008), "Globalisation or regionalistion? The strategies of the world's largest food and beverages MNEs", *European Management Journal*, No. 26.

Fung, K.C., A. García-Herrero and A. Siu (2009), "A comparative empirical examination of outward foreign direct investment from four Asian Economies: People's Republic of China, Japan, the Republic of Korea, and Taipei, China", *Asian Development Review*, No. 26.

GAIN Report (2010), *Japan: Biofuels Annual*, USDA Foreign Agricultural Service, Washington, D.C.

Gereffi, G. and J. Humphrey (2003), "The Governance of Global Value Chains: an analytical framework", unpublished.

Gereffi, G., T. Sturgeon and J. Humphrey (2005), "The governance of global value chains", *Review of International Political Economy*, vol. 12, No. 1.

Girado, G.G. (1999), "Evolución y perspectivas de la inversión extranjera directa asiática en el Mercosur y Chile", *Panorama del Mercosur*, No. 4, Secretaría de Relaciones Económicas Internacionales Centro de Economía Internacional, Ministry of Foreign Affairs and International Trade of Argentina [online] www.asiayargentina.com.

Government of Japan, "Advancing the Initiative on Responsible Agricultural Investment" [online] www.farmlandgrab.org [date of refrence: 15 October 2010].

Government of the United States (2010), "Roundtable on Responsible Agricultural Investment (RAI)".

Greenpeace (1999), "Face a Face com a Destruição", May [online] www.greenpeace.org.

___(1997), "Desflorestando a Planeta: Madeireiras Asiáticas invadem nossa últimas fronteiras floestais", São Paulo.

___(2005), "Our Role in Stopping the Illegal Mahogany Trade", 2003 updated [online] http://www.greenpeace.org/usa/news/our-role-in-stopping-the-illeg.

Gutiérrez, H. (1998), "Asian conglomerates and regionalism in the Southern Cone of Latin America" Project on Latin America and the Pacific Rim University of California, San Diego.

Harago, Y. (1993), "Mitsubishis´s Investments in Brazil: a case study of Eidai do Brasil Madeiras S. A.", Rainforest Action Network, San Francisco.

JICA (Japan International Cooperation Agency) (2010), "JICA development model to encourage increased agricultural production in Africa" [online] farmlandgrab.org/11756.

Latin American Herald Tribune (2010), "Brazil's Petrobras Eyes 2011 Start-up for Ethanol Pipeline", [online] www.laht.com/article.asp?ArticleID=359968&CategoryId=14090.

Lederman, D. and W. F. Maloney (2007), "Trade Structure and Growth", *Natural Resources, Neither Curse nor Destiny,* D. Lederman and T. N. Srinavasan (eds.), Palo Alto, Stanford University Press.

Lederman, D., M. Olarreaga and G.E. Perry (eds.) (2009), *China's and India's Challenge to Latin America. Opportunity or Threat,* Washington, D.C., World Bank.

Lentini, M. A. Verissimo and D. Pereira (2005), "The Expansion of Logging in the Brazilian Amazon", May [online] www.imazon.org.

Luo, Y. and R.L. Tung (2007), "International expansion of emerging market enterprises: A springboard perspective", *Journal of International Business Studies*, vol. 38.

Macqueen, D. (2003), *Growing Exports*, Herfordshire, Earthprint Ltd.

Malamud, C. (2007), "Outside players in Latin America: China", Working Paper 50/2007, Madrid, Real Instituto Elcano.

Mongabay.com, "Brazil-Japan Ethanol Investment worth US$ 8 billion" [online] mongabay.com [date of reference: 15 October 2010].

Nazareth Satyanand, P. (2011), "India's agriculture and food multinationals: a first look", *Transnational Corporations Review,* No. 3.

Nicolas, F. and S. Thomsen (2008), "The rise of Chinese firms in Europe: Motives, strategies and implications", Asia Pacific Economics Association Conference, Beijing.

Pietrobello, C. and R. Rabelotti (2004), "Upgrading in clusters and value chains in Latin America: the role of policies", *Sustainable Department Best Practices series,* New York.

Putzel, L., C. Padoch and M. Pinedo-Vasquez (2008), "The Chinese Timber Trade and the Logging of Peruvian Amazonia".

Rama, R. (1992), *Investing in Food*, Paris, OECD Development Centre Studies.

___(1998), "Growth in food and drink multinationals, 1977-94: an empirical investigation", *Journal of International Food & Agribusiness Marketing*, No. 10.

Rama, R and J. Wilkinson (2008), "Foreign direct investment and agri-food value chains in developing countries: a review of the main issues", *Commodity Market Review*, No. 2007-8, FAO.

Rosas, R. (2009), "Petrobras produz Gasolina com Estanol no Japão", *Valor Econômico*, 3 March.

Saavedra-Rivano, N. (1999), "Trade and foreign direct investment between Asia and Latin America", *Asian Journal of Latin American Studies*, No. 2.

Santiso, J. (2006), "¿Realismo mágico? China e India en América Latina y Africa", *Economía Exterior*, No. 38.

Scaramuzzo, M. y V. Dezem (2009), "ETH e Brenco vão se unir para criar nova empresa", *Valor Econômico*, 10 September.

Seedlings (2007), "Snapshot of the agrofuel situation in some Asian countries", July [online] www.grain.org.

Sethi, D. (2009), "Are multinational enterprises from the emerging economies global or regional?", *European Management Journal*, No. 27.

Sim, A.B. (2007), "Emerging Southeast Asian and Taiwanese Multinational Firms and their Internationalization Strategies" Oxford Business & Economics Conference, United Kingdom.

Soares, P. (2007), "Petrobras e Japão fazem Parceria no Álcool" 3 March [online] folha.com.

Stopford, J.M. and J. H. Dunning (1983), *Multinationals. Company performance and global trends*, London, McMillan Publishers.

Tozanli, S. (2005), "The rise of global enterprises in the world's food chain", Multinational Agribusinesses, R. Rama (ed.), New York, Haworth Press Inc.

Viana, G. (1998), "Relatório da Comissão Externa destinada a averiguar a aquisição de madeiras, serrarias e extensas porções de terras brasileiras por grupos asiáticos", Câmara de Deputados, Governo do Brasil, Brasília.

UNCTAD (United Nations Conference on Trade and Development) (2006), *South-South Commodities Trade Quantitative Report*, Geneva.

___(2009), *World Investment Report 2009. Transnational corporations, agricultural production and development*, Geneva.

Wilkinson, J. (2004), "The food processing industry, globalization and developing countries", *Electronic Journal of Agricultural and Development Economics*, No. 12.

Zanatta, M. (2006), "Japão Investe em Etanol e Biodiesel", *Valor Economico*, 31 June.

Chapter II

The changing nature of Asian investment in Latin American manufacturing: a value chain analysis

Jae Sung Kwak

Introduction

This chapter assesses the changing nature of Asian foreign direct investment (FDI) in Latin American manufacturing, with a focus on the position of Latin America within Asian global value chains. Value chain analysis helps to evaluate the local benefits of participating in the global economy. The study also identifies the policies that have enabled individual producers and countries to increase their shares in these gains. At the same time, the report seeks to depart from the dichotomy of whether globalization benefits or harms the poor within the context of bilateral relations between Asian and Latin American countries.

Current trans-Pacific investments are largely dominated by Asian investment in Latin America, which is concentrated in four areas of the manufacturing sector (steel, automobiles, electronics and textiles); investment in the other direction is still minimal. To begin with, Japanese firms have a long history —since the mid-1950s— of involvement in the production of steel products in Latin America, and in more recent times Korean companies have begun to invest in Latin America as well. Second, increasing demand for automobiles and the strengthened global competiveness of Chinese, Korean and Japanese firms have resulted in large-scale investment projects in Latin America. Japanese companies such as Toyota, Honda and Nissan have paved the way for their Korean and Chinese peers to follow. Third, Asian brands are leading the global market as the principal innovators in the field of electronics. Here, the trend is twofold: efficiency-seeking investment in Mexico for the United States market, and market-seeking investment in Brazil. Fourth, the Central American and Caribbean subregions have become export platforms of the textile and garment industry for the United States market. The main investors are Korean firms.

The focus on value chains is particularly useful for analysing the position of Latin America in the FDI and trade strategies of Asian multinationals. Value chains are "the full range of activities which are required to bring a product or service from conception, through the different phases of various producer services, delivery to final consumers, and final disposal after use." (Kaplinsky and Morris, 2000). A simple model of a value chain shows that production is only one of the elements in value added links. The present research focuses on the flow of multiple inputs and services in the production life cycle (see diagram II.1).

Diagram II.1
VALUE ADDED LINKS WITHIN A VALUE CHAIN

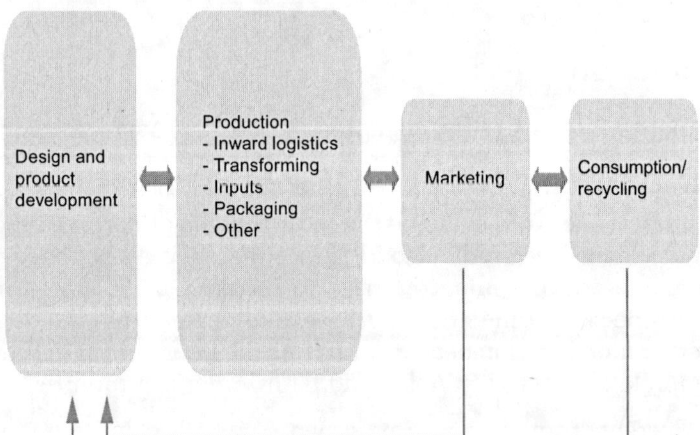

Source: Kaplinsky and Morris (2000).

An important dimension of value chains and global production networks is their power relations, in which one or a few firms dominate the overall chain or network (Gereffi, 1994). Two types of governance can be distinguished: those chains dominated by buyers (BDC: buyer-driven chains), and those dominated by producers (PDC: producer-driven chains) (Kaplinsky and Morris, 2000). Nevertheless, these two systems usually work together when it comes to FDI. This is exemplified in Korean FDI in the textile sector in Central America: initially, Korean clothing companies produced directly for the United States market. When Korea lost price competitiveness owing to rapidly rising labour costs in the 1990s, entrepreneurs changed their function in the value chain, subcontracting production to third countries like China, Viet Nam and Guatemala, and delivering these clothes to the buyers in the final market. In this example, it was the buyers that forced contractors to supply goods at minimum prices, whereas the decision to relocate production was made by the producers.

A case provided by Kaplinsky and Morris exemplifies the importance of value chains. The core competence of a firm in an export-processing zone in the Dominican Republic during the early 1990s was the sewing of materials designed and cut in the United States, which were then sold under the brand name of a major international company. That local firm received US$ 2.18 per pair of jeans sewn. As neighbouring countries devalued their currencies, the Dominican Republic firm was forced to systematically reduce its fee charged per pair. However, in the end, that was not enough and the work was eventually outsourced elsewhere. The vulnerability of this firm was its specialization in a narrow function (sewing) within a particular segment (production) of the value chain. Its value added was too low to improve efficiency, since most value was appropriated in the design and branding segments of the chain.

A. The steel industry

The steel industry's value chain has eight distinctive activities. It starts with the transformation of natural resources into an array of steel by-products used for the production of automobiles, housing appliances, industrial machinery, and many other commonplace devices. The first phase (I) includes mining exploitation of key inputs such as pig iron, coke and limestone. These three elements together are used to cast cold iron ingots and constitute the basis of every steel by-product involved in the fourth section. Both production phases (II and IV) are closely related to research and development (R&D) and have the two highest value added contents and returns on investment within the entire chain. Steel by-products can be commercialized directly for industrial use or further transformed by subjecting the final products to the fifth (V) section of the chain, in which final products are cut and undergo a finishing process; this step is chosen mainly when there is a demand for highly-specialized goods, as in the case of automobile components. Finally, distribution and sales are performed mostly by producers and retailers. In this industry, Latin America is sought chiefly for its natural resources and large markets for steel by-products.

Table II.1
FDI MOTIVATIONS OF ASIAN FIRMS INVESTING IN LATIN AMERICA IN THE STEEL, AUTOMOBILE, ELECTRONICS AND TEXTILE INDUSTRIES

	Venture	Home	Host	Entry mode	Start-up of operations	Sales target	FDI motives
Steel industry	POSCO Altamira	POSCO Republic of Korea	Mexico	Full ownership	August 2009	Mexican auto market and exports to the United States and to Latin America and the Caribbean	Resource-seeking: cheaper skilled labour compared to that in the United States. Market-seeking: with a clear objective to serve its clients in the United States and expand its presence throughout Latin America.
	Companhia Coreano-Brasileira de Pelotização (KOBRASCO)	POSCO Republic of Korea	Vale Brazil	Joint venture	October 1998	Mainly Korean market	Resource-seeking in the form of cheaper, higher quality of raw material to supply POSCO's manufacturing sites located in Korea. Strategic Seeking: The company was ultimately assuring a steady supply for its own home production, at a lower cost by dividing the risk with its Brazilian partner.
	NIPPON Steel USIMINAS	NIPPON Steel Japan	USIMINAS Brazil	Joint venture	October 1962	Brazilian market	Resource-seeking: NIPPON Steel sought a secure source of raw materials, while USIMINAS was after the achievement of technology and knowledge. Strategic-asset-seeking: the ultimate goal of both partners was market expansion and being able to serve the growing needs of a fast-developing Brazil, while also establishing a long-term relationship between downstream and upstream partners.
	BAOSTEEL Victoria Iron & Steel	BAOSTEEL People's Republic of China	Vale Brazil	Joint venture	An agreement was signed in 2007, but the investment never materialized		

Table II.1 (continued)

	Venture	Home	Host	Entry mode	Start-up of operations	Sales target	FDI motives
Automobile industry	Chery Socma	Chery People's Republic of China	Socma. Argentina and Oferol of Uruguay	Joint venture	March 2008	MERCOSUR market, especially Brazil and Argentina	Market-seeking: establish production in Latin America. Strategic-asset-seeking: Chery is China's number one automobile producer with a comparatively younger history. Thus, as the company grows, there is a pressing need to catch up and establish a presence within international markets.
	Moto Honda da Amazonia	Honda Japan	Brazil	Full ownership	1972, strictly imports, and from 1976 as producer	Brazilian market	Market-seeking: as a first comer, the company became Brazil's number one motorcycle brand.
	Honda Automoveis do Brasil	Honda Japan	Brazil	Full ownership	August, 1997	Brazil's market and the rest of MERCOSUR	Market-seeking: establishing a production base to serve the South American market.
	Nissan Mexicana	Nissan Japan	Mexico	Full ownership	September 1962	Latin America, the United States market and the global market in general	Resource-seeking: Mexico has a pool of skilled and comparatively cheaper labour. Moreover, the access to components is possible both through local vendors and imports. Market-seeking: Nissan Mexicana initially sought to enter the Latin American market and intensify its presence in the United States. However, nowadays, it exports to more than 90 countries. Efficiency-seeking: localizing global production to guarantee quality and better use of resources.

Table II.1 (continued)

	Venture	Home	Host	Entry mode	Start-up of operations	Sales target	FDI motives
Electronics Industry	Panabras	Panasonic Japan	Brazil	Full ownership	1967, as an importing branch, and from 1974 as a producer	Local market. Exports to Mercosur, Panama, Mexico & the United States	Market-seeking: the company first initiated operations to expand within Brazil and South America. However, since the establishment of its plant in Manaus, its exports have diversified to several countries in and outside the American continent.
	Toshiba	Toshiba Japan	Brazil	Full ownership and a joint venturea	1968	Brazilian market and an export hub for the rest of the American continent	Market-seeking: the company is nowadays a main provider of the electric power sector for many Latin American countries. Strategic-asset-seeking: In recent years, its home appliance brand has grown considerably, thanks to its alliance with Brazilian Sociedade Eletro Mercantil Paulista (Semp).
	Huawei	Huawei People's Republic of China	Brazil	Full ownership	1999. It operates branch offices, marketing, maintenance and overall customer service; without actual production facilities	Brazilian market and the rest of South America	Market-seeking: Huawei is perhaps a perfect example of market-seeking FDI. Its internationalization strategy has led to the establishment of branch offices around the world. Brazil and Mexico host the company's branch offices on the American continent.
	Samsung da Amazonia	Samsung Republic of Korea	Brazil	Full ownership	1995	Brazilian market and the rest of South America	Market-seeking: The company has managed to rank second in the Brazilian LCD TV market and has a strong presence in mobile phones and home appliances throughout the region.
	Samsung Mexicana	Samsung Republic of Korea	Mexico	Full ownership	1988	Mexican market. Exports are mainly directed to the United States, Central America and the Caribbean	Resource-seeking: cheaper labour and access to components. Market-seeking: Samsung has established an international operation in Mexico with broad networks that allow the company to serve not only Latin America, but also the United States and European markets
	LG Electronics do Brasil	LG Republic of Korea	Brazil	Full ownership	1995	Brazilian market	Market-seeking: The company was looking to expand its market share inside Brazil. However, tariffs were too high to do it through imports.

Table II.1 (concluded)

	Venture	Home	Host	Entry mode	Start-up of operations	Sales target	FDI motives
Textile Industry	Sae-A	Sae-A Republic of Korea	Central America	Full ownership	1998, starting in Guatemala	The United States market	Resource-seeking: vast pool of cheap labour. Market-seeking: the company needed to keep serving its American clients from a third country, since costs of doing so from Korea were too high.
	Hansoll	Hansoll Republic of Korea	Central America	Full ownership	1998, starting in Guatemala	The United States market	Resource-seeking: vast pool of cheap labour. Market-seeking: the company needed to keep serving its American clients from a third country, since costs of doing so from the Republic of Korea were too high.
	Hansae	Hansae Republic of Korea	Central America	Full ownership	1998, starting in Nicaragua	The United States market	Resource-seeking: vast pool of cheap labour. Market-seeking: the company needed to keep serving its American clients from a third country, since costs of doing so from the Republic of Korea were too high.

Source: Prepared by the authors.

[a] Toshiba runs factories in five locations in Brazil, of which three are a joint ventures with the local company Sociedade Eletro Mercantil Paulista (Semp) for the production of television sets, DVD players, telephones and other computer components.

POSCO and NIPPON Steel Corporation are both successfully operating similar activities in Brazil and Mexico. They differ, however, in terms of how they entered the region: POSCO entered in a mix of greenfield investment in Mexico and joint venture in Brazil, whereas NIPPON Steel formed an exclusive joint venture with a local company in Brazil. POSCO oversees its entire operation within Mexico, with a strong presence of Korean nationals in almost every key decision-making position. NIPPON Steel depends on its Brazilian partner for all its operations in Brazil. Finally, both groups retain most of their R&D activities in their home bases.

The Korean company POSCO has invested in Brazil and Mexico for different motives. In Brazil, the POSCO affiliate Companhia Coreano-Brasileira de Pelotização (KOBRASCO) has tried for more than a decade to secure access to low-cost, high-quality raw materials to feed its steelmaking operations in Korea. Its partnership with the Brazilian mining giant Companhia Vale do Rio Doce (Vale) has afforded it access to one of the world's largest mines. The KOBRASCO plant produces iron ore pellets which are shipped to Korea to be made into steel slabs and steel by-products. In Mexico, the company seeks to serve the northern hemisphere automobile market. For this purpose, POSCO has two mineral processing centres (MPCs, stage V), in Puebla and San Luis Potosi, where galvanized sheets are cut and stamped. It also has a continuous galvanized line (CGL, stage IV), which converts hot rolled coils into galvanized sheets. It also has two distribution centres for logistics and customer service.

Diagram II.2
STEEL INDUSTRY VALUE CHAIN

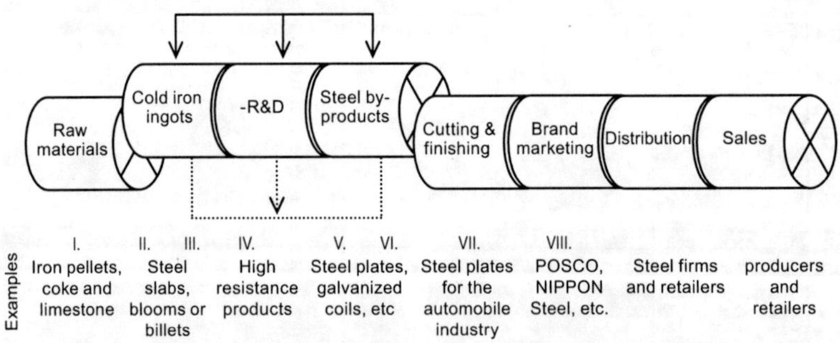

— High value added activities ...... Closely related with R&D

POSCO MEXICO
Stage IV: CGL Altamira.
Stage V: MPC in Puebla and San Luis Potosi
Stage VII: MESDC.
Stage VI - VIII: POSCO main branch Mexico, D.F.

NIPPON STEEL
Stage II: Raw steel production.
Stage IV-V: USIMINAS and Unigal.
Stage VII: Distribution centre.
Stage VIII: USIMINAS main office.

KOBRASCO BRAZIL
Stage I: KOBRASCO. Iron ore pellet plant.

Source: Prepared by the author.

The NIPPON Steel investment in Brazil, a joint venture with the Brazilian company USIMINAS, is completely vertically integrated along the entire value chain. Initially, the company focused on raw steel production (stage II), but later diversified product lines into the fourth and fifth sections of the value chain. It recently introduced an advanced production centre for hot-dip galvanized steel sheets for sale to the South American automobile sector. NIPPON Steel can access high-quality, low-cost raw materials through the domestic mining activities of its partner, USIMINAS. The company has a distribution centre (stage VII) to facilitate delivery from production centres to clients. NIPPON Steel depends largely on its Brazilian counterpart for its operations in Brazil, as it has few Japanese on the board or in other strategic positions.

There are two other Asian steel companies with significant investments in Latin America: Jindal of India and the Shougang Group of China. Jindal works the world's largest iron ore mine (El Mutun) in the Santa Cruz region of the Plurinational State of Bolivia, which has reserves of over 40 billion tons that are apportioned between Jindal and the Bolivian State (Lesova, 2007). The Shougang Group is the largest iron ore producer on the west coast of the Americas, in Peru (at Marcona, about 500 km south-east of Lima), and its operations include an open pit mine, beneficiation plants and a port, producing over 7 million tons. The company's product range comprises blast furnace pellets, direct reduction pellets, pellet chips, high-grade pellet feed, calibrated sinter feed, high-grade sinter feed and dolomite (Campbell, 2009).

1. POSCO CGL Altamira, Mexico

The Korean company POSCO is one of Asia's most profitable steelmakers, the world's third largest steel producer by total output and the second largest in terms of capital. It possesses a combined capacity of 35.5 million metric tons of crude steel, and reported sales over US$ 24 billion in 2009 (POSCO, 2010).

The Mexican affiliate of POSCO, POSCO CGL Altamira, produces steel products for the automobile industry, including processed products of cold rolled, hot-dip galvanized steel goods, and galvanized steel sheets.[1] The investment in Mexico was the first step in its

[1] Cold rolled products are used in the production of car body panels, while hot-dip galvanized steel products are used in civil engineering and construction, and in the fabrication of electrical and automobile parts. Galvanized steel sheets are also used in diverse areas, especially in the production of auto parts.

overseas expansion, following from the company's goal of becoming the world leader in automobile steel products. The POSCO approach has been gradual; two processing centres for cutting and stamping galvanized sheets were opened in 2007 and 2008, respectively, the first in Puebla and the second in San Luis Potosí. With an initial investment of US$ 25 million at each location, both plants have been processing 170,000 tons of auto steel sheets annually. In 2009, POSCO opened a continuous galvanized line (CGL) facility in Altamira. Map II.1 shows the strategic location of the plant vis-à-vis its major markets. This plant produces 400,000 metric tons of galvanized sheets per year (POSCO Mexico, 2009).[2]

The company's investments in Mexico are strategic for three reasons. First, Mexico is a major supplier to large automobile companies worldwide. For several decades, Mexico has been producing car parts for a range of automobile models and brands, in parallel with car assembling. Nowadays, the country has both low-cost, experienced labour and more than 1,000 parts suppliers to offer, which enhance the potential of automobile clusters and value chains. Second, Mexico has a free trade agreement with the United States and Canada. Third, national and local governments grant tax exemptions to foreign investors.[3] Its investments in Mexico have helped POSCO to gain a strategic position within the global market by placing its automotive steel production right on the doorstep of its major clients in Mexico and the United States, such as GM, Toyota, Mercedes, Volkswagen and Hyundai. Moreover, the company offers a full service package —sales, production and processing— to automakers throughout the region (POSCO Mexico, 2009).

POSCO Mexico currently employs 215 workers directly, and 450 indirectly. Of these, 47 have been trained in the Republic of Korea, in areas such as quality control, production, administration and marketing. Within the POSCO corporate organization in Mexico, most heads of department are Korean expatriates, which runs the risk of underutilizing local expertise.

---

2 The Altamira facilities complement the POSCO steel sheet processing plant in Birmingham, Alabama, which produces 120,000 metric tons per year. This combination strengthens the company's presence in the United States auto parts market, in addition to the strategic alliance of POSCO with US Steel.

3 For example, the Tamaulipas state government granted the CGL plant a three-year tax exemption and a 50% reduction in registration taxes (POSCO Mexico, 2010).

Map II.1
POSCO: LOGISTICS FOR AUTOMOBILE INDUSTRY IN MEXICO

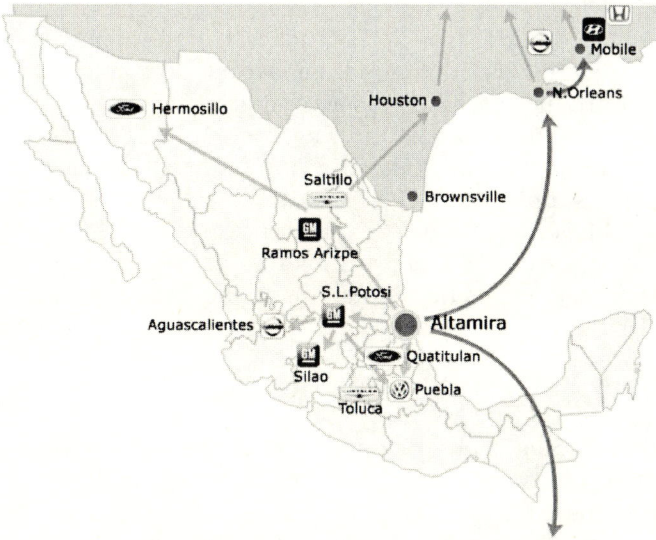

Source: Prepared by the author, on the basis of data from POSCO Mexico.

2. Companhia Coreano-Brasileira de Pelotização (KOBRASCO)

The Korean multinational POSCO and Vale, Brazil's largest mining company and world leader in iron ore pellet production, sealed a joint venture named KOBRASCO under equal ownership in October 1998. KOBRASCO operates an iron ore pellet plant with an annual production capacity of 4 million tons. Iron ore pellets are the raw material used inside blast furnaces to produce steel. Through this joint venture, POSCO has secured a stable provision of raw materials (pellets) for domestic steel and iron production. In the case of Vale, the move has represented an opportunity to increase its presence in Asian markets, while assuring a large, stable customer for its products.[4] As part of this joint venture, the KOBRASCO International Trading Company (KOBIN) was created to act as an intermediary for trade and financial transactions on the global market. Overall, KOBRASCO has been very profitable, except for

[4] Vale has other joint ventures for pellet production with Italian, Japanese and Spanish steel companies which are in close geographical proximity to one another and operate under similar lease agreements.

a setback as a result of the global crisis, when production fell by 30% during the first nine months of 2009.

About a decade ago, POSCO set about securing its supply of iron ore pellets in order to maintain a leading position in regional and global steel production. This was accomplished through joint ventures with the world's three largest mining companies: Rio Tinto and BHP Billiton in Australia, and Vale in Brazil, which together represented 70% of global supply. POSCO also joined forces with DONGKUK Steel (of the Republic of Korea) and Vale to build a steel mill in Ceará, Brazil, with a production capacity of 6 million tons a year. The fact that POSCO has strengthened its position in the region shows its strategic interest in Latin America.

3. NIPPON Steel USIMINAS, Brazil

NIPPON Steel Corporation is one of the largest steel producers in the world. In order to expand its production base, NIPPON foresaw the need to ensure access to raw materials and diversify its production geographically. It established joint ventures to ensure access to raw materials with major raw-material providers around the world, such as Rio Tinto and BHP Billiton in Australia, and Vale in Brazil.

In 1957, NIPPON sought to spread its production around the globe through strategic collaboration with the Brazilian State-owned company, USIMINAS. Together, they built a plant in the city of Ipatinga in the mineral-rich state of Minas Gerais. From 1962 to 2010, the joint venture expanded its annual production capacity from 0.5 million tons to 5 million tons in crude steel and to 11 million tons in steelworks (see table II.2). In 1991, USIMINAS was privatized, and the joint venture decided to diversify production: crude steel production fell from 96% to 80%, while other products grew from 4% to 20% in the 1990s.

Table II.2

USIMINAS AND UNIGAL – FOUNDATION, SHARES, PRODUCTION AND SALES

	Foundation year	NIPPON shares *(percentages)*	Production capacity [a] *(thousands of tons)*	Total sales *(millions of dollars)*
USIMINAS	1957	27.5	5 637 of crude steel 11 050 of steelworks	5 051
UNIGAL	1998	30	480 [b]	119.7

Source: Prepared by the author, on the basis of data from USIMINAS and NIPPON Steel Corporation.

[a] Total production for USIMINAS includes the consolidated production of the Ipatinga and Cubatão plants.

[b] With the initiation of the second UNIGAL plant in 2012, total production is expected to double by the end of that year.

The global crisis of 2009, the subsequent swift recovery of Brazil and other emerging markets, and the merger of ArcelorMittal increased the pressure on NIPPON Steel to strengthen its production bases and upgrade its technologies.[5] In this context, NIPPON and USIMINAS have built two plants: UNIGAL and UNIGAL 2. UNIGAL produces hot-dip galvanized steel sheets for automobiles, with an annual production capacity of 400,000 tons. UNIGAL 2 is expected to start operations in 2012 with a capacity of 550,000 tons per year. It has also invested in the production of new value added products for pre-salt oil exploration on the coast, such as Sincron (USIMINAS, 2010a). For this purpose, the company has invested in new accelerated cooling technology for plate production at its Ipatinga mill. Most of the USIMINAS production is for the domestic market while 20%-30% of its production is sold abroad.[6]

Most employees of USIMINAS and UNIGAL are locals, with the exception of some Japanese nationals holding senior positions. Both companies are headed by Brazilian nationals, and both vice-presidencies are held by Japanese citizens. During the early stages of the joint ventures, extensive training and internship opportunities in Japan were made available to key Brazilian engineers.

Increasingly diversified operations have made these joint ventures between NIPPON Steel and USIMINAS successful cases not only in Brazil, but also in Latin America.[7]

4. BAOSTEEL Victoria Iron & Steel Co., Brazil

In 2010, BAOSTEEL Group Corporation was the world's second largest crude steel maker after ArcelorMittal. The company produces mainly premium steel and operates in six sectors: steel industry, resource

---

5 USIMINAS was relatively well prepared for the crisis, having restructured the company and reduced its debt. NIPPON, for its part, strove to "enhance its manufacturing skills, capabilities and platform; sharpen its technological edge; bolster its global sales and marketing capabilities; and enhance its global production and supply structure to facilitate integrated, more strategic Group management" (NIPPON Steel Corporation, 2010a).

6 USIMINAS exports to Asia (China and Republic of Korea) and the Americas (Chile, the United States and Argentina). Surprisingly, the company sells little to Japan, notwithstanding the share of NIPPON in USIMINAS.

7 In 2010, USIMINAS established another joint venture (Mineração USIMINAS) until 2015 with a Japanese company (Sumitomo Corporation), to improve access to raw materials through an investment of up to US$ 4.1 billion in industrial plant, dams and loading terminals. It owns four mines in the Serra Azul region in the state of Minas Gerais, and land in the state of Rio de Janeiro for the construction of a port terminal. This partnership is strategic for USIMINAS, due to Sumitomo's expertise in selling iron ore as well as its global presence, especially in the Chinese market (USIMINAS, 2010c).

development, steel processing, technology service, and finance and production services. BAOSTEEL has been aggressively merging with other steel companies to expand its production capacity (BAOSTEEL, 2010). Unstable prices and increasing dependency on iron ore to supply its mills have been big concerns for the company.

Nonetheless, a joint venture initiative between BAOSTEEL and Vale failed in 2009. Seeking a more stable and less costly supply of raw materials, BAOSTEEL had established BAOSTEEL Victoria Iron & Steel in Anchieta, in the state of Espírito Santo, in partnership with Vale, Brazil in 2007, with an ownership split of 60% for BAOSTEEL and 40% for Vale, Brazil. The joint venture was intended to build a plant between 2009 and 2011, with a US$ 3 billion initial investment. Production was projected to grow from 5 million to 10 million tons annually and to create at least 3,000 direct jobs (Mofcom, 2007). However, the project encountered two obstacles: demand for steel dropped in the context of the global economic crisis in 2008, and the company failed to obtain an environmental licence. In 2009, both companies agreed to dissolve the joint venture. Vale acquired the shares of BAOSTEEL and changed the company's name to Ubu Steel Company (known by its Portuguese acronym, CSU). This new plant is scheduled to start operations in 2014.[8]

B. The automobile sector

The automobile industry value chain is complex, but may be summarized through the main activities that constitute the industry's backbone. The first section of the value chain relates to raw materials, including steel and rubber by-products. All the products and processes in this first category themselves form part of other value chains corresponding to different industries. The second section of the value chain is the production of parts and components. In this stage too, the array of component producers includes a multilayered system of providers. The present study only considers the first tier of component providers, as this receives the most investment from brand automakers.

The remainder of the value chain creates the most value, in particular the third and fourth sections. R&D and design are critical to the assembly process and final product. Once the product is developed and

8 Vale finally obtained the environmental licence in March 2011, after scaling down production plans to 5 million tons annually. Although the US$ 6.2 billion Ubu Steel Company is fully owned by Vale, the Brazilian group is looking for a partner to develop the project.

ready for sale, each brand spends heavily on marketing, as this, together with the quality of the product, determines customer preferences and loyalty. Producers and authorized dealers both participate in the final stages, including distribution and sales. These activities bridge the gap between producers and final buyers and are indispensable, regardless of whether the vehicle has been produced locally or procured through imports. After-sales activities, such as repair and inspection, reinforce the companies' traditional marketing channels.

Latin America's large and growing market makes it an attractive destination not only for companies seeking to export outside the region, but also for firms wanting to sell within the region itself. Most automobile companies that are already well established in Latin America are highly integrated along the value chain, while newcomers such as the Chinese Chery Automobile Co. Ltd. seem eager to follow the example of their peers, such as Nissan in Mexico and Moto Honda da Amazonia Ltda. in Brazil.

Chery, one of the China's fastest growing automakers, saw a market niche in an equally fast-growing Latin American region. Chery cars were so well received by the public that the company decided to expand its activities in the region by forming a joint venture with the Argentine group SOCMA. The two companies hired OFEROL S.A. to assemble sports utility vehicles (SUVs) and A1 compact cars in Uruguay (stage IV), to taps the benefits of producing within the Southern Common Market (MERCOSUR). About 60% of all parts come from China, Brazil and Argentina, while the rest is procured locally. The joint venture represents the largest FDI project in Uruguay, consolidating a local value chain. As sales have exceeded expectations, the plant has not been able to meet demand and the Chinese carmaker plans to expand production by building a new plant in São Paulo state, Brazil by 2013.

Given its active participation in the motorcycle market in Latin America in general, and Brazil in particular, Honda began operations in Brazil in 1971 by importing motorcycles through the establishment of Moto Honda do Brasil. Five years later, Moto Honda da Amazonia was created to produce stationary engines (stage II), motorcycles and all-terrain vehicles (stage IV). In addition, two more firms were created: one to produce and import motorcycle parts (stage II) and the other to work on innovation (stage III). Moreover, one warehouse and two distribution centres were established (stage VI). Finally, as a part of the company's brand creation and marketing efforts, Honda Access was established as a source of original parts, apparel and other services for Honda motorcycle riders.

Diagram II.3
AUTOMOBILE INDUSTRY VALUE CHAIN

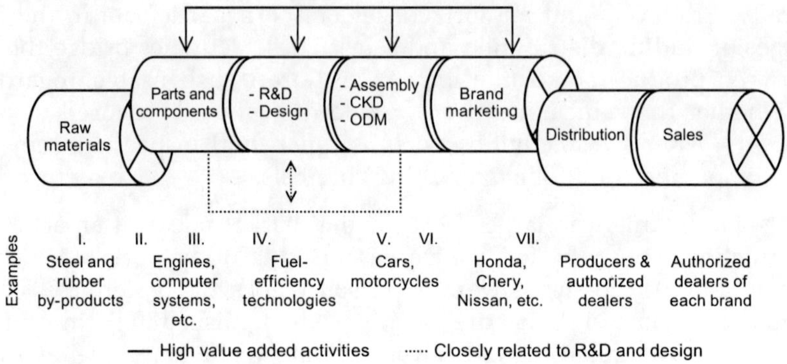

Chery-Socma Uruguay
Stage IV: CKD assembly plant.
Stage V-VI-VII: Marketing and sales dealerships.

Honda Automoveis do Brasil
Stage IV: Civic, City and Fit production.
Stage V: Marketing and brand creation
Stage VI -VII: Distribution networks and dealers.

Moto Honda da Amazonia Brazil
Stage II: Production of engines & power products.
Stage III: R&D innovation.
Stage IV: Motorcycles production.
Stage V: Honda Access and advertising
Stage VI -VII: Distribution centres and dealers.

Nissan Mexicana, S.A
Stage II: Engine manufacturing centre.
Stage III: R&D and prototype design centres.
Stage IV: Two automobile assembly plants.
Stage V: Marketing and brand creation
Stage VI -VII: Distribution networks and dealers.

Source: Prepared by the author.

In 1997, Honda entered the automobile-producing business in Latin America with a production plant (stage IV) for specific models (Civic, City and Fit models). Other car models were imported from Japan or the United States. Although Honda's automobile distribution network was smaller than its motorcycle network, the sixth and seventh sections of the value chain have clearly been in place since the company started its initial importing phase. Marketing and brand creation have likewise formed crucial components of Honda operations in Brazil.

Nissan also first explored Latin America through imports, starting with a network in Mexico, together with a warehouse and a distribution centre for Datsun cars and auto parts in 1959 (stage VI). Two years later Nissan started producing automobiles, and continues to do so today at two factories located in Aguascalientes and Cuernavaca (stage IV). Its entire operation revolves around the importance of R&D, for which a technological development centre, a prototype-modelling centre, and an emissions laboratory were set up. That section of the value chain was essential to the development of key components such as engines (stage II). Stages V through VII of the value chain are controlled by the main Nissan Mexico regional offices located in Mexico City.

1. Chery Socma S.A. Uruguay

In contrast with Brazil and Mexico, Uruguay only recently started manufacturing auto parts and assembling vehicles. Currently, there are around 40 manufacturers of automobiles and auto parts in Uruguay. Uruguay has struggled to make a name for itself within MERCOSUR and to attract foreign automobile investors successfully.

Chery Socma S.A. is a joint venture set up in May 2007 between Chery Automobile Co. Ltd. of China, Socma of Argentina and Oferol of Uruguay, with an initial investment of US$ 12 million.[9] Chery holds 51% of the total shares and the Macri Group (Socma) of Argentina holds the remaining 49%. Oferol of Uruguay acts as the assembler. The creation of Chery Socma was intended to combine Socma knowledge of the automobile market in MERCOSUR and assembly plants for Fiat and Peugeot in Uruguay and Argentina, with the innovative technologies and products of Chery.[10] Nowadays, Chery Socma produces 25,000 units per year.

The joint venture assembles SUVs and A1 compact cars in Carrasco, Uruguay, through a complete knocked-down or CKD process,[11] utilizing imported parts from China, Brazil and Argentina and local parts manufactured in Uruguay. Chery Socma targets mostly the Argentine and Brazilian markets. Initially, 40% of auto parts were procured within the region to meet the MERCOSUR rules of origin for tariff-free exports to other member countries. A special agreement between Brazil and Uruguay obliged the company to increase local content to 60% within a three-year period in order to continue to receive preferential treatment. If Chery were unable to meet the local content threshold, it would still be able to export a limited number of automobiles to Brazil tariff-free provided at least half of all parts had been procured locally.[12]

---

9 Chery reported remarkable growth: its first unit was produced in 1999, while its mass production grew from 50,000 to 1 million units between 2002 and 2007. Today, Chery is the fourth largest producer on the domestic automobile market in China and the leader among Chinese-owned groups abroad. Chery has formed alliances with large international automobile manufacturers such as Chrysler and Fiat.

10 In 2007, Chery also entered into a joint venture with Uruguayan firms Bognor and Socma to produce bulletproof automobiles at the Oferol facilities in Uruguay.

11 Complete Knocked-Down refers to a dismantled kit coming from the home country, to be reassembled at a subsidiary in the host country.

12 The 2008 automobile agreement between Uruguay and Brazil has been extended until 2014.

Diagram II.4
PROCESS PRODUCTION AND SALES OF CHERY SOCMA

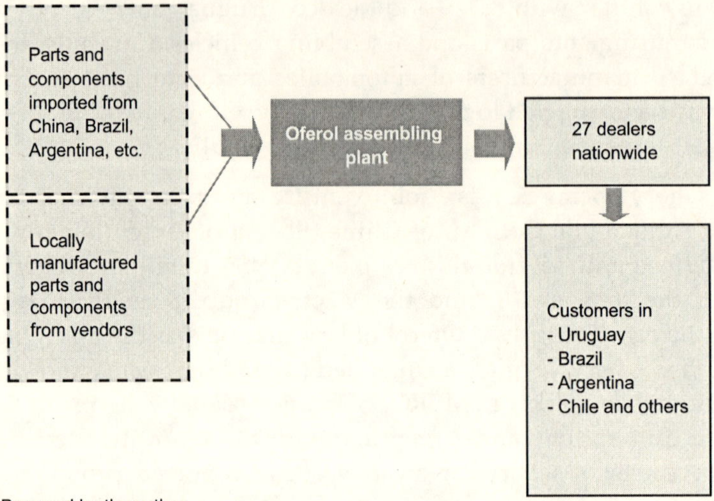

Source: Prepared by the author.

Moreover, Chery Socma constitutes the largest Chinese FDI project in Uruguay and is the first Chinese operation in the auto industry in Latin America. Apart from assembly companies, several foreign investors have entered the auto parts manufacturing industry in Uruguay, which reinforces the local industry's value creation and assures Chery of the procurement of raw materials. Examples of foreign investors with significant equity shares include Bader, ArcelorMittal, GKN Driveline, Dana Corporation, and Yazaki Corporation (Uruguay XXI, 2011).

Uruguayan automobile assembly lines had gained expertise after the creation of MERCOSUR, but subsequently suffered from the crises that hit Argentina, in particular, and the world economy in general (Bittencourt and others, 2010). The slacker demand following the crisis has proven disastrous for sustaining previous production levels. The World Investment Report stated that, by December 2009 alone, "production [in the automobile sector] fell year-on-year by over 51% in Brazil and 47% in Argentina" (UNCTAD, 2009). Several assembly plants had to shut down and, in the case of Oferol in Uruguay, had their focus redirected to armoured cars, with the plant using 30% of its installed capacity.

Despite the success of its SUV model Tiggo[13] on the Brazilian market after the 2009 crisis, the plant had trouble expanding production

13 The model was nominated (but finally not chosen) as "SUV of the Year" by Brazilian magazine Auto Sporte, which demonstrates the way the Chinese brand is valued in the Brazilian market.

to the degree expected by Chery (El País, 2010). In 2010, the Chinese group announced an agreement with the São Paulo state government in Brazil to build the first Chinese automaker plant in the city of Jacarei, with a total investment of US$ 400 million. The plant should produce 50,000 units annually by 2013.

2. Moto Honda da Amazonia

Honda Motor Co. Ltd. has several affiliated companies producing motorcycles, automobiles and power products, mostly located in Japan and other Asian countries. It has many subsidiaries on other continents, including Latin America: one in Argentina and three in Brazil.

In Brazil, Honda launched its activities in 1971 with Honda Motor do Brasil. It first imported motorcycles and two years later expanded its business to power products. In 1976, Honda built a plant called Moto Honda da Amazonia Ltda (HDA) to produce motorcycles, quads (all terrain vehicles – ATVs) and stationary engines, in Manaus, Amazonas state. HDA also controlled two other companies located in the same area: Honda Componentes da Amazonia Ltda (HCA), producing parts, and Honda Tecnologia da Amazonia Indústria e Comércio Ltda. (HTA), responsible for R&D. In 1992, Brazil began to liberalize imports, including automobiles and parts, and Honda started importing its cars. High demand for its imported cars led to the establishment of Honda Automóveis do Brasil (HAB) in 1997, in Sumaré, São Paulo state. By 2009, HAB had produced 700,000 automobiles and HDA 13 million motorcycles in Brazil.[14]

Despite the growing competition led by Yamaha, HDA has retained the leading position in the Brazilian market, with a 70%-80% market share. The most successful model has been the Honda CG FAN 125cc, which enjoys great popularity on account of its fuel economy, resale value and low maintenance cost. Although the domestic market constitutes its priority, HDA also exports motorcycles to other Latin American countries, its only exporter competitor within this sector being Yamaha.

HDA has subsidiaries in most parts of the value chain to satisfy its growing demand. Moto Honda da Amazonia runs a non-stop production plant in Manaus to meet the demand for motorcycles in Brazil. HDA has 742 dealers nationwide both for the sale of motorbikes and spare parts, and for providing after-sales service and repairs. HDA has also established an

[14] As expected, domestic sales and exports were affected by the international crisis in 2009. Nevertheless, projections by the Brazilian Association of Producers of Motorcycles and other two-wheelers (ABRACICLO) pointed to a recovery in 2010 and 2011 to levels similar to those of 2008.

R&D centre called Honda Tecnologia da Amazonia Indústria e Comércio Ltda (HTA).[15] In addition, Honda Componentes da Amazonia Ltda. (HCA) manufactures genuine parts and imports components needed for use elsewhere in the manufacturing process from Japan. HDA has a warehouse in Sumaré, and two distribution centres elsewhere, which maintain inventories and ensure the distribution of motorcycle spare parts nationwide. Honda Access Ltda. is a subsidiary that provides genuine parts and apparel for Honda motorcycle customers. Diagram II.5 depicts the relationships among the group's companies, offering an overview of Honda supply chain management.

Diagram II.5
SUPPLY CHAIN MANAGEMENT

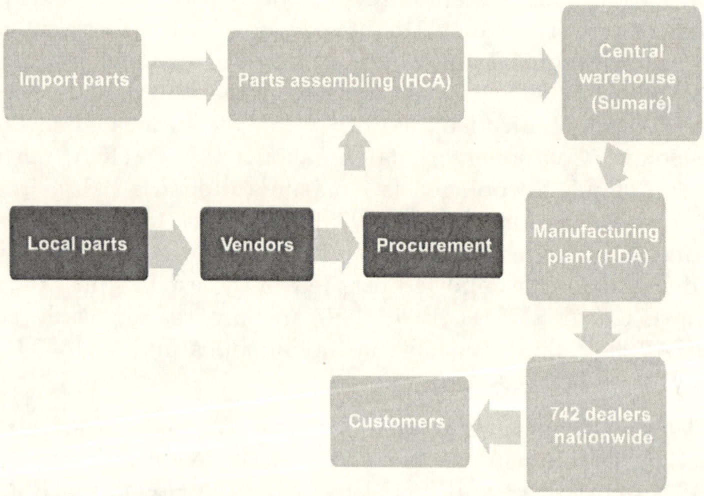

Source: Prepared by the author.

3. Honda Automóveis do Brasil Ltda.

After importing Honda automobiles for five years, HAB set up its first factory in 1997, in Sumaré, São Paulo. After 12 years of production, Honda ranked fifth (with a 5% market share) in the highly competitive Brazilian automobile market, behind Volkswagen, Fiat, GM and Ford, but ahead of Renault, Peugeot, Mercedes-Benz and Toyota. The company has adopted and introduced new production processes to maintain high quality standards.

15 In 2009, Honda started manufacturing and selling the world's first flexible motor fuel engines, equipped with a Mix Fuel Injection System in the new model CG150 TITAN MIX, which runs on a combination of ethanol and gasoline. This technology reduces carbon dioxide (CO_2) emissions and fuel costs.

So far, the company has focused on the production of three types of vehicle (City, Civic and Fit), which has enabled economies of scale. Honda's focalized production strategy within a single category has made its achievements in Brazil even more interesting. The latest model produced at the HAB plant is the City FFV (fuel flexible vehicle). Imports from production bases in Japan, Mexico and the United States cater for domestic demand for other models of Honda (SUVs and sedans). The four largest automobile producers have also dominated exports and yet, apart from Volkswagen —which has a much longer history in Brazil— Honda exports a smaller share of automobiles to other countries in the Americas than companies as Ford and GM (see figure II.1). The MERCOSUR countries are an important destination for Honda exports, accounting for up to 94% of exports of the Civic model.

Figure II.1
AUTOMOBILE EXPORTS FROM BRAZIL, PER COMPANY, 2011

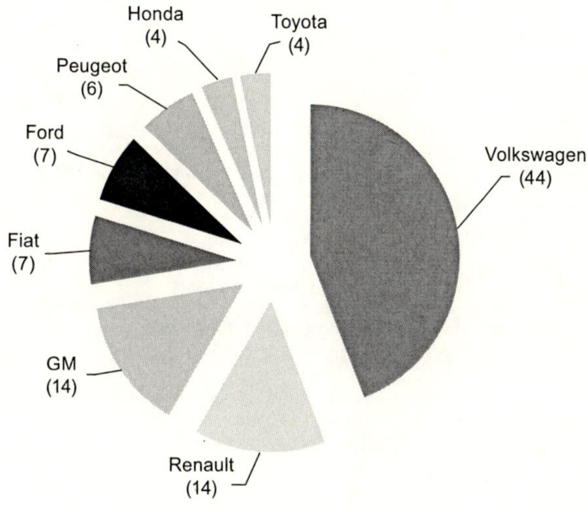

Source: National Association of Motor Vehicle Manufacturers (ANFAVEA) of Brazil, 2012.

4. Nissan Mexicana S.A.

Nissan Motors is a Japanese company (established in 1933) operating in auto manufacturing, sales and related activities, along with industrial and marine equipment businesses. Working in a strategic alliance with Renault for the past decade, the company's global production and sales were about 3.4 million units in 2009 (Nissan, 2010). Nissan has three production sites in Latin America, in Mexico and Brazil, and two sales networks in Chile.

Nissan Mexicana has become Asia's largest automobile producer in Mexico, and constitutes an important asset to the Japanese automaker. It has fully integrated production facilities for design, R&D, manufacturing, sales and management, at nine locations throughout Mexico, to meet the high demand from the United States and European markets (see table II.3). The latest addition to its value chain was a prototype-modelling centre located in Mexicali.

Table II.3
FACILITIES OF NISSAN MEXICANA

Facilities	Date (Location)	Main operation	Capacity
Corporative offices	May 1990 (Mexico city)	Management of general operation of marketing, service, logistics, design, domestic and overseas sales, customer service.	
Assembling plant	December 1982 (Aguascalientes)	Production of automobiles, (aluminum) parts, engines, etc.	202,500 automobiles and 648,000 engines are produced in two shifts. At the components plant, 168,000 transmissions are produced per shift.
Assembling plant	May 1966 (Cuernavaca)	Production of automobiles, parts, engines, etc.	140,000 automobiles and 90,000 light trucks
Test centre	June 1992 (Manzanillo)	Monthly audit on gas emissions for export Durability test for export	
Service and sales training centre	October 1970 (Mexico City)	Training centre for service personnel and sales	
Emissions laboratory	June 1975 (Mexico City)	Research for gas emissions reduction Certification and verification of gas emissions	
Auto parts distribution centre	June 1992 (Toluca)	Storage of automobile parts in 20,208 m^2 sites	75,102 parts in stock
Technological development centre	November 1994 (Toluca)	Design and development of suppliers	
Prototype modelling centre[a]	January 2010 (Mexicali, BCal)	Design and modelling of automobiles	

Source: Prepared by the author, on the basis of data from Nissan Mexicana.

[a] This facility is considered an investment by Nissan Design America in Mexican territory.

The group owns two production plants at Aguascalientes and Cuernavaca, with a production capacity of 350,000 units and 250,000 units, respectively.[16] Cuernavaca was the first Nissan plant ever established outside Japan. In 2010, the company announced a plan to increase its production capacity from 22,450 units to 134,000 units by March 2011. The Aguascalientes plant was established in 1982 as part of Nissan's strategic plan to strengthen its internationalization strategy. This plant was so successful that Nissan has used it as a benchmark for other production sites within the region and beyond. Competitive labour costs and State support have also contributed to its success. In 2006, the plant introduced a system of rotating three groups of workers in two shifts per day to keep operation at optimal capacity. As a result, annual production jumped from 203,000 to 350,000 units without any new investment in infrastructure.

The Aguascalientes plant has three sections: engine production, vehicle assembling and warehousing. The first section has two types of systems operating.[17] In the second section, the vehicle assembling process is divided into four stages. Steel plates are manufactured through press forming processes and then welded and processed in a vehicle bodyline. For this stage, the company adapted the Nissan Integrated Manufacturing System (NIMS) line, seeking to improve its operation while reducing the likelihood of error. Along with low labour costs, NIMS has helped to improve product competitiveness by achieving a 72% automation rate. After each unit has undergone the painting stage, the processed vehicle plates are moved to the assembly line.

After the North American Free Trade Agreement (NAFTA) came into force, the Government of Mexico eliminated several protectionist policies, including the Automotive Decree and minimum local content requirements (Moreno, 1996). Moreover, domestic manufacturers were allowed to import up to 10% of their total production into Mexico tariff-free. Most of the parts and components supply is still heavily concentrated with Japanese producers.[18]

---

16 The company may see production rise in the coming years due to the introduction of three subcompact models (*The Economic Times*, 2010).

17 One is a mixed production system that produces a large number of engines. The other, a caravan production system, manufactures fewer engines in a shorter time.

18 There are significant risks when production is highly concentrated in one country, in this case, Japan. Following the devastating earthquake and tsunami of March 2011 in Japan, several production processes across the globe have been affected by shortages of parts.

C. The electronics industry

The electronics value chain resembles that of the automobile industry in terms of its extensive nature and the key role of the procurement of raw materials. It includes several layers of parts and components producers. They sell not only amongst themselves, but also directly to the brand or company operating the final assembly. In the third section of the value chain, firms undertake R&D and design in an effort to enhance the scope and quality of the product line. Therefore, these activities are closely related to the manufacturing processes of main components and final assembly lines. Brand marketing is vital in promoting the public's acceptance of a given product. Its activities are intense, given the highly competitive electronics market and the rapid pace of technological change towards the offering of new products. Finally, distribution and sales are conducted by parent companies and authorized dealers.

With the exception of two companies, Asian investors in Latin America have integrated their operations throughout the entire value chain, except for the stages dealing with the production of raw materials and the creation of R&D centres. The first exception is LG Brazil, which has completely internationalized its operations and relies heavily on local human resources to develop regional business[19] So far, LG is the only electronics company to run a local R&D centre in São Paulo to strengthen its presence in the mobile market (stage III). The second exception is the Chinese group Huawei, which has a production plant for telecommunications products in Brazil, together with a manufacturing management support centre, a training centre for its employees, a spare parts centre and a logistics centre (stages V to VII). These additional investments have helped to create an extensive customer-oriented service network that enhances the Huawei market position in the mobile phone, USB modem, and mobile broadband markets.

Other FDI investors include Panasonic and Samsung. Panasonic has factories in two locations: in São José do Campos (São Paulo state) where it produces and exports batteries, flashlights, mechanical components for audio and video, and microwave components (stage II); and in Manaus (Amazonia), where it has a production plant (stage IV) and a component manufacturing plant (stage II). The other company is Samsung, for whom Latin America is the second most important continent in terms of investments. Samsung has operations in Manaus and Campinas in Brazil, where it assembles mobile phones, monitors, AV products and hard disk drives (stages II and IV). In 2011, Samsung added a new air-conditioner

[19] LG Brazil operates factories in the Manaus, Paulinia and Taubate regions. The first location produces televisions, videocassette recorders (VCRs) and A/C stations (stage IV), the second, home appliances and the third, mobile telephones and monitors (stages II and IV).

production line, while a laptop computer factory is expected to start operations shortly. Samsung has become a main provider of electronic goods within Brazil, with strong exports to the rest of Latin America (stages VI and VII). In Mexico, Samsung has production sites in Tijuana (on the Baja California Peninsula) and in Queretaro. Both plants produce liquid crystal display (LCD) and plasma display panel (PDP) televisions, mobile handsets and LCD monitors (stage IV). The Samsung distribution network covers the entire Mexican territory, guaranteeing local sales and exports to its most important market in the United States, and to other Latin American countries (stages VI and VII).

Diagram II.6
THE ELECTRONIC INDUSTRY VALUE CHAIN

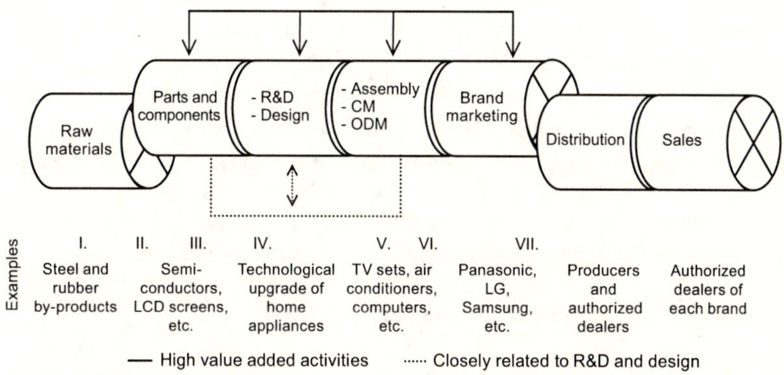

Panasonic Do Brasil (PANABRAS)
Stage II: A/C and home appliance components.
Stage IV: Two manufacturing plants.
Stage V: Marketing and brand creation
Stage VI -VII: Distribution networks and dealers

Samsung Electrónica da Amazonia (SEDA)
Stage II: Produces CRTs, monitors and HDDs
Stage IV: Runs two home appliance factories
Stage V: Marketing and brand creation
Stage VI -VII: Distribution networks and dealers

LG Electronics do Brasil
Stage II: Monitor production in Taubate
Stage III: R&D centre in São Paulo
Stage IV: Runs two factories in Manaus & Taubate
Stage V: Marketing and brand creation
Stage VI -VII: Distribution networks and dealers

Toshiba Brazil
Stage V: Marketing and brand creation
Stage VI -VII: Distribution networks and dealers

Samsung México
Stage II: CRT production line
Stage IV: Processing plants, Tijuana & Queretaro
Stage V: Marketing and brand creation
Stage VI -VII: Distribution networks and dealers

LG Electronics Mexico
Stage II: CRT production
Stage IV: Manufacturing of TVs and monitors
Stage V: Marketing and brand creation
Stage VI -VII: Distribution networks and dealers

Source: Prepared by the author.

1. Panasonic do Brasil Ltda. (PANABRAS)

In 1967, the Japanese company Matsushita Electric Industrial Corporation launched its first operation in Brazil, with a sales office in São Paulo. At that time, the company imported batteries from Japan and commercialized them locally. In 1974, it established a factory in São José dos Campos (São Paulo state), under the name of National do Brasil Comercial Ltda. and produced batteries under the brand name National. By 1980, the company was exporting batteries to Bolivia and televisions to Argentina, Paraguay, Uruguay and Panama. National do Brasil inaugurated an air-conditioner factory in 1984, and a home appliances division in 1987 (see table II.4).

Table II.4
CHRONOLOGY OF PANASONIC DO BRASIL (COMPANY STRUCTURE), 1967-2006

Year	Event
1967	Matsushita Electric Industrial Corporation opened an office in São Paulo
1974	The Matsushita Group established National do Brasil Comercial Ltda., a battery factory in São José dos Campos
1981	Springer National da Amazônia Ltda. was created in Manaus
1982	Springer National Componentes S.A. was established in Manaus
1984	National do Brasil inaugurated the air-conditioner factory in São José dos Campos
1987	National do Brasil created the Home Appliances Division
1988	National do Brasil became Panasonic do Brasil; Springer National da Amazônia and Springer National Componentes became Panasonic da Amazônia
2001	Springer sold its shares of Panasonic da Amazônia to Panasonic do Brasil
2006	Panasonic da Amazônia S.A. unified the name to Panasonic do Brasil Ltda. (PANABRAS)

Source: Matsushita Electric Industrial Corporation, 2008.

Matsushita expanded its operations to Manaus in 1981 as an export base to other countries in the Latin American region and to the United States. It opened a factory through a joint venture between National do Brasil and Springer Amazônia Indústria e Comércio. Springer had just finished a two-decade contract with a United States company (Admiral), which had provided the company with expertise in refrigerators and air conditioners. The production also made it necessary to establish Springer National, a parts factory, nearby. In 1988, the Matsushita Group changed the brand name from National to Panasonic, following an international strategy of brand unification. The company in Manaus proceeded to incorporate the parts factory and changed its name to Panasonic da Amazônia. In 2001, Springer sold its shares to Panasonic do Brasil, which now controls the entire production and sales process. Panasonic do Brasil in Manaus has made the most of its geographical location and the benefits of its special fiscal regime to boost exports to Colombia, the Bolivarian Republic of Venezuela, Panama, Mexico and the United States.

Adapting to the growing number of middle-income consumers in Brazil, Panasonic has become more aggressive in its sales strategy, advertising accessories for luxury cars and high-end home appliances. Today, Panasonic do Brasil employs around 2,000 people and plans to build another factory in Brazil before 2016. It produces batteries (manganese and alkaline), flashlights, mechanical components for audio and video, and microwave components at its São José dos Campos production site, and televisions, audio appliances, recorders, watches, microwave ovens, DVD players, cell phone batteries, digital cameras and LCD screens at its Manaus location.

2. Toshiba T&D do Brasil Ltda.

Toshiba T&D do Brasil Ltda. (TTB) is a subsidiary of Toshiba Corporation, and is located in the city of Contagem, Minas Gerais state. In 1968, TTB started off producing distribution transformers in Contagem. Today, the company produces a wider range of transformers, such as power, furnace, rectifier and cycle-converter transformers, as well as step voltage regulators, derivation shunt reactors, pressure relief valves and fans. This Brazilian Toshiba affiliate is strategically important to the Japanese headquarters, as it contributes to the development of the electrical power sector in countries within South, Central and North America. The company conducts business with clients in Colombia, Argentina, Paraguay, Guatemala, Mexico and the United States, in addition to Brazil.

The Toshiba Corporation also established another subsidiary in Curitiba (Paraná state), Toshiba Sistemas T&D do Brasil Ltda. (TSTB), which focuses on manufacturing equipment to supply energy generation, transmission and distribution, as well as on industrial and infrastructural goods. Its main products are SF6 gas circuit breakers, disconnect switches, protection and control systems, surge arresters, gas insulated or GIS substations, medium voltage or MV cubicles and vacuum circuit breakers. In sum, TTB (Contagem) produces transformers, targeting industries as clients, while TSTB (Curitiba) produces larger energy systems that target governments and infrastructural projects.

Toshiba Corporation also has a joint venture with Sociedade Eletro Mercantil Paulista (SEMP) in the industrial zone of Manaus, named SEMP Toshiba Amazonas S.A. This joint venture has become one of the main television manufacturers in Brazil. Over the past three decades, the company has diversified and modernized its production, including LCD televisions, digital television converters, DVD players, stereos and (fixed and mobile) phones. In 1998, the company entered the computer business by establishing Semp Toshiba Informática (STI) in Salvador, Bahia state. The growing demand for computers, especially notebooks, in Brazil, has led STI to expand its production constantly, employing over 400 people in Bahia alone. Another joint venture, Semp Toshiba Componentes, also located in Manaus, produces parts for both Semp Toshiba Amazonas and Informática.

3. Huawei do Brasil

Huawei Brazil was founded in 1999, with offices in Rio de Janeiro, São Paulo, and Brasilia. By 2005, its investment had grown to US$ 100 million (Huawei do Brazil, 2008). The Campinas facility includes a technical support centre, training centre, and a spare parts and logistics centre. Huawei employs about 400 staff, 75% of whom are local employees. It is the market leader in fixed and mobile broadband goods, holding about 70% of the USB modem market with more than 1 million terminals sold. The company also leads the supply of infrastructure for fixed and mobile telephone services in Brazil, serving other markets such as the Global System for Mobile Communications (GSM), Code Division Multiple Access (CDMA), Synchronous Digital Hierarchy (SDH) and Datacom. Most Huawei clients in Brazil and Latin America are local telecom providers, including Telemar.

By 2007, Latin America had become Huawei's most significant market. The company has no production sites in Brazil. It is mainly a service provider, focusing on the development and implementation of communications technologies, for which marketing and customer services are key areas. The company has partnerships with major national operators such as Telemar, Brasil Telecom and some government departments and major financial companies. Huawei has established four training centres in Latin America (in Campinas, Mexico City, Bogota and Caracas) with the capacity to train 380 trainees simultaneously. A wide range of high-quality technical training sessions have been made available. By May 2008, 12,000 trainees had been trained at these facilities.

Huawei Brazil has a threefold strategy: innovation, partnership and localization. The first, innovation, includes the introduction of next-generation technology such as voice-, data-, and multimedia services in emerging markets. The second, partnership in Brazil, is a long-term goal that seeks cooperation in logistics, engineering and support services. It may also go further to include strategic alliances with industrial leaders. The company's third strategy, localization, seeks to incorporate local entities and investment, hiring local staff, cooperating with local partners, logistics and support infrastructure, and establishing cross-cultural communication (Huawei do Brazil, 2008).

4. Samsung Electrónica da Amazonia Ltda. (SEDA)

Samsung Electrónica da Amazonia Ltda. (SEDA) was established in Manaus, Brazil in 1996 as a subsidiary of Samsung Electronics Corporation (SEC). Nowadays, it operates one plant in Manaus and another in Campinas, employing around 5,000 workers, producing electronics products such as television sets, mobile phones, monitors, as well as audiovisual (AV) products and hard disk drives (HDDs) for the domestic and overseas markets. SEDA sales grew rapidly to reach US$ 2.7 billion by 2008.

Brazil is attractive to Samsung not only because of its vast market, but also for its great potential as a production platform for the rest of the Americas. Traditionally, Samsung produced cheap home appliances, mainly in Brazil, Mexico and China, and concentrated the production of premium goods for the United States market at its Korean facilities (Park, 2010). However, in view of the need to satisfy the rapidly increasing domestic demand of middle- and high-income consumers in Brazil, Samsung decided to produce better-quality goods within Brazil, thereby reducing distribution costs and enabling a faster response to changing market conditions. With this goal in mind, SEDA invested heavily in the local production of leading Samsung products, such as mobile phones and television sets.

SEDA is a key player in the domestic market for television sets and mobile phones; it has now entered the market for air conditioners and computers as well. It ranked second in terms of market share of LCD television sets in Brazil in 2008. The SEDA Manaus plant produces 300,000 television sets per year. As Brazil produces only a few of the components of LCD and plasma television sets, most parts are imported from Samsung subsidiaries and other companies abroad. SEDA was the first company to introduce LED television sets in Brazil, and monopolized sales for about a year before competitors appeared. SEDA is also an important player in the mobile phone market. The company had planned to operate a new manufacturing line within the Manaus plant to meet increasing demand, with an annual production of about 500,000 mobile phones by 2011 (Jung, 2011). It is also entering new product markets: its Manaus plant began producing air conditioners in September 2010, and the Campinas plant will soon start producing computers.

The success of SEDA can be attributed, in part, to the creation of an innovative supply network. This system detects detailed global market changes by region and product, in real time, and distributes the information to supply and sales networks. In turn, production quantities are constantly adjusted to sales records. This system thus allows Samsung to adjust quickly to customers' needs (Park, 2010). Another reason for its success is that Samsung involves local human resources in running the business, including in management positions.

Table II.5
SAMSUNG ELECTRÓNICA DA AMAZONIA: PRODUCTION HISTORY, 1995-2011

Year	Production
1995 (December)	Started production of CRT TVs and VCRs
1996 (January)	Started sales
1998 (July)	Started production of computer monitors
1999 (March)	Started production of mobile handsets
1999	Stopped production of TVs
2002 (March)	Started production of HDDs
2004 (January)	Relocated mobile handset plant to Campinas
2004 (March)	Started production in Campinas
2004 (October)	Resumed production and sales of TVs
2007 (February)	Started production of mobile handsets (CDMA à GSM)
2011 (March)	Started laptop production

Source: Prepared by the author, on the basis of data from Samsung Electrónica da Amazonia Ltda. (SEDA).

5. Samsung Mexicana S.A. de C.V. (SAMEX)

Samsung established two subsidiaries in Mexico: Samsung Mexicana (SAMEX) in Tijuana, Baja California in 1988 and Samsung Electronics Mexico (SEM) in Queretaro. Prior to this, SAMEX had mainly produced cathode-ray tubes (CRT) for televisions, computers and cellular phones. Nowadays, SAMEX focuses on producing LCD and PDP television sets, LCD monitors and mobile handsets. Its plant in Tijuana produces over 1.3 million LCDs per month. Samsung is a leading electronics multinational, especially in the United States and European markets. Samsung's annual sales have increased by a 26% average since 2003, based on a market strategy of high quality and advanced technology. In addition, most products manufactured by SAMEX are exported to the United States and Canada (80%) benefiting from NAFTA, while the remainder is sold to the rest of Latin America (12%) and the Mexican domestic market (8%).

SAMEX uses large amounts of imported parts and components, such as casings, screens, panels, mother boards, semiconductors and other critical parts, from Chinese, Korean and Japanese suppliers. Many local suppliers are subsidiaries of other foreign firms. In Tijuana, 30 out of 53 supply companies are of Korean origin, and among those 30 companies, 70% are in partnership with SAMEX (see table 6). Few products and services are purchased from Mexican suppliers, as they often do not meet the strict quality standards established by SAMEX.

Table II.6
SAMSUNG MEXICANA: KOREAN SUPPLY PARTNERS, 1991-2007

Name of corporation	Year of entry	Handling area
Cobuy	2007	Electronic components
KOMEX	2006	TV & MNT cabinet
NOSCOM	1999	Electronic injection and assembly
Taewoo Mexico	1999	TV monitor stand base
Daedong Corp.	2000	Plastic moulding (TV)
Chemtronics	2007	PBA for LCD/PDP
Daewon	1991	Van-trailer parts
Daeha Cable	1997	TV and industrial wire harness, cable assembly
Samsung SDI	1995	Display device
Dongchul Mexico	1994	Bracket, heat sink
Seshin electronics	2001	EPS resin
Han-il electronics Mexico	1998	PCB assembly

Source: Samsung Mexicana (SAMEX), 2009.

6. LG Electronics do Brasil

In 1995, LG Electronics (LG) established production plants in Brazil, both to avoid high import tariffs on finished goods and to reduce the distance between production centres and the Brazilian market.[20] The firm has three production plants. The first is LG Electronics da Amazonia (LGEAZ) located in Manaus, which started operations in 1995 and produces home appliances such as TVs, VCRs, and air conditioners. The second is LG Electronics de São Paulo Ltda. (LGESP) operating in Taubate, which started in 1996 and manufactures mobile telephones and monitors. The third plant opened in Paulinia[21] in October 2011. Between 1996 and 2010, LG invested US$ 28 billion in its Brazilian plants, and plans to invest another US$ 5.8 billion for the production of LCDs and plasma television sets, aiming to produce 2.55 million television sets by 2012. However, LG products are manufactured with minimum local content. The Manaus plant reported that local supplies (plastic front and back covers and boxes) represent 6%-10% of all inputs in the case of CRTs, and 3%-4% in the case of digital television (D-TVs). In 2008, sales of LG Electronics do Brasil reached US$ 28 billion, with exports accounting for less than 7% of all sales.

[20] LG Electronics was founded in the Republic of Korea as Goldstar Co. Ltd. in 1958. In 1995, the company changed its name to LG. It has 114 subsidiaries around the world, employing 82,000 people. In Latin America, LG has sales offices in 12 countries, and production sites in Brazil and Mexico.

[21] The city of Paulinia donated the construction site and provided tax concessions for the operation of this new plant. In return, LG should employ at least 20% of the local work force.

The success of LG in Brazil can be explained, in part, by its emphasis on hiring local employees in every business area, including marketing and production. Korean workers take on only the role of connecting the subsidiary with the parent company in the Republic of Korea (Kim, 2010). LG aims to locate all stages of its production chain within the Latin American region, from R&D to production, sales and customer services.

D. The textiles and apparel sector

The global textile sector and apparel industries are both part of the same global value chain, but are situated in different groups of countries. Most apparel firms are in developing countries, benefiting from cheap, unskilled labour. In contrast, textile production has remained in developed or transition economies, as it is intensive in capital and R&D. High value added activities are concentrated in R&D, design and brand creation.

This section looks at Korean-owned apparel production affiliates in Central America serving the United States market. Being original equipment manufacturing (OEM) contractors for major brands, these companies also subcontract to smaller Korean small and medium-sized enterprises (SMEs) located in and outside the region, for such activities as procurement of raw materials (fabrics and trims) and shipment to final clients in the United States. Therefore, the value chain processes performed in Latin America are limited to design (mostly part of a full package deal), assembly and distribution activities.[22]

Over the past two decades, Korean companies have focused on OEM services, i.e. mass production of pre-ordered designs for their customers. However, lately, these large producers have entered the original design manufacturing (ODM) business, where companies participate in the entire production process and serve the final market by creating their own brands. Entering the design phase, while seemingly an upgrade of the Korean firms' participation in the value chain, is mostly intended to create their own collections for their home market. That is, the bulk of design projects are concentrated in the Republic of Korea.

In terms of production, exports and investment in Central America, the three largest Korean companies are Sae-A, Hansae and Hansoll. Sae-A is by far the largest Korean operation in the subregion, with six production lines located in Guatemala and four in Nicaragua. As part of its production facilities, Sae-A also owns printing technology for more

---

[22] There are other Chinese and Korean apparel producers in South America. However, their production capacity is smaller than that of producers in Central America, and produce for domestic markets.

sophisticated goods. The company's production consists mainly of crews, polo shirts, pants and graphic tees (stages V and VI). Hansoll, the smallest of the three Korean apparel firms in Central America, produces apparel at one location in Guatemala and another in Honduras, and works with several subcontractors to increase its production capacity. Hansae manages sewing factories in Nicaragua and Guatemala which, about a decade ago, had rapidly become Hansae's major sources of revenue. Recently, however, the company's expansion has been mostly in South East Asia, particularly in Viet Nam. Nonetheless, Central America remains an important contributor to Hansae's total revenues.

Diagram II.7
TEXTILE INDUSTRY VALUE CHAIN

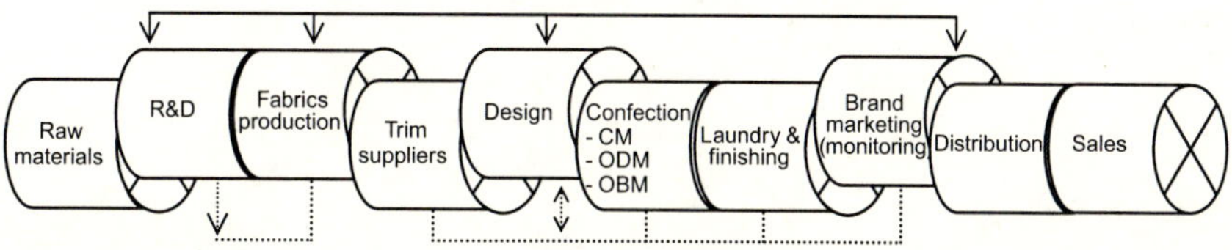

	I.	II.	III.	IV.	V.	VI.	VII.	VIII.	IX.	X.
Examples	Cotton, wool, synthetic fibres, etc.	Intelligent fabrics for sports	Denim, knit, woven, industrial fibres, etc.	Button, labels, zippers, etc.	Fashion design based on season & target group	Jeans, shirts, pants, shoes, etc.	Washed denim	Levi's, Liz Claiborne, Adidas, etc.	Producers, retailers and brands	Brand stores and retailers

— High value added activities ...... Closely related to R&D and design

Hansae
Stage V: Design
Stage VI: Factories in Nicaragua and Honduras.
Stage IX: Distribution networks within the United States.

Hansoll
Stage V: Design
Stage VI: 3 sewing factories in Guatemala and Honduras.
Stage IX: Distribution networks within the United States.

Sae-A
Stage V: Design
Stage VI: 10 sewing factories (Guatemala and Nicaragua).
Stage IX: Distribution networks in Latin America and New York City.

Source: Prepared by the author.

1. Sae-A

Sae-A was founded in the Republic of Korea in 1986 and rapidly expanded its operations abroad with a focus on the United States market. After consolidating its position at home, in the mid-1990s Sae-A invested in new production plants in developing countries and sales offices in the United States. The company invested mainly in production sites in Central America, geographically closer to its United States customers, starting with several factories in Guatemala and later adding new facilities in Nicaragua. Recently Sae-A investment efforts have shifted towards South East Asia (Indonesia and Viet Nam), both to maintain price competitiveness as labour costs in Central America have risen, and to serve the rapidly growing consumer demand in Asia. Nevertheless, half of its global production has remained in the Central American subregion.

From 2000 to 2010, Sae-A export revenues expanded at an average annual rate of 20%. They grew from US$ 21 million in 1995 to US$ 126 million in 2000 and US$ 980 million in 2010. As an acknowledgement of its performance, the company has received two awards from the Government of Korea as part of a programme monitoring the performance of the nation's exporting firms. Most Sae-A clients are located in the United States and, therefore, its trading offices in New York and Los Angeles play a strategic role in its global operations. Recently, the company has expanded its list of clients to include prominent brands such as Adidas, Oshkosh B'Gosh, Levi's, Pacific Sunwear of California (Pac Sun), Express, Forever 21, and K-mart (see table II.7).

Table II.7
SAE-A, HANSOLL AND HANSAE: MAIN BUYERS

SAE-A		HANSOLL		HANSAE	
Buyer	Country	Buyer	Country	Buyer	Country
Target	United States	La Senza	United States	Gap	United States
Wal-Mart	United States	Liz Claiborne	United States	Kohl's	United States
Gap	United States	Adidas	Germany	Old navy	United States
Kohl's	United States	American Eagle	United States	Nike	United States
Liz Claiborne	United States	Old navy	United States	Target	United States
Aeropostale	United States	Delias	United States	The limited	United States
Lane Bryant	United States	Express	United States		
Adidas	Germany	Gilly Hicks	United States		
Gymboree	United States	Hollister	United States		
Abercrombie & Fitch	United States	The Limited	United States		
Bcbg Maxazria	United States	Gap	United States		
Carter's	United States	Pink	United States		
Oshkosh B'gosh	United States	Reebok	United States		
Levi's	United States	Kohl's	United States		
Pacific Sunwear	United States	Justice	United States		
Express	United States	JC Penny	United States		
Forever21	United States	Victoria's Secret	United States		
K-mart	United States	Eddie Bauer	United States		
		New York & Company	United States		
		Abercrombie & Fitch	United States		
		Uniclo	Japan		
		Muji	Japan		

Source: Prepared by the author.

In Central America, the company first invested in Guatemala in 1998, and a few years later opened facilities in Nicaragua. Guatemala has become the site of six production facilities equipped with sewing machinery and printing technology in one factory. All together, there are 67 production lines for knitwear (mainly crews, polo shirts, pants and graphic tees) with a monthly capacity of 10.5 million units. By 2010, the Guatemalan plants accounted for 31% of overall Sae-A production. In Nicaragua, the company has grown from two to four factories. These have 106 production lines for knitwear (mainly basic crews and pants) with a monthly capacity of 4.3 million units. By 2010, the Nicaraguan plants accounted for 16% of global Sae-A production.

2. Hansoll Textile

Hansoll Textile, established in 1992, is a Korean consortium of companies devoted to textiles, processing and final apparel-making. After opening its first overseas location on the island of Saipan in 1997, the company invested in Central America: first in Guatemala in 1998, and later in Honduras in 2000. During the past decade, Hansoll also expanded its production base to Asia, especially India and Cambodia. Rising costs led the company to shut down factories in Saipan (after 10 years of operation) and Honduras (after three years).

Hansoll exports have grown impressively from about US$6 million in 1993 to about US$ 580 million in 2009. Its exports grew every year except 2005, when new competitors arrived following the liberalization of the global textile and apparel trade, upon the expiration of the Arrangement Regarding International Trade in Textiles (Multifibre Arrangement). After rapidly restructuring its operations, Hansoll regained export growth with a 30% rise in 2006. As in the case of other large textile groups, its major buyers are mainly located in the United States, even though certain brands served by the company are originally from Germany and Japan (see table II.7).

Hansoll's Central American operations started in Guatemala in 2000. With a monthly capacity of 1.1 million pieces and 12 sewing lines, it has been serving a diverse range of clients, including Kohl's, Liz Claiborne and Walmart. The second Hansoll factory in Guatemala opened in 2003, with eight production lines, increasing production to 730,000 pieces per month. Similarly to other Korean apparel producers in Central America, this firm increases its production capacity for large orders by outsourcing to smaller Korean factories also located in the subregion, in order to guarantee timely delivery to United States clients.

3. Hansae

The firm was established in the Republic of Korea in 1982, where it has produced textiles for more than 15 years. In 1998, Hansae started overseas production in Central America, first in Nicaragua and later in Guatemala in 2005. From 2003 to 2007, the company tripled its exports from US$ 193 million to US$ 530 million. All buyers are located in the United States, including Gap, Old Navy and Nike, among others.

Hansae investments in Asia expanded much faster than in Central America. It invested in countries such as China, Indonesia, Cambodia and, in particular, in Viet Nam, whose share in total Hansae exports grew from 18% in 2003 to 45% in 2007. As a consequence, Central America's share in Hansae global production began to decrease from 2006 onwards (see figure II.2).

In summary, for most of the 1990s and in the previous decade, Korean companies provided mainly OEM services, which basically meant mass production of pre-ordered designs. However, lately, large producers such as Sae-A, Hansoll and Hansae have started to enter the ODM business, in which a company participates in the entire process, from the development of fabrics and fashion designs to the creation of its own collections.

Figure II.2
HANSAE: CONTRIBUTION OF COUNTRIES' FACTORIES TO TOTAL EXPORTS, 2003-2007
(Percentages)

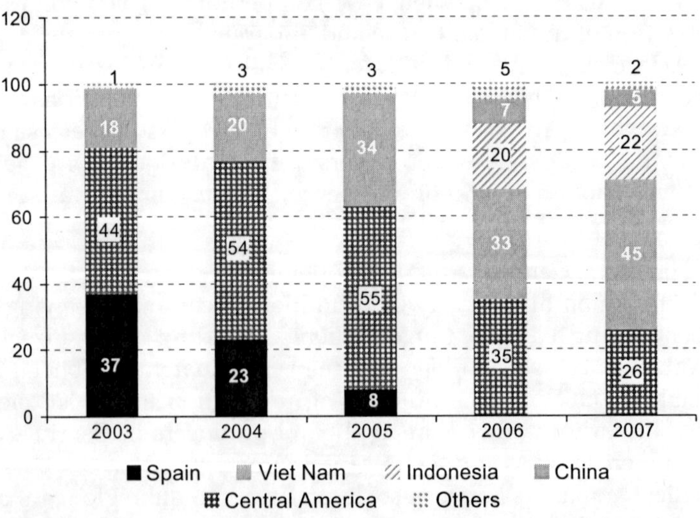

Source: Hansae.

E. Concluding remarks

Emerging markets, once an arena of marginal importance, have now become essential to the competitiveness and growth of many foreign companies. Despite the mixed results of studies on the effectiveness of FDI incentives, there seems to be a consensus that foreign investment benefits the local economy (Farrell, 2004). For this reason, governments, both central and local, are eager to have their share of foreign capital, along with the transfers of technology and management skills that accompany it. Furthermore, the forward and backward linkages that FDI generates in local value chains are regarded as important benefits.

Many countries hosting manufacturing investments, especially the larger economies in Latin America, do require foreign investors to obtain supplies from local sources. Mexico imposes higher tariffs on products imported from countries without a free trade agreement, thereby strengthening local content requirements. In Brazil, imported products are subject to a higher tariff unless a company can prove that particular parts and materials are not available locally.

However, foreign investors are often not satisfied with local supplies in Latin America. Common complaints include delayed deliveries, low quality and high cost. The presence of China, the most competitive manufacturer in the world, has given foreign investors little incentive to source from local supply chains. Even ever-rising trans-Pacific shipping costs are no impediment to goods made in East Asia in terms of delivery speed, quality and price.

How do Asian investors respond to the dilemma of host-government demands and local supply problems? The current report has identified company responses in two directions: importing "raw" parts and enhancing them by in-house assembly to categorize production as local (Brazil) or persuading Asian SMEs in the home-production network to invest locally (Mexico). For example, the Samsung Tijuana plant successfully lined up 22 local vendors in the area for digital television manufacturing, comprising mostly parts suppliers already existing in their Korean production network. Therefore, although as much as 43% of parts and materials may be locally supplied, many of them actually come from Korean SMEs in the maquila industry that supply large manufacturers like Samsung and LG. Either way, the spillover effects to local R&D and innovation are minimal when the core parts are imported from Asia.

Therefore, the failure to build technology-intensive local supply chains has diminished the positive impact of Asian investments, leaving the creation of low-skilled employment by such multinational corporations (MNCs) as the only local benefit.

Is it possible for local Latin American suppliers to join the more sophisticated parts of the value chain? Should governments put more effort into strengthening innovation and capacity-building in local industries? Can they compete with their Asian counterparts? Unfortunately, the tentative answers may not be that positive.

The most typical regulations on MNCs are the strengthening of joint venture requirements and the local-contents requirement to purchase a certain percentage of inputs locally. However, it has been repeatedly argued that these regulations are of dubious effectiveness. MNCs in India and China source many contents locally even though they are not subject to local contents requirements. These two countries provide a large supply of relatively low-wage, skilled labour and a strong industrial base. Similarly, "Mexico began phasing out local-content requirements for automakers in 1994 but still has seven times more jobs in companies that make components" (Farrell, 2004).

It is worth recalling that most FDI entered Brazil only after the government stabilized its economy through the 1994 Real Plan. In this regard, host economies should concentrate on strengthening their economic foundations to maximize the benefits of FDI, by stabilizing the economy and promoting competitive markets, rather than relying on microeconomic incentives and regulations.

Bibliography

ANFAVEA (National Association of Automotor Vehicle Producers) (2010), "Statistics" [online] http://www.anfavea.com.br/tabelas.html [date of reference: December 2010].

BAOSTEEL Group Corporation (2010), "The Outline of the Development Plan 2010-2015", Shanghai, BAOSTEEL Group Corporation.

Bittencourt, Gustavo, Rosario Domingo and Nicolás Reig Lorenzi (2010), "The Uruguayan Case", *The Automobile Industry in Mercosur*, Uruguay, Red Mercosur de Investigaciones Económicas.

Campbell, Keith Campbell (2009), "Chinese group ups mining investment in South America", *Sector News, Iron Ore*, February, [online] http://www.miningweekly.com/article/chinese-group-ups-mining-investment-in-south-america-2009-02-13

Creamer Media's Mining Weekly.com

El País (2010), "Chery analyzing the possibility of leaving Uruguay in the face of low productivity" [in spanish] *Economy*, February [online] http://www.elpais.com.uy/100204/pecono-469346/economia/chery-analiza-dejar-uruguay-por-la-escasa-productividad/.

Farrell, Diana and others (2004), "The truth about foreign direct investment in emerging markets", *The McKinsey Quarterly*, No. 1, February [online] https://www.mckinseyquarterly.com/The_truth_about_foreign_direct_investment_in_emerging_markets_1386. McKinsey & Co.

Gereffi, Gary and Miguel Korzeniewicz (eds.) (1994), *Commodity Chains and Global Capitalism,* Westport, CT, Praeger.

Huawei do Brazil (2008), "Brazil Telecom Market Presentation", presented at Telecom Headquarters, Brasilia.

Jung, Sangkyun (2011), "Open a bigger market in Brazil - (1) Invest in infrastructure industry in advance" [in Korean] *Financial News*, 1 January.

Kaplinsky, Raphael and Mike Morris (2001), "A Handbook for Value Chain Research", Canada, International Development Research Centre (IDRC).

Kim, Myungsu (2010), "To succeed in business-unfriendly Brazil" [in Korean] December, Mae Kyung Economy.

Lesova, Polya (2007), "Jindal Steel to invest $2.1 billion in Bolivian iron ore mine", *Emerging Markets Report*, July [online] http://www.marketwatch.com/story/jindal-steel-to-invest-21-billion-in-bolivian-iron-ore-mine.

Matshushita Electric Industrial Corporation (2008), *Annual Report 2008, We are Panasonic*, Osaka, Japan.

MOFCOM (Ministry of Commerce People's Republic of China) (2007), "BAOSTEEL to invest in Brazil" *Significant News,* August [online] http://english.mofcom.gov.cn/static/column/newsrelease/significantnews.html/1.

Moreno Brid, Juan Carlos (1996), "Mexico's Auto Industry after Nafta: A succesfull experience in restructuring?", *A Working Paper of the Kellogg Institute*, No. 232.

NIPPON Steel Corporation (2010a), *Annual Report 2010, Steeling for Global Competition*, Tokyo, NIPPON Steel Corporation.

Nissan Motor (2010), *Business Report 2009*, Yokohama, Nissan Motor Corporation.

POSCO-Mexico (2009), "News Release" [online] http://www.poscomexico.com.mx/S919/jsp/front/en/board/board.jsp?cmd=view&mid=E0401&document_seq=25.

___(2010), "News Release" [online] http://www.poscomexico.com.mx/S919/jsp/front/en/board/board.jsp?cmd=view&mid=E0401&document_seq=25.

SAMEX (2009), Interview with SAMEX

The Economic Times (2010), "Nissan to assemble three subcompacts in Mexico", *International Business*, July [online] http://economictimes.indiatimes.com/news/international-business/Nissan-to-assemble-three-subcompacts-in-Mexico/articleshow/6221152.cms.

UNCTAD (United Nations Conference on Trade and Development) (2009), *World Investment Report 2009,* New York.

Uruguay XXI (2011), "Automotor and Autoparts sector's investment report" [in Spanish], Montevideo, Institute of investment and export promotion of products and services.

USIMINAS (2010a), "Press Release" [online] http://eng.usiminas.com/irj/portal?standAlone=true&anoNoticia=2010&windowId=WID1302598479140.

___(2010b), "2T10", Brazil.

Chapter III

Global services models for promoting economic integration between Asia and Latin America [1]

Joaquín Piña

Introduction

This study looks at specific services sectors which could be instrumental in promoting and strengthening economic integration between Asia and Latin America. The focus is on the global services industry, which offers a higher integration potential than traditional services sectors.

The global services industry grew out of three main trends: outsourcing, information technology (IT) development and offshoring. Outsourcing refers to a type of business restructuring in which a non-core process formerly performed in-house is contracted to a third party or company. Offshoring refers to the overseas migration of certain operations, with or without outsourcing (National Academy of Public Administration 2006).

Market deregulation and integration in the 1990s forced multinational companies to shift specific operations to less developed nations based on cost-saving opportunities. In the early stages of this

1 The views expressed in this document, which has been reproduced without formal editing, are those of the author and do not necessarily reflect the views of the Organization.

process, India secured a privileged position due to its rich pool of highly skilled, low-cost human resources in IT. Early offshoring/outsourcing involved low complexity tasks such as accounting and basic customer services. Growing IT capabilities supported a new range of higher-value-added contracts, allowing multinational companies to save operational costs while concentrating on their core business.

In the past decade, many emerging countries saw the opportunity and adopted active policies to promote their offshoring capacities, offering subsidies and other benefits to attract foreign investment and develop infrastructure. By 2012 this competitive scenario included South-East Asia, China, the Middle East, Eastern Europe and Latin America. There is an ongoing debate in developed countries about offshoring's overall costs and benefits, as well as its motives and projections. This is particularly the case for higher-value-added segments; research has yet to determine whether R&D offshoring is a strategy to secure access to global talent or merely another form of labour- cost arbitrage (Lewin and Couto, 2006).

No official global services data are available. Such data are considered a subset of the commercial services account which individual countries register in their balance of payments. The services account includes three main items: transportation services, travel-related services, and other commercial services (also known as non-traditional services). The World Trade Organization (WTO) has estimated the total current volume for other commercial services, leaving global services to private estimates which lack official status.

A. Analysis of offshoring industries in Latin America and Asia

1. Definition and international trends

Offshoring (offshore sourcing) has been defined as an international business strategy that enables companies to shift manufacturing or service activities overseas, sourcing high-skilled human resources with cost advantages (Bhide, 2005). The offshoring of services is a recent development: a few decades ago services were considered non-tradable and offshoring possibilities were limited to the sourcing of manufacturing components. IT development has been signalled as one of the key factors in international trade in services. Significant process improvement through new communication platforms, automation tools, supply chain and inventory management, and simulation technologies were the main drivers of business process outsourcing and offshoring, enabling value-chain fragmentation in vertically integrated industries. The global services industry is related to the vertical integration of industries, and has shown unprecedented growth in terms of business segments, market size, country positioning, corporate strategies and revenue, and trade volumes.

(a) Main services segments

Services offshoring is a by-product of software offshoring in the early 1990s and has evolved since then to include a wider range of services for a variety of industries with specific levels of technology. Currently there are three main areas:

- Information Technology: IT infrastructure services, software applications and IT consulting.
- Business: accounting and finance, human resources, sales and customer services (in horizontal processes) and vertically specialized applications in finance, healthcare and telecommunications.
- Knowledge development: specialized financial services, engineering services, architecture, clinical trials and R&D activities.

(b) Market highlights

According to estimates by the Boston Consulting Group (2009), offshoring-related flows reached an overall value of US$ 132 billion in 2008, of which the United States represented 70%, followed by the European Union (18%) and Asia (9%). Current market volume is the result of average annual growth rates of 35% reflecting geographical expansion of the industry.

Recent data and estimates lend support to the notion that a new stage of slower growth rates and consolidation has begun within the industry. According to AT Kearney (2009), in the first half of 2009 new offshoring contracts fell by 25% in value terms. Annual growth rates of 15% are not expected until the global economy fully recovers from the current crisis.

In Latin America, services data show a slightly countercyclical response to the crisis. Chile's exports of goods fell 19% in 2009, while total services exports fell 21% (mainly owing to a sharp fall in export-associated transport). Other services (which include offshoring and global outsourcing) decreased only 13%.

In the first quarter of 2010 traditional services, such as travel and tourism, suffered the immediate impacts of the earthquake which struck Chile on 27 February, with a loss of 16%, while other services grew by 15%.[2]

[2] IT and financial services grew by 12% and 11%, respectively, while sales and purchase services increased by 18% possibly due to post-earthquake reconstruction efforts (for more details see Central Bank figures www.bcentral.cl).

(c) Main offshoring services provider countries

India, Ireland and the Eastern European countries are the main providers of offshoring services today.

India shows a higher level of maturity owing to early creation of back-office centres by companies such as British Airways, American Express and GE in the 1980s. These companies were attracted by the availability of low-cost, highly skilled human resources. Since then, many of these centres have been spun off, while local companies have developed aggressive international strategies. According to current market estimates, India's offshoring companies employ 700,000 people and produce revenues of US$ 11 billion (1% of GDP). The industry's main driver is India's vast high-skill labour pool, with 2.5 million graduates per year. However, industry dynamics are such that the increase in wages is eroding former comparative advantages vis-à-vis other providers.

Ireland's offshoring industry is similar to India's in terms of multinational presence, although more recent in development. Rather than human resource availability, Ireland's success in offshoring is related to public policies, including attractive tax legislation. Language and cultural affinity to the United States, European Union membership and proximity to Europe's continental markets were also instrumental in attracting foreign investment.

Eastern Europe became an outsourcing and offshoring alternative after the fall of the Berlin Wall in 1989. Central planning was abandoned for free-market policies and foreign investment. Industry drivers were similar to those in India (labour pool, cost arbitrage) and in Ireland (European Union membership), with German companies playing a significant role owing to geographical proximity and cultural affinity. Poland, Hungary and the Czech Republic are currently the main players in terms of project development.

(d) Corporate strategies

Process outsourcing was a private sector response to market deregulation, which started in the United States and the United Kingdom with a series of public policies designed and adopted to address growth and productivity stagnation after the crisis of 1973-1975. In the 1990s outsourcing and offshoring gained momentum driven by trade liberalization, international finance deregulation and capital account liberalization in many emerging economies. Multinational companies in the manufacturing, telecommunications, transport and retail industries seized the opportunity and adopted aggressive services-offshoring strategies to cut costs and increase efficiency and competitiveness in a new global scenario.

According to a survey conducted by AT Kearney (2006), the percentage of multinational companies considering services operations overseas increased from 50% to 70% between 2003 and 2005, with the proportion rising fastest among United States companies (from 62% to 87%). Sectors with a substantial outsourcing and offshoring potential are IT (68%); customer service centres (50%); R&D (40%); shared services (40%) and knowledge centres (23%).

Significant foreign investment growth in services is a consequence of both national promotion policies and a wider range of location alternatives for multinational companies, including through direct investment, joint ventures with local partners and outsourcing. According to the United Nations Conference on Trade and Development (UNCTAD) (2008), foreign investment in corporate services reached US$ 2.05 trillion in 2006, with financial services accounting for US$ 2.5 trillion of US$ 7.7 trillion in overall services. As of 2006, foreign investment in services represents 62% of total foreign investment, against 30% in manufacturing (UNCTAD, 2008).

A significant feature in this trend is R&D internationalization (Couto and Sehgal, 2007) in a context in which multinational companies account for 50% of world expenditure on R&D. A survey of top executives by Booz & Allen and Duke University's School of Management identified decision-making patterns of European and United States multinational companies. European companies tend to outsource transactional, low-cost operations, while United States companies outsource higher complexity processes. European companies select locations by language and cultural affinity, hence their preference for Eastern Europe and Latin America, while United States companies prefer India, China and locations in South-East Asia such as the Philippines, based on large-scale, high-skilled labour supply. In terms of offshoring models, German and Spanish companies tend to establish captive centres, while United States companies are more disposed to outsource. European firms are sensitive to risk related to cultural differences; United States companies are concerned with IT security.

In a context of international financial turmoil, offshoring will maintain its role in a globalized world economy, but corporate strategies and growth dynamics will evolve. Some analysts forecast slower growth, as well as higher concern for risk, a tendency towards consolidation of operations and smaller geographical expansion. Global operational models will balance complementary offers from India and Eastern Europe and providers will aim towards higher specialization. Current global providers tend to combine operations 30% in higher- to medium-cost countries such as the United States, Canada and Western European countries, and

70% in lower-cost regions such as Asia-Pacific, Eastern Europe and Latin America. This follow-the-sun model allows for balancing near-shore and offshore alternatives, securing access to talent, language skills and cultural affinities, reducing operational costs and profiting from time-zone differences to accelerate project cycle development.

In addition, competition among top technology companies has become so fierce that that they cannot afford to rely solely on domestic markets for their R&D teams. This is why companies such as Yahoo! and chip-design software developer Synopsis are tapping talent in countries like Chile. The key concept is Ready-to-Market[3] (Couto and Sehgal, 2007), speed in developing new products in a more competitive context and restriction of work visas in the United States even for IT specialists. This is forceing IT companies to source R&D from overseas centres.

(e) Public policies and support

Almost all the Latin American countries have developed policies to attract foreign investments in contact centres, business process outsourcing (BPO), information technology outsourcing (ITO) or knowledge process outsourcing (KPO) (Gereffi., Castillo and Fernandez-Stark, 2009). They have designed schemes that combine promotion with incentives to support foreign investors, directly or indirectly, in these services (ECLAC, 2009). Indirect estimates of the impact of offshoring on overall economic activity are given in ECLAC (2011). This publication quotes Latin American software services exports from Argentina, Brazil, Chile and Mexico as having reached US$ 4.4 billion in 2010.

Brazil and Mexico combine international promotion programmes with national and State incentives. Brazil's Apex and Mexico's Bancomext are the agencies responsible for international marketing and promotion. Brazil offers lower taxation incentives at the national level for investments, IT-related R&D activities and technological park development. Mexico's national maquiladora endorsement and operation law allows foreign companies to operate as industrial free trade zones. In both countries, subnational entities have some autonomy in promoting investment through tax breaks, infrastructure provision and training subsidies. Brazil's top destinations are Campinas and metropolitan São Paulo; in Mexico foreign companies are located in Monterrey, Guadalajara and Mexico City.

In Spanish-speaking South America there are several investment promotion agencies such as Argentina's ProsperAr, Chile's CORFO and CINVER, Colombia's PROEXPORT and Uruguay XXI. Argentina has

---

3 Competitive edge measured as critical speed in transforming R&D investments into goods marketable worldwide.

a range of national incentives similar to Brazil's, with tax incentives for the software industry. Argentina's provinces have their own programmes consisting of special taxation and infrastructure and public service subsidies. Buenos Aires, Córdoba, and Rosario have attracted a range of offshoring providers from Spain, India and the United States. Chile offers training incentives instead of special taxation to foreigners. It also offers co-financing for IT infrastructure and free, long-term office rent, as well as English courses for engineers and technicians. Colombia has an industrial parks scheme operating as a free-trade-zone regime, as well as a set of tax breaks for BPO companies and English-language training for BPO and contact centre professionals. In Uruguay, services exports must obtain official recognition as such to be exempted from VAT. Software companies are also eligible for income tax exemption. Uruguay's free-trade-zone regime also covers services exports, including zero import-tax for equipment, raw materials and semi-processed goods, as well as VAT and corporate net wealth taxes.

Central America's main investment promotion agencies are Costa Rica's CINDE, El Salvador's PROESA and the Dominican Republic's CEI-RD. Costa Rica's free trade zone is flexible and not limited to specific regions or cities. Any company can apply to a location of its choosing and obtain a government decree granting free-trade-zone status. The system exempts firms from all kinds of taxes for a certain period, including VAT and tax on remittances. English and other language training schemes are also offered. El Salvador has a law exempting global services centres from VAT, as well as relevant goods and equipment custom taxes. The Dominican Republic has a free-trade-zone regime as well as English training programmes and is currently overhauling its educational system.

2. Services offshoring in Latin America

Latin America is currently an emerging offshoring destination for a host of European and United States multinationals. It also has a high development potential and offers the conditions to become a world leader through the industry's transition to a new, post-boom stage. But countries must address policy issues and closely coordinate at the regional and multilateral levels, if they wish to develop the necessary conditions to seize this unique, temporary opportunity.

(a) Latin America's offshoring industry profile

There are no official figures for this industry, and private estimates vary. Taking the Boston Consulting Group's worldwide estimate of US$ 132 billion (2008) in services exports, Latin America's market share would be approximately 7%, that is US$ 9.2 billion in offshoring contracts, mainly in IT and BPO.[4] This is the result of a six-year run of double-digit growth in the number of new projects being located in Latin America by offshoring companies. According to fDi Markets, more than 6,000 BPO or KPO projects came to Latin America between 2003 and the first quarter of 2009, representing a twofold increase over that period. Latin America's market share in total foreign direct investment (FDI) for offshoring projects is still modest (5%) compared to Asia-Pacific (49%) and Eastern Europe (10%) (OCO Global & fDi Markets, 2009). But it was the fastest-growing region in the world in this respect, even against a backdrop new projects falling worldwide by 15% in 2009.

Latin America was first seen as a potential global services hub after the terrorist attacks of 11 September 2011 in the United States. The subsequent national security measures have made it increasingly difficult and cumbersome for Indian IT professionals to obtain work visas in the United States. (Chu and Herrero, 2005) Furthermore, increasing demand has pushed up the costs of Indian engineers. Latin America's growing relevance in the offshoring industry can be measured in export volume as well as in terms of international positioning. Business environment, cost structure, skilled labour availability and government support are the main factors.

Table III.1
LATIN AMERICA: BASIC DATA ON OFFSHORING

Country	BPO project (2003-2004/2009)	AT Kearney (2009)	Gartner country ranking (2009)	50 best cities for outsourcing
Argentina	39	Top 30	Leader	Buenos Aires
Barbados		New player		
Brazil	92	Top 15	Leader	São Paulo, Curitiba, Brasilia
Chile	29	Top 10	Leader	Santiago
Colombia	22	New player	To follow	
Costa Rica	25	Top 25	Leader	San José
Dominican Republic		New player	With potential	
Ecuador			With potential	
El Salvador	5	New player	With potential	
Guatemala		New player	To follow	
Jamaica		Top 25	With potential	
Mexico	59		Leader	Monterrey, Juárez
Nicaragua			With potential	
Peru	5		To follow	
Panama	6	Top 45	Leader	
Uruguay	9	Top 40	To follow	
Venezuela (Bolivarian Republic of)			To follow	

Source: Economic Commission for Latin America and the Caribbean (ECLAC), on the basis of fDi Market, AT Kearney, Gartner & Global Services.
Note: Top player: countries in AT Kearney's offshoring ranking.
New player: countries in the process of reaching AT Kearney's offshoring ranking.
Leader, to follow and with potential: Classification by Gartner according to the conditions offered in each country for attracting offshoring activities.

4 IDC, BCG, and AT Kearney.

According to AT Kearney's Global Location Index (2009), eight Latin American and Caribbean countries are among the world's top competitive locations: Argentina, Brazil, Chile, Costa Rica, Jamaica, Mexico, Panama and Uruguay. The Global Location Index identifies new players with active promotion strategies such as Colombia, Guatemala, El Salvador, the Dominican Republic, and Barbados (AT Kearney, 2009). According to a model developed by Gartner (2009),[5] which evaluates critical industry factors, Argentina, Brazil, Chile, Costa Rica, Mexico and Panama are leaders. Countries to follow are Bolivarian Republic of Venezuela, Colombia, Guatemala, Peru and Uruguay, and the territory of Puerto Rico. Countries with potential are Cuba, Dominican Republic, Ecuador, El Salvador, Jamaica and Nicaragua.

Offshoring development in Latin America shows different levels of maturity, but common factors are identifiable in terms of four categories: (i) countries with large domestic markets such as Brazil and Mexico; (ii) Spanish-speaking South American countries; (iii) Central America and Spanish-speaking Caribbean countries; (iv) English-speaking Caribbean countries (ECLAC, 2009; Gereffi, Castillo and Fernandez-Stark, 2009).

(i) Brazil and Mexico

Offshoring was first observed in the information and communications technologies (ICT) sector in Brazil and Mexico in the late 1990s. The clients of these sectors were manufacturing and electronics producers. Both countries had large domestic markets and were close to the United States. As industrial activities migrated to China, several hardware companies in Mexico and Brazil transformed their facilities into services centres, capitalizing on their infrastructure and skilled labour supply. United States ICT and BPO companies also explored new locations south of their borders. They located low-added-value centres for transaction processing and data entry facilities mainly in Mexico.

The large Indian providers came later, with contact centres, shared centres and IT applications development. Early United States providers were EDS and ACS. Also, Tata, Inofsys and Wipro from are India. But both Mexico and Brazil have significant local services providers which are also active in offshoring: Mexico's Softek, Neoris, and Hildebrando (Mexico); Brazil's CPM, Politec, Ci&T, Tivit, and Stefanini.

(ii) Spanish-speaking South America

Offshoring in IT/BPO has developed fairly recently in South America and varies greatly between countries. Three hundred new

---

5 Evaluation criteria: English advanced skills, government support, labour availability, infrastructure, educational system, costs, political and economic context, cultural affinity, law enforcement, personal data protection and IP protection.

offshoring centers have been registered as FDI projects in South America in the past six years: 39 in Argentina, 29 in Chile, 22 in Colombia, 9 in Uruguay and 5 in Peru (fDi Market, 2010). The region is seemingly succeeding in capitalizing upon its geography as a near-shore destination. It also offers competitive qualified-labour costs and several government programmes to support FDI projects.

Argentina is the offshoring leader in South America. It has an extensive network of graduate universities in Buenos Aires, Córdoba and Rosario. National currency devaluation in 2001 increased Argentina's cost advantages, which boosted investment in new projects and expansion of existing capacity throughout the industry's whole value chain. Teleperformance, Convergys, Atento and TeleTech are active players in the contact centre industry. IT and BPO firms include Accenture, IBM, Motorola, Intel, Tata, Microsoft and EDS (ECLAC, 2009).

Chile and Colombia are recent, high-growth players which entered the market after 2005. Chile has a national policy for attracting FDI through CORFO, and this facilitates basic infrastructure for call centres. Higher-value-added centres are a more recent phenomenon. Chile's main assets are political stability, human resources and costs. The country also offers specific capacities for different value chain segments, provided by firms such as Teleperformance, Transcom, Capgemini, Citigroup, Oracle, Pioneer, Synopsis and Yahoo! Colombia is offering voice and data applications for contact centres and BPO, and is gaining presence in IT-associated higher-value-added areas, attracting firms such as Convergys, SITEL, Atento, Digitex and EDS.

Uruguay spearheaded software exports from Latin America in the 1990s. After developing an internationally-oriented domestic industry, the conditions were in place to attract international firms such as Tata, Trintech, IBM and Microsoft. In 2007 Uruguay exported US$ 120 million in IT services to Latin America, North America and Europe (Cuti, 2007). According to Tata executives, the firm picked Uruguay to host its Latin America headquarters because of its image of neutrality among the region's animosities (see chapter II) (Chu and Herrero, 2005). Peru is a new player. Economic growth, pro-market policies and qualified-labour cost advantages make Peru a country "to watch", according to the Gartner Index.

(iii) Central America and the Caribbean

In Central America and the Caribbean subregion, offshoring has developed in certain countries, including the Dominican Republic and Costa Rica. Of the 36 new foreign centres located in Central America between 2003 and 2009, 25 were located in Costa Rica, 6 in Panama and 5 in El Salvador.

Costa Rica had a headstart in the 1990s in attracting IT, BPO and contact centres, and is now the regional leader. Some of the landmarks were Intel's assembly facility (1998), Procter & Gamble's shared services centre (1999) and offshoring centres operated by companies such as Western Union, HP and IBM. Since 2001 other countries have adopted offshoring strategies based on three main factors: increasing demand for near-shore, customer and BPO services focusing on the United States; the migration of manufacturing operations to China; and greater availability of bilingual human resources as a result of national training programmes, as well as the return of emigrants from the United States (ECLAC, 2009). This sort of strategy was adopted first by Panama, El Salvador, and the Dominican Republic, followed by Guatemala, Nicaragua and Honduras.

(iv) English-speaking Caribbean

The English-speaking Caribbean has a smaller-scale offshoring industry, owing mainly to population factors. However, offshoring has helped to provide these countries with a diversification strategy to compensate for the cyclical fluctuations in tourism, the region's main export service (ECLAC, 2008). Language, culture and geography played a role in the establishment of early offshoring ventures in the 1980s, with data entry and customer service centres for the United States market. The sector enjoyed a resurgence after 2005, with significant developments in Jamaica (where offshoring employs 10,000 people), Barbados, Guyana, and Trinidad and Tobago.

(b) Asia's offshoring industry profile

Some very successful offshoring initiatives have been developed in Asian countries, especially India, the Philippines, Viet Nam and China. These countries have attracted large European, United States, Japanese and Korean multinationals, which outsource or locate in-house centres based on cost considerations or other benefits offered by host countries.

(i) Philippines

The Philippines is one of the most competitive offshoring destinations thanks to its attractive labour and operational costs and bilingual human resources.

The Philippines has a population of 90 million[6] and per capita income of US$ 3,515 (PPP). Different Western and Oriental cultures merge in its many islands, and languages spoken include Malay (95% of the population), English (the official and business language) and Spanish (in the Catholic religion). As well as the local population, an estimated 11 million Filipinos live overseas. They are often referred to as Overseas Filipino Workers (OFWs) and send home US$ 15 billion in bank remittances, almost 13.5% of GDP, per year.

6 United Nations Population Division, 2009 estimates.

Some 788 call centres are currently operating in the Philippines: 35% are located in Makati city,[7] a metropolitan Manila municipality considered to be the business and financial capital. Another important location is Origas Center, also in Metropolitan Manila, which hosts United States, Canadian and French operators such as Sitel, Telus and Teleperformance. According to the main private sector organizations, Business Process Association of the Philippines (BPAP) and BPO Services Association, in 2008 offshoring employed some 435,000 and generated revenues of US$ 6.1 billion. Accordingly, the Philippines is the third largest offshoring destination in the world after India and Canada.

To sustain industry growth the government offers significant fiscal and non-fiscal incentives through its Board of Investments (BOI), a public agency responsible for promoting foreign investment in the context of a medium-term development plan.

Apart from traditional call centres, several BPO companies offer legal and medical file transcription, financial and accounting services (the Philippines is one of South-East Asia's largest back-office and shared services centre locations), and software and digital animation. Companies such as Disney, Marvel Comics, Warner, Hannah Barbera, Universal and Cartoon Network, as well as Japanese manga and animé[8] producers, are outsourcing with Filipino animators.

(ii) China

China could hardly be other than an important industry player, given its vast resources pool and unparalleled economic growth. The Government of China is promoting services sector development in keeping with the country's industrial and technological stature. Several multinationals, including Dell, Motorola and HP, have located customer service centres in China, alongside local such as Bank of China, China Mobile and Huawei.

This growing supply targets mainly the domestic market, however, with some provision for neighbouring countries. While labour costs are exceedingly competitive, China lacks India's (and to a lesser extent the Philippines') bilingual and English skills.

Several cities, including Dalian, Hangzhou and Chengdu, compete for foreign investment, offering a large graduate pool and tax and infrastructure benefits. Dalian is a seaport located in North-East China. It was nicknamed "China's Bangalore" because of its extraordinary growth in IT-related offshoring activities. GE, Microsoft, Dell, HP and Accenture

---

7 See [online] www.callcenterdirectory.net.

8 Manga are comics and cartoons produced in Japan. Animé refers to Japanese animation films, usually based on manga characters and products. For animation offshoring and outsourcing in the Philippines, see Animation Council of the Philippines (2008).

are currently operating in Dalian, but the main players are Japanese, due to geographical proximity and the availability of Sino Japanese bilingual technicians. There are 22 universities and a student population of about 220,000 (Friedman, 2004). Dalian also has a tax and infrastructure incentive programme in the form of its technology parks (Dalian Software Park and Dalian High-Tech Zone), where the main activities are software development, BPO, programming, circuit design, R&D and digital animation. Chengdu, the capital of Sichuan province in South-East China, is one of the most dynamic cities in the country as regards private investment. IT outsourcing and offshoring are concentrated in Chengdu Hi-Tech Zone and Tianfu Software Park. This is a long-term project which will reach 1.2 million m^2 by 2010 and an overall capacity of 50,000 employees.[9] About 100 companies operate in Chengdu Hi-Tech Zone, of which 40% are foreign: they include IBM, Accenture, Symantec, Huawei, SAP, Nokia-Siemens, EMC, Alcatel-Lucent, Siemens, Synnex, Maersk, Tencent and China Mobile.

(iii) Viet Nam

In recent years Viet Nam has become a new player in Asia's offshoring industry, specifically in IT services. Companies such as Intel, Honda, BP and Prudential have outsourced IT services to Quang Trung Software Park and Saigon High Tech Park, located close to Ho Chi Minh City, Viet Nam's largest city. Viet Nam has a population of 85 million and a per capita income of US$ 2,793. The country adopted a market socialism model in 1986, with notable results. Viet Nam's economy is now the second fastest-growing in the world after China and it is more open in terms of foreign trade and investment. In 2006 Viet Nam acceded to WTO and adapted its intellectual property laws to conform to the Agreement on Trade-Related Aspects of Intellectual Property Rights (TRIPS).

Viet Nam's main asset is a generous pool of skilled labour, with 80,000 IT-related graduates each year. This is fewer than China and India, but still significant from a national point of view (CNN, 2007). Viet Nam also offers a stimulus package similar to that provided in several Latin American countries: four-year VAT exemption, special import tariffs for equipment and income tax liberation (Wilson, 2007). Another asset is the Vietnamese-American community, located mainly in California, which operates as a powerful broker in filling the business-culture gap between the United States and Viet Nam.[10] Weak points, however, are the country's telecoms infrastructure and poorer bilingual-English skills than the Philippines.

---

9 See [online] www.chengduinvest.gov.com.

10 Phil Tran created Egg Digital in 1995, a design and 2D animation company in Ho Chi Minh City. In 2002 he started designing race cars for Forz Motorsport, a Microsoft Xbox videogame. TMA Solutions, founded by Canadian-Vietnamese Nguyen Huu Le, outsources software development for Nortel, Comsys and Alcatel-Lucent (see also Balfour, 2006).

(c) Labour and competitiveness

Costs are among the key factors for offshoring decisions (AT Kearney, 2009), while ITO and KPO demand higher and specific skills.

There are no common indicators or labour costs estimates for all the countries analysed in this study, and still less information concerning specialized services. AT Kearney has constructed a labour competitiveness index (see figure III.1) on the basis of specific costs for offshoring.

Figure III.1
SELECTED COUNTRIES: LABOUR COST COMPETITIVENESS INDEX, 2009

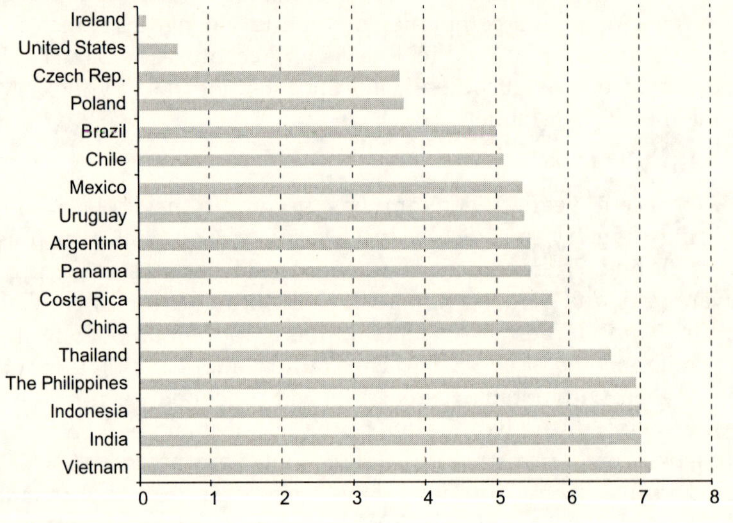

Source: AT Kearney.

The AT Kearney index weighs country data on average wages and compensations for call centre operators, BPO analysts, IT programmers and local managers. In this index Viet Nam is the most competitive country, followed by India, Indonesia and the Philippines, all of which have a labour supply consisting of thousands of college graduates per year. At the other extreme is Ireland, where salaries are paid in Euros and the labour supply grows only marginally.

The Latin American countries are situated in between. Costa Rica leads the region, followed by Panama. Both are more competitive than Ireland and even some Eastern European countries, including Poland and the Czech Republic.

3. Services integration between Latin America and Asia

(a) World market share

WTO estimates the share of different regions in world services exports on the basis of individual countries' balance of payments. According to this information, Asian countries account for 26% of total services exports, while Latin America represents just 3% (see figure III.2).

Figure III.2
REGIONAL SHARE IN WORLD SERVICES EXPORTS, 2010
(Percentages)

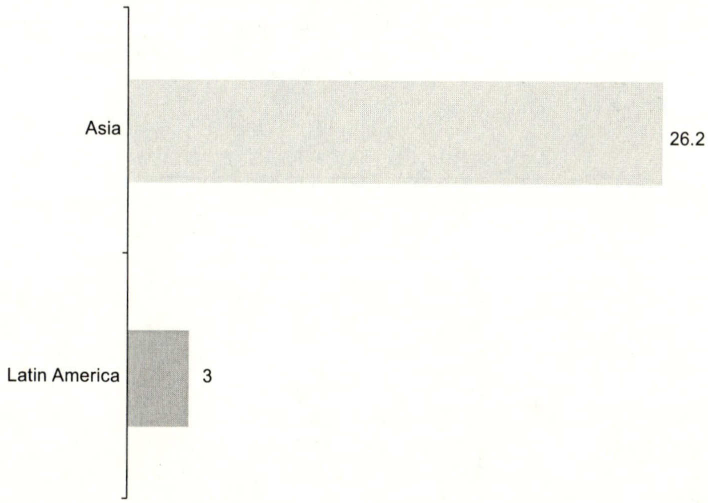

Source: World Trade Organization (WTO).

Services exports represent a relatively new field for Latin America's commodity-based, export-oriented economies. In trade negotiations Latin American governments still treat merchandise exports as the priority, including in their negotiations with Asian countries. Only a handful of public institutions responsible for trade promotion and negotiation have taken on board the importance of global services industries and even those responsible for services trade have been slow to react. Latin American countries thus still tend to be seen as providers of raw materials. Geographical and cultural distances also explain the region's lack of allure in terms of attracting investments in global services.

Relative to world services exports, Latin America's exports of other commercial services represent a lower share (2%) than traditional services such as transport (3%) and travel (5%). Services trade in Asia and Latin America involves different sectors: Latin America's main exports are in transport and travel (61%) while other services represent only 39%. In Asia, the latter represent 50%.

The European Union is the world leader in global services or offshoring (a subset of other commercial services) with 46% of the world's exports, followed by the United States with 16%. Three large Asian economies —India, China and Japan— rank third, fourth and fifth, respectively. Singapore, Hong Kong Special Administrative Region, Republic of Korea and Taiwan Province of China range from sixth to eleventh. Brazil is the only Latin American country among the main services exporters, with about 1% of the world's "other services" exports.

Table III.2
MAIN SERVICES EXPORTERS, 2010-2011

Country	Exports (billions of dollars)		World market share	
	2010	2011	2010	2011
European Union (27)	925.5	1 030.9	45.8	46.0
United States	326.7	352.3	16.2	15.7
India	95.9	101.5	4.7	4.5
China	90.2	98.3	4.5	4.4
Japan	86.6	93.1	4.3	4.2
Singapore	65.1	72.7	3.2	3.2
Switzerland	61.0	70.0	3.0	3.1
Hong Kong, China	54.0	61.1	2.7	2.7
Canada	40.1	44.3	2.0	2.0
Republic of Korea	36.9	44.4	1.8	2.0
Taipei, China	21.6	25.3	1.1	1.1
Russian Federation	20.7	24.9	1.0	1.1
Norway	19.3	21.6	1.0	1.0
Brazil	19.4	24.1	1.0	1.1

Source: World Trade Organization (WTO).

(b) Double taxation agreements

Double taxation occurs when a single economic activity is taxed by more than one jurisdiction, i.e. when more than one State taxes the same income.

In the world income approach,[11] the principle behind most tax legislations, any person situated or residing in a specific country will

[11] There are other double taxation systems such as the "territorial" one, in which taxation is levied only on territorially-generated income. Most countries have adopted the world income approach.

pay taxes on any kind of income, disregarding its domestic or foreign origin. The result is an over-taxation which affects capital, investment, services and technology flows between countries. There are cases of even triple or fourfold-taxation depending on the number of tax administrations involved, and this is a strong deterrent of trade between foreign partners/taxpayers.

Many countries negotiate and sign bilateral double taxation agreements (DTAs) to avoid double taxation. There are three main kinds of DTAs: the model developed by the Organization for Economic Cooperation and Development (OECD), the model developed by the United Nations, and the Andean Community model. Of these, the OECD model is the most widely used. The main difference between the models is the way by which the "fiscal sacrifice" is shared between tax administrations, i.e. between the country where the economic activity takes place and the one where the head office is located. Preferences between models depend on whether the country is a capital exporter or importer. Only five Latin American countries have signed double-taxation agreements with Asian countries.

(c) Services agreements between Asia and Latin America

In the past two decades several countries have signed agreements to liberalize trade in services. With different coverage and depth, these agreements take either a positive or a negative list approach.

Agreements set forth relevant information for companies willing to explore foreign markets, specifically concerning local legislation affecting the national treatment principle, with which every country must comply. However, this is not sufficient to actually export a service.

Global services perform high-tech, value-added international transactions through ICT networks, which necessarily involve technical assistance and support. Physical presence of foreign technicians is sometimes required in the country where the service was contracted. Agreements in trade in services include important chapters on business travel, temporary entry and work visas. Usually these issues are part of the negotiating agenda, but to date agreements between Asian and Latin American countries show no significant improvement on previous conditions. Labour legislation is a sensitive issue virtually everywhere.

Services trade integration between Asia and Latin America is also limited, with only 11 service agreements signed as of 2009. Chile has the largest share of agreements with specific service chapters, followed by Mexico, Panama and Peru. Guatemala and Honduras have bilateral agreements with Taiwan Province of China.

Asia-Pacific Economic Cooperation (APEC) is a platform that has potential to promote services integration. APEC has created a services group (GOS) to promote and facilitate cooperation and investment in the services trade; however, only three Latin American countries, Mexico, Chile and Peru, are participating.

In 2001, GOS created an operational framework for the voluntary liberalization of trade in services. This includes an indicative list of possible measures for that members may adopt in their individual action plans. However, no significant developments have taken place, owing to restrictive policies on services in individual countries, as well as the non-mandatory nature of APEC agreements. Nevertheless, a services negotiation "model chapter" was designed in 2007-2008, which could be used as a model for a regional agreement.

Even though market liberalization in the context of APEC is not substantial compared to the Doha Round of trade talks, it is a positive sign. Asia-Pacific is the world's most dynamic region in terms of innovation and economic and trade growth, so services trade integration is a relevant issue. It could materialize in a new-generation trade agreement called the Trans-Pacific Partnership (TPP) between Australia, the United States, Peru, Viet Nam, Malaysia and the group known as the Pacific 4 (Brunei Darussalam, Chile, New Zealand and Singapore. Japan, Canada and Mexico may also join the group.

Consolidation of niche services might be a reasonable target. Technological and scientific cooperation between Latin American universities and R&D-intensive Asian companies has the potential to become a spearhead for services integration between the two regions (see chapter III).

B. Asian offshoring services firms in Latin America: case studies

Global services centres in Latin America are subsidiaries of United States and European firms. The Asian presence, especially from India, Japan and the Republic of Korea, is concentrated in a limited number of projects and countries. However, there are several successful experiences which may serve as an example for Latin American countries willing to reproduce and enhance them.

Between 2003 and 2009, approximately 62 centres were set up by Indian, Japanese and Korean companies in Latin America. Brazil and Mexico were the main target markets followed by Argentina, Chile and Costa Rica (see table III.3). Indian companies form an emerging group of large offshoring service providers, while the pattern among Japanese and Korean firms is establishment of in-house centres for large hardware and electronics companies.

Table III.3
LATIN AMERICA (SELECTED COUNTRIES): ASIAN OFFSHORING SERVICES CENTRES, 2003-2009

Country	India	Japan	Republic of Korea	Total
Argentina	4	2	1	7
Brazil	6	7	5	18
Chile	4	3	3	10
Colombia	1	-	2	3
Costa Rica	2	2	-	4
Guatemala	1	-	-	1
Mexico	9	5	2	16
Panama	-	-	2	2
Uruguay	1	-	-	1
Total	28	19	15	62

Source: Prepared by the authors on the basis of data collected by fDi Markets and Off-shoring Times.

Indian service companies are international providers offering near-shoring under the concept of a "global delivery model". They combine and complement capacities located in Asia, Europe and Latin America. Their business models focus on BPO and ICT services for vertically integrated sectors such as retail, finance and banking, and telecommunications. Indian services leaders such as Tata, Infosys, Wipro and HCL are the trendsetters in this industry.

By contrast, Japanese and Korean companies follow an offshore/in-house model. These are centres run directly by hardware components, network equipment, semiconductors and electronics companies in general.

Centres operating in Latin America under this rationale focus on post-manufacture (distribution, logistics, sales and marketing, customer support and technical support); internal process support such as shared services, software development; and pre-manufacture services such as R&D, testing and design (KPO). Samsung, LG, Mitsubishi, Fujitsu and NEC are important players.

1. Indian firms

India is one of the largest players in the offshoring industry. Different sources estimate India's market share in the range of 6% to 7% (Nasscom) and agree upon the country's absolute leadership in offshoring

(63%). Companies operating in high-tech parks such as Bangalore, Hyderabad, Kolkata, Mumbai, Pune, Chennai and New Dehli export an average of US$ 10 billion per year. They employ 10,000 people in their Latin American centres.

Indian services companies were created by large industrial conglomerates or by independent entrepreneurs. Domestic markets were closed to foreign competition during the 1970s and 1980s, facilitating the development of these companies. They gained experience and volume that would later be instrumental to their success in the global scene. Other players in India are multinational companies such as GE, IBM and American Express. Main services providers are TCS, Infosys, Wipro Technologies WNS Global Services and Genpact. Several were created as back-office centres for local companies or multinationals, and later opened their resources to third party customers. Indian competitiveness is based on human capital (especially IT talent at competitive costs), and English skills, a great advantage vis-à-vis other Asian countries.

Tata Consultancy Services (TCS) is part of the Tata Group, one of India's largest conglomerates, founded in 1868 as a textile company. Today Tata Group is a diversified holding with interests in the automotive, telecoms, food and steel industries. TCS was the group's IT services unit. During the 1970s and the 1980s it gained visibility in IT outsourcing and offshoring, especially for the financial sector. In the second half of the 1990s TCS took advantage of the approach of the millennium bug and the adoption of the euro. Since then it has become the largest Indian global services provider, with annual sales of US$ 5.7 billion (2008). Tata's arrival may be considered a milestone and a spearhead in Latin America's offshoring industry. Currently Tata has operations throughout Latin America and employs 9,000 people, including IT professionals. Its business model combines a local market focus in Argentina, Brazil, Chile, Colombia, Ecuador, Mexico and Peru, and global sourcing from Mexico and Uruguay.

WNS was created in 1996 as a small-scale back-office centre for British Airways, with 30 employees located in Mumbai. Six years later it was acquired by an American investment fund. In June 2006 it was the first Indian company to be listed in the New York stock exchange. Initially specialized in tourism and air travel, it has expanded into retail, banking and insurance, among other areas. WNS has 23 thousand employees and has recently set up in Latin America with a bilingual shared-services centre in San José, focusing on the United States market.

Wipro (Western India Products) was created as a food company in 1947, the year of India's independence. Like other industrial conglomerates, it took advantage of the protectionist years to explore and develop IT hardware. Its software services unit was created in 1992. Since then, Wipro has become one of the largest global services providers. It arrived in Latin America in 2008, establishing two shared-services centres in Curitiba, Brazil, providing services to financial institutions as well as entry management, customer services and human resources management on behalf of local clients. In 2010 it opened an IT services centre in Brazil with 350 professionals, and another in Monterrey, Mexico, aimed at the United States, Latin American and European markets.

Infosys is one of the youngest companies in India's global services industry. It was created in 1981 by seven entrepreneurs from Pune. In 2008, sales reached US$ 4.6 billion, of which 97% were service exports. It stands out among its Indian peers for its academic links and recruiting and training policies. Infosys runs one of the largest corporate training centres in Asia, the Mysore campus, in Karnataka state. In 2007 Infosys established its first Latin American subsidiary in Monterrey, Mexico, focusing on banking, financial services and retail. The following year it opened a development centre in Belo Horizonte, Brazil. There the focus is on banking, financial services, insurance, manufacturing, retail, telecoms and energy.

HCL was founded in the 1970s as a hardware and electronic equipment manufacturer. In the 1980s it ventured into system development. With offices in São Paulo, Brazil, it serves customers in telecommunications, IT, healthcare, financial services and government. It also runs an IT application and development centre in the state of Rio Grande do Sul.

Genpact was founded in 1997 as a GE subsidiary. It has sales of more than US$ 1 billion and 37,000 employees. In Mexico Genpact operates two centres in Ciudad Juárez in the state of Chihuaha, and in Caborca in the state of Sonora. These offer bilingual English-Spanish customer service, document management and financial-accounting registry storage. In 2008 Genpact bought a call centre from GE Money in Guatemala.

Apart from these large BPO and ITO companies, there is a new generation of smaller-scale companies such as Evalueserve, Axial Analytics and Crisil-Irevna, whose focus is KPO, including market research, financial and patenting analysis.

Table III.4
INDIAN GLOBAL SERVICES PROVIDERS IN LATIN AMERICA, 2003-2009

Company/ service	Business process outsourcing	Information technology outsourcing	Knowledge process outsourcing	Annual sales 2008 *(dollars)*
Tata Consultancy Services	BPO (Santiago)	Application development, infrastructure support and consultancy (Buenos Aires; Guadalajara, Mexico; Montevideo, São Paulo, Brazil)		5.7 billion
Infosys Technologies		ICT consultancy, packaged solution management, infrastructure management (Monterrey, Mexico; Belo Horizonte, Brazil)		4.6 billion
Wipro	Shared services in finance, accounting, customer support and human resources (Curitiba, Brazil)	Design centre, development and testing centre (Monterrey, Mexico)		4.9 billion
Patni Computer Systems		Design, development and testing center (Querétaro, Mexico)		719 million
HCL Technology		Corporate application services, customized application management, remote infrastructure management (Rio Grande do Sul, Brazil)		2.3 billion
Genpact	Shared-services centre (Chihuaha and Sonora, Mexico) Customer support (Guatemala)			1.004 billion
Oracle Financial Services (I-flex)		Financial sector software solutions (Santiago)		478 million
Tech Mahindra		Design, development and testing centre (São Paulo, Brazil)		...

Table III.4 (concluded)

Company/ service	Business process outsourcing	Information technology outsourcing	Knowledge process outsourcing	Annual sales 2008 *(dollars)*
Mphasis	Contact centre (Baja California, Mexico)			...
WNS Global Services	Accounting, finance, customer service, research and analysis (San José)			360 million
Hewarare		Software development, application and maintenance (Coahuila, Mexico)		...
Polaris		Software solutions for banking and finance (Santiago)		
Zensar Technologies	Technical support centre (São Paulo, Brazil)			200 million
Firstsource	Back-office and shared services (Buenos Aires)			...
Essar Group	Customer support and telemarketing (San José)			...
Sasken		Software development and support centre, (Mexico)		142 million
Usha Martin		Software development centre (São Paulo, Brazil)		...
Evalueserve			Financial services KPO for banking, insurance and retail (Valparaíso, Chile)	...
Axial Analytics			KPO (Buenos Aires; Bogotá)	...
Crisil-Irevna			KPO (Buenos Aires)	...

Source: Prepared by the authors on the basis of data collected by the Boston Consulting Group, fDi Markets and Off-shoring Times.

2. Japanese firms

Hardware has become one of the most globalized industries in the world, and Japanese companies have gained leadership in each of its segments, including electronics, telecoms and network equipment and personal computing.

Japanese companies have expanded worldwide creating manufacturing centres in Asia (China and Viet Nam), in Eastern Europe (Czech Republic, Hungary and Poland) and in Latin America, (Mexico and Brazil). Between 2003 and 2009, Japanese companies were responsible for 80% of all hardware industry projects in both countries, second only to the United States in terms of foreign investment.

Brazil and Mexico offer different location advantages. Projects in Mexico target the United States, while those in Brazil focus on the large domestic market (ECLAC, 2008).

These investments have strengthened Japanese firms' world-class manufacturing capacity, and are gradually widening their range of activities to include different value-added services. Japanese companies operate several sales, marketing and technical support services, while gradually developing testing and software centres. Some specific R&D activities are also performed in industries such as telecoms (NTT), automotive (Nissan), chemicals (Takasago), pharmaceuticals (CMIC) and mining (Nippon Mining & Metals). Interestingly these are joint ventures with local companies and research centres.

Japan has not developed a global services industry such as India's, due to high labour costs and a more centralized, risk-adverse corporate culture. However, recessions and the ensuing cost-saving needs have forced Japanese multinationals, such as Sony, Nissan and Toyota, to outsource BPO services to China and, to a lesser extent, to the Republic of Korea, Viet Nam and India. Japan's main BPO providers are Fujitsu, IBM Japan, NEC and Nihon Unisys.

Fujitsu provides global services through Fujitsu Consulting, with operations in the United States, Canada and India, and a call centre in Costa Rica. NEC operates through NEC Solutions, NEC India and joint ventures with Indian companies such as HCL.

Japan has a strong competitive advantage in telecoms services, particularly Internet and digital television. NTT America, the United States subsidiary of NTT, is an active IP service provider. In the 1990s NTT created Access Nova, an R&D scheme with the University of Chile's School of Engineering. Initially focused on application development for wideband platforms, Access Nova has become an independent company while strengthening its relationship with NTT and a network of Japanese R&D

centres. Access Nova has an agreement with NTT DoCoMo to develop software applications for third and fourth generation mobile phones.

Another Latin American subsidiary of NTT is Micomo, a joint venture with Chile's State-owned mining giant CODELCO. Micomo develops IP telecoms solutions for large mining operations, integrating developments from other institutions such as University of Chile's Mathematical Modelling Centre (CMM,12 see chapter III), MIRS Robotics, ABB Chile and several R&D centres in Australia and the United States.

Another domain with Japanese involvement is R&D in specific areas, such as mining and resource-based industries. A prominent example is Biosigma, a joint venture between Nippon Mining & Metals and CODELCO. This is a case study for R&D offshoring services integration between Asia and Latin America.

Biosigma comprises a team of 12 Chilean and Japanese doctoral graduates specialized in molecular microbiology, bio-metallurgy and mineral characterization, working on developing biotech applications. According to the CREAX database, they have registered 42 patents, including mineral bacteria-based bioleaching technologies. Biosigma may be considered an in-house research centre and one of the main players in international research in this domain, which includes BHP Billiton, South Africa's Mintek and Colorado-based Geobiotics.

Table III.5

JAPANESE COMPANIES OPERATING IN-HOUSE CENTRES AND JOINT VENTURES IN LATIN AMERICA

Company/ service	Business process outsourcing	Information technology outsourcing	Knowledge process outsourcing	Annual sales 2008 *(millions of dollars)*
Fujitsu	DSL Technical Support Centre, San José	Software & IT services sector in a design, development and testing project, São Paulo, Brazil		46
NEC		Software development centre, São Paulo, Brazil		41
Sharp	Sales, marketing and support project for consumer electronics and office equipment, Mexico City			28
Nikon	Sales, marketing and technical support project for photography equipment, Mexico City			60

12 CMM provides Micomo with design and mathematical modelling services to perform tasks such as structural stress monitoring and modelling and prediction of environmental impact.

Table III.5 (concluded)

Company/ service	Business process outsourcing	Information technology outsourcing	Knowledge process outsourcing	Annual sales 2008 *(millions of dollars)*
Olympus	Sales, marketing and technical support, Santa Ana, Costa Rica			12.4
Casio Computer	Sales, marketing and technical support, Brazil and Mexico City			7
Furukawa (Japanese cable supplier)	Logistics, distribution and transportation for electronic components, Pernambuco, Brazil Sales, marketing and technical support, Argentina			...
Omron	Sales, marketing and technical support for industrial automation, Nuevo León, Mexico			...
Panasonic	Sales, marketing and technical support for consumer electronics, Santiago			77
Nidec	Logistics, distribution and transportation for home appliances, São Paulo, Brazil			...
Canon	Sales, marketing and technical support, Argentina			35
Mitsubishi Electric	Technical support centre for factory automation devices, São Paulo, Brazil			32
NTT (joint venture with University of Chile)			Development centre for high-speed network and broadband applications, Santiago	103
Takasago International			R&D and product development for Latin American customers, São Paulo, Brazil	1
CMIC			Clinical trial support services for drug and food development, Brazil	...
Nissan			Design, development and testing projection, Baja California, Mexico	83
Nippon Mining & Metals (joint venture with CODELCO)			R&D centre for bioleaching in mining, Santiago	...

Source: Prepared by the authors on the basis of data from the companies and fDi Markets.

3. Korean firms

The Republic of Korea has a similar services outlook to Japan. Large Korean conglomerates (known as chaebol) and their subsidiaries in electronics and automobiles operate in-house centres in key markets, including Latin America. Foreign multinationals such as IBM also provide outsourcing to the Republic of Korea's domestic and Asian markets from high-tech centres such as Incheon and Songdon International City. Korean large service providers include conglomerates such as LG, Samsung and Korea Telecom.

LG is a chaebol with 52 subsidiaries in electronics, chemicals and telecoms. Its global service companies include CS Leader and AIN Teleservices, in-house support service for LG Telecom customers; as well as LG CNS, an IT service provider whose subsidiary Ucess Partners is a Philippines-based BPO provider. In Latin America, LG operates an in-house call-centre and a training centre in Panama, as well as sales, marketing and technical support in Brazil, Chile and Colombia (see table III.6).

Table III.6
KOREAN IN-HOUSE CENTRES IN LATIN AMERICA, 2008

Company/ service	Business process outsourcing	Information technology outsourcing	Knowledge process outsourcing	Annual sales (*millions of dollars*)
LG	Customer contact centre in consumer electronics products, Panama City Education and training project in air conditioning, Panama Sales, marketing and technical support, Rio Grande do Sul (Brazil), Colombia and Santiago			82
Samsung	Maintenance and servicing centre for consumer electronics, Pereira (Colombia), Santiago, Buenos Aires and Mexico City	Software and IT services, São Paulo (Brazil)	R&D centre in mobile solutions, Recife (Brazil) R&D centre in communications, Campinas (Brazil)	110
KT&G			Design, development and testing project on tobacco (Brazil)	...
Sinil	Logistics, distribution and transportation centre for the telecoms industry, Tijuana (Mexico)			...
Daewoo	Sales, marketing and technical support, Santiago			...

Source: Prepared by the authors on the basis of data from fDi Markets.

Samsung is one of the world's largest providers of call centre equipment and technology, including IP telephony and office servers. Samsung has manufacturing operations in Manaus, Brazilian Amazonia (hard disks and LCDs) and Campinas, São Paulo (printers and cell phones). It operates in-house call centres in Mexico City, Buenos Aires, Santiago and Pereira (Colombia). High-value-added services (mobile technology development) are located in São Paulo, Campinas and Recife. Highly skilled human resources are the key factor in these investment projects, particularly Brazil's public and private universities such as the State University at Campinas (UNICAMP),[13] one of Latin America's foremost research institutions.

Korea Telecom is a global, diversified telecoms conglomerate present in all significant industry segments, including high-tech consultancy and network management. Its natural area of influence is Asia. In contrast with Japan's NTT, it does not have significant operations in Latin America, though it has some prospective operations in Chile.

4. Chinese firms

Trade and financial exchanges between China and Latin America focus on raw materials, which are increasingly important for the region. In this context, Chinese large-scale investments are meant to secure and consolidate the supply of minerals, energy and other fundamental materials.

One exception is Huawei, one of the world's most prominent high-tech companies. Huawei was created in 1988 and provides mobile Internet access solutions for large telecoms operators. It is one of the world's largest 3G technology providers, with US$ 11 billion in local sales (2006).

Huawei has a commercial presence in Brazil with offices in São Paulo, Rio de Janeiro and Brasilia. It also operates a training centre in Campinas with more than 1,000 employees. In 2008 Huawei sold US$ 1 billion in services, reflecting growth in Latin America's largest mobile market.

There are no Chinese offshoring projects in Latin America. Being a labour-intensive economy, China promotes foreign investment in its own domestic services sector. Chinese companies investing in Latin America usually need work visas not only for engineers and top executives, but also for unskilled workers.

---

13 The second largest city in the state of São Paulo.

5. Challenges to integration between Latin America and Asia

Research shows that Latin America cannot achieve a large-scale competitor status against large Asian services providers from India, the Philippines or China. Latin America cannot compete with Asia's cost structure, labour supply, or market and industry scale.

However, there is scope for integration and complementarity which can be promoted to achieve a critical mass of successful initiatives.

Robust Indian expansion in Latin America reveals a strategic vision to provide near-shore services to the United States market. Japanese and Korean in-house centres are part of a support network for large electronics and automobile clusters. Policymakers should target these two segments with fine-tuned initiatives, especially in ITO, KPO and value-added, higher-complexity centres. Current support mechanisms, including tax breaks and subsidies, have succeeded in attracting a first wave of investments, but should be updated to adjust to a new stage of industry development. Relevant strategy issues can be drawn from the experience of Eastern Europe and South-East Asia.

For example, there are still few joint Asian-Latin American R&D centres, which have the potential to become a major building block in Latin America's nascent knowledge-based economies.

C. Policy outlines for promoting the integration of offshoring services between Asia and Latin America

In the medium and long terms, Asia will be the world's leading economic zone. In terms of policy, China and India will base their leadership on strategies focused not on export promotion, but on creating the right conditions for the internationalization of their companies.

In terms of trade in services, Asia and Latin America are very different. Several Asian countries are the world's largest players, while Latin America is only marginal in this field.

Analysis of recent trends and medium-term perspectives show some competitive elements that might eventually allow Latin America to gain a better position in the global services trade. Whether this actually occurs will depend on a combination of public policies and corporate vision.

1. Latin America's perspectives in the offshoring industry

Latin America has a newly-gained role as a near-shore services provider for the United States market and a growing one as support centre hub for Japanese and Korean hardware manufacturers. Competitive advantages have been built up to offset historical prejudices and perceptions of Latin America as a politically and economically high-risk region. Some global services firms see Latin America not as a competitor to Asia, but rather as a complementary provider.

To take advantage of the current scenario, Latin American countries need to consolidate a set of advantages and skills. Current offshoring providers are not necessarily forced to choose between Asia, Europe or Latin America; instead, they seek a well balanced mix of operations on the three continents, allowing them to develop a truly global services supply in at least three time zones. In the case of R&D, this combination of different teams working simultaneously shortens the access-to-market of knowledge-based goods and services, from Internet search engines to chip-design software or biotech applications.

India's leadership in offshoring has been contested by a set of challenges such as increasing country risk, higher staff turnover and permanent wage inflation. The appreciation of the rupee, terrorist strikes, geopolitical risk and corporate malpractice are also increasing the need for India's providers to diversify geographically.

Eastern Europe, an alternative location to India, has also shown signs of stagnation. Rising labour costs, stalled labour supply and workforce mobility within Europe are eroding competitive advantages as far as estimated growth rates are concerned.

In this context, Latin America has a clear value to offer in the form of its skilled labour and cultural and geographical proximity to the United States and Western European markets. Though costs are higher than in India, they can be offset by higher productivity due to lower staff turnover, a smaller time-zone gap and a relatively stable business environment.

India's and Eastern Europe's offshoring development are the result of national efforts to simultaneously promote a skilled labour supply and develop consistent labour markets for engineers, finance specialists and accountants, quantitative analysts, biotech researchers, physicians, nurses and support teams.[14] From that point of view, Latin America has

---

14 The McKinsey Global Institute (2005) estimates that global demand for skilled workers specialized in services by main global industries (automobile, financial services, healthcare, insurance, IT services, software development, pharmaceuticals and retail) grew by more than 1.2 million worldwide between 2003 and 2008.

enormous potential. On the basis of information from McKinsey's Global Institute (2005), Latin America's labour supply is estimated at 50% of India's (in volume terms), larger than other countries and regions such as China or Eastern Europe. The offshoring industry has not viewed this skilled labour availability from a regional perspective yet, but has rather seen it in terms of individual countries such as Argentina, Brazil, Chile, Costa Rica, Mexico and Panama. A regional positioning strategy could create a powerful, human-resources-driven, near-shore service supply.

Latin America's cost advantages are consistent with the concept of a near-shore service platform for the United States market. Travel costs to the United States are significantly lower than from India or Eastern Europe, and travel times are shorter. A narrower time-zone gap is also a strong point. Costs savings lie between those of India and Eastern Europe.

Table III.7
LATIN AMERICA, INDIA AND EASTERN EUROPE: CHART OF COMPARATIVE ADVANTAGES, 2009
(Averages)

Factor	Latin America	India	Eastern Europe
Cost savings from the United States (percentages)	25-40	30-50	10-20
Time-zone gap with respect to the United States (hours)	2.5	13	7
Travel times from the United States (hours)	8	21	10
Travel costs from the United States (dollars)	2 750	8 500	5 400

Source: AT Kearney.

2. Public policies and productivity

The quality of public policies has been signalled as a key factor in economic growth and development in any given scenario. From the point of view of this study, attention must be given to policies that could stimulate factor productivity and promote the services industry.

Labour productivity is practically stagnant in Latin America (Farrell and Remes, 2007), precisely because of low productivity in the services sector,[15] which is currently the largest employer and focus of investment in the region. Services industries in Latin America are lagging behind owing to an institutional environment which lacks a pro-innovation and pro-entrepreneurial drive.

15 Brazil's food retail productivity is only 16% of that of the United States. In more capital-intensive services such as retail banking, Latin American productivity is less than half that of the United States (Farell and Remes, 2007).

Latin American governments have spent many years focusing on manufacture and industrial promotion policies, both capital-intensive industries that were losing competitiveness vis-à-vis Asian products. Only recently have they turned to policies to promote services and capitalize on their potential. Future developments should address company creation and closure, and promotion of market and factor flexibility.

3. Policies to promote the services industry

Several Latin American countries have adopted services promotion policies. Policy studies show both successes and shortcomings (Gereffi, Castillo and Fernandez-Stark). Issues that need to be addressed include:

- Infrastructure improvement: ICTs are central to the development of trade in services, based on cost-competitive quality broadband availability.
- Skill availability: A critical mass of skilled, bilingual professionals is central to cash in as a near-shore powerhouse.
- Institutional coordination: Export promotion is usually the responsibility of industry, trade or foreign relations ministries. Services export promotion is somehow diluted in a number of agencies such as customs, tax administrations, industrial promotion and investment attraction.
- Incentives: Several Latin American countries offer a set of incentives to attract foreign investment into offshoring and outsourcing projects. There is a risk of discrimination against local companies, which should be eligible if WTO rules allow it.
- Intellectual property rights and privacy: Call centre operation involves personal data management, which requires mandatory legislation to protect it. KPO also requires intellectual property rights protection.

There is broad scope to improve the regulatory environment in Latin America, including by eliminating restrictions and harmonizing standards as a means to make the region more attractive to Asian investors. Trade agreements are important for creating certainties and reducing risk, but they are not enough to promote actual business. A combination of policies is needed to improve bilateral trade regulation:

- Promotion of services agreements with Asia and implementation of agendas included in free trade agreements. The goal of services agreements should be to promote greater integration in value-added segments such as innovation and technology. If Latin America is to be perceived as a stable, attractive and low-risk economic zone, services integration within the region is central. This involves new and prompt mechanisms for obtaining work visas for technical and managerial staff, flexible rules for new start-ups, and international services trade without mandatory commercial presence.

- Agreements to avoid double taxation between Latin America and Asia. Governments should evaluate the real trade-offs between the initial decrease in tax flows versus new tax income from economic growth and job creation.
- Latin America-Asia mutual recognition agreements. Obstacles to skilled labour mobility are a major limitation to services integration. Some professional services require diploma recognition. In other services, professionals must stay in a foreign country for lengthy periods, making it all the more important to adopt mechanisms to avoid double taxation and double contributions to retirement funds.

4. Policy on research and development

Another key area for promoting integration and complementarity between Asia and Latin America is scientific research. Patent, investment and R&D data confirm that Latin America is lagging behind in knowledge creation, which does not mean that the region lacks world-class researchers.

Table III.8

SELECTED COUNTRIES: INVESTMENT IN R&D AS A PERCENTAGE OF GDP, 2006

Country	Public	Private	Total
Japan	0.60	2.20	2.80
Republic of Korea	0.60	1.90	2.50
Brazil	0.63	0.42	1.05
Mexico	0.23	0.23	0.46
Chile	0.36	0.31	0.67
Argentina	0.35	0.15	0.50

Source: Prepared by the authors on the basis of Organization for Economic Cooperation and Development (OECD) and information provided by the International Monetary Fund.

R&D levels in Latin America are lower than in Asia, and similar to some European countries, but most R&D expenditure is made by the public sector. In Japan and the Republic of Korea the largest share in R&D expenditure is made by private industrial conglomerates. In Latin America the public sector is the largest sponsor of scientific research, through government R&D promotion agencies such as CONICET (Argentina),

CONICYT (Chile) and COLCIENCIAS (Colombia). Japanese private investment in R&D amounts to US$ 95 billion yearly, i.e. equivalent to 2.2% GDP; by contrast, the Government of Brazil provides US$ 6 billion, or 0.63% of GDP, in R&D grants and subsidies.

Integration between the two regions could be sought through potential complementarity between private resources (Japan, Republic of Korea) and State subsidies by Latin American R&D agencies. Today, R&D cooperation between Latin America and Asia is scarce.

Mexico and Argentina show the highest levels of cooperation in terms of patented knowledge. However, Chile is the only country to have developed cooperation projects with an Asian country. As of 2006, Chile had a single shared patent with Japan, though the work of Biosigma should help to raise this number in the coming years. This Japanese-Chilean joint venture has achieved significant advances in bioleaching bacteria. Biosigma is an interesting case study, inasmuch as it has created new capital flows through patented knowledge.

Another relevant factor in R&D country indicators , is the role of foreign companies. In Ireland, Hungary and the Czech Republic this percentage varies from 40% to 60% of overall R&D investment. In Mexico it is almost nil, which confirms that industrial offshoring (maquila) is not a significant source of knowledge development or technology spillover (OECD, 2006, p.41). Individual government actions in Latin America should be informed by these models, whose lessons could be of value in assembling a set of skill-promoting subsidies for attracting R&D investments from Asia.

Under law 11.196 of 2005, Brazil allows national and foreign companies to accelerate depreciation and treat R&D as operational expenses and thus reduce income tax payments (including contracts with universities and small companies). Further deductions are possible by contracting scientists and patenting inventions. What is more, federal agencies will finance up to 40% of a researcher's salary (60% if the contract is in the Amazon region or in the Northeast) (Brito Cruz, 2011). The promotion agency of the State of São Paulo, Fapesp, covers from 20% to 70% of R&D expenditure to promote cooperation between companies and universities. Federal funds are also available to sponsor projects in telecommunications, ICTs, petroleum, aeronautics, healthcare, mining, water treatment and transport, among others. In this context, Brazil is strengthening links with other countries, including Japan, to promote research in areas such as health care and bio-fuels, in which it has world-class capacities and competence. It also has a large immigrant community of Japanese origin, with individuals active in research, production and politics.

A case study for exports of R&D services is the Mathematical Modelling Centre (CMM) in Chile, which has built up an impressive client portfolio of large mining and services companies, Chilean as well as foreign.[16] CMM offers world-class R&D outsourcing and an offshoring base of state-of-the art mathematical modelling. As seen in figure 20, CMM has several R&D projects and joint ventures with local companies, both private and State-run, as well as with foreign companies, mainly from Europe and North America.

Figure III.3
CLIENT NETWORK OF THE MATHEMATICAL MODELLING CENTRE, CHILE

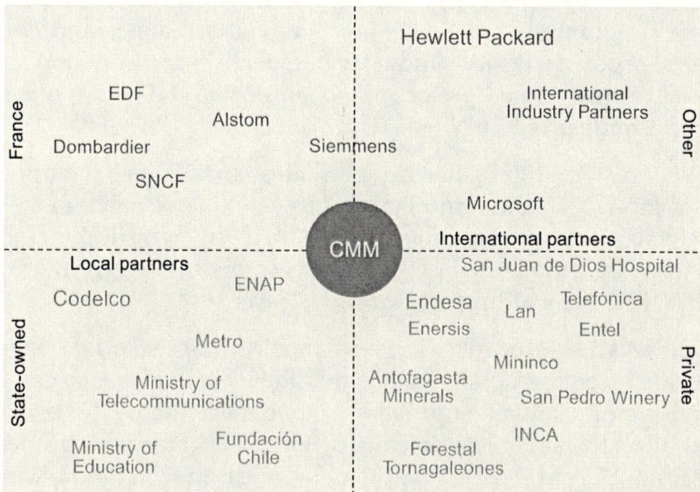

Source: Center for Mathematical Modelling, Universidad de Chile [online] www.cmm.cl.
Note: CMM clients not shown in the figure include the CODELCO subsidiaries Micomo and Biosigma, and Chuquicamata and Teniente mines.

Chile has an R&D promotion law which is part of a comprehensive national strategy to promote innovation and science, financed by a royalty tax levied on mining activities. Under the law, companies which hire a research centre registered with the development agency (CORFO) are eligible for credit (35% of total payments) and a 65% tax refund. In the past four years, emphasis has been given to collaborative university-run research centres focusing on specific areas, as well as

16 CMM has KPO contracts with Biosigma for biomining technology development and with Micomo for IP solutions. Chile's R&D support system is promoting this kind of interaction.

technological consortiums with private companies, in order to create ad hoc solutions for industry-specific problems. Agencies involved in this process are CONICYT (Ministry of Education), ICM (Ministry of Planning), FIA (Ministry of Agriculture) and Innova (CORFO). Under a systemic approach (Ministry of Economic Affairs of Chile, 2010, pp. 53-58), these agencies provide capital for collaborative or individual, theoretical or applied research. Several of the R&D projects mentioned in this study were supported by Conicyt.

5. Education, training and social capital

Asia and Latin America are separated by geography, time zones and cultural factors. Policies could help bridge these gaps by promoting Asian language programmes, academic and student exchanges and circulation of cultural products. Positive industry perspectives in near-shore and KPO (for United States-related projects) lend support to the notion of culture as a powerful trade promoter.

Visa restrictions in the United States since 2003 have affected the influx of foreign IT and engineering professionals. Unable to stay in the United States, foreign students return to their countries in increasing numbers. They ultimately operate as promoters of foreign investment in trade in services, including offshoring projects.

Chile is a significant example. Yahoo!, Synopsis and AirSage's R&D centres are a policy achievement, but they also reflect larger cultural issues. Several Chilean engineers who participated in these projects trained at universities in the United States, a factor which operates as trust-capital. CMM has an agreement with the National Centre for Scientific Research (CNRS) of France, and several of its mathematicians trained in that country, which helps to explain a number of contracts with large French industrial conglomerates. There are few examples of such links links between Latin America and Asia, however. Latin American engineers, designers and scientists could eventually follow graduate programmes in Japan, China or the Republic of Korea and act as integration brokers in the future.

Universities could play a key role in Asian-Latin American integration in relation to services exports and offshoring. Agreements between governments and universities have the potential to stimulate professional and scientific training, creating knowledge networks and building trust.

6. Regional initiatives

National policies have been enacted to promote and attract investment, and to facilitate bilateral trade between Asia and Latin America. There are fiscal incentives as well an attractive supply of human resources. But there is still space for regional and subregional action to produce a coherent and effective strategy to support Asian companies willing to offshore and outsource in Latin America.

A joint regional approach is a major policy challenge for Latin America, because a coordinated strategy implies major breakthroughs in two key areas:

- Services must gain top priority on national agendas, avoiding seizure and co-option by the bureaucratic interests of services promotion policies.
- Services integration within Latin America is central to promote a free flow of professionals. Intraregional agreements should be implemented to grant work visas and recognition of diplomas and qualifications.

Significant efforts could be made within the region to double taxation agreements, of which there are only 14 in the region thus far.

Agreements must act as effective support mechanisms for companies willing to internationalize. Offshoring project planning and design requires specialists to travel, supervise and hold meetings with local partners. These professionals also need health insurance and pension-fund mechanisms, whether long- or short-term. Agreements must bring tangible and practical trade benefits, as well as operational flexibility, thus leading to robust integration in R&D, innovation and development.

Regional integration institutions have been slow to adopt trade in services as a priority on their agendas. Members have not shown the necessary commitment to this end. Attention has been given to the study and follow-up of national policies, downplaying the possibility of coordinating a systematic agenda.

Bibliography

Animation Council of the Philipinnes (2008), Pinoy Animation Defined [online] http://www.animationcouncil.org/news.php?p=88.

AT Kearney (2006), "Chile Offshore Objectives Assessment Study", Working document.

___(2009) , "The Shifting Geography of Offshoring", Chicago.

Balfour, Frederik (2006), "Vietnam's Growing Role in Outsourcing", *Business Week*, December.

Bhide, D. (2005), "Strategic Offshoring: Decision Analysis, Best Practices, and Emerging Trends", *Technology and Offshore Outsourcing Strategies*, P. Brudenall, , London, Palgrave Macmillan.

Boston Consulting Group (2007), "Estudios de competitividad en clusters de la economía chilena", Documento de referencia Offshoring, Santiago, Chile.

Boston Consulting Group (2009).

Brito Cruz, C.H (2011), "Support for Business R&D in Brazil", presentation, unpublished.

Chu, Michael and Gustavo Herrero (2005), CASES "Tata Consultancy Services Iberoamerica", Harvard Business School.

CNN (Cable News Network) News (2007), July.

Couto, V. and V. Sehgal (2007), *Offshoring 2.0, Contracting Kowledge and Innovation to Expand Global Capabilities*, Duke University School of Business, Booz & Co.

ECLAC (Economic Commission for Latin America and the Caribbean) (2011) *Foreign Direct Investment in Latin America and the Caribbean 2010* (LC/G.2494-P), Santiago, Chile.

___(2009), *Foreign Direct Investment in Latin America and the Caribbean 2009* (LC/G.2447-P), Santiago, Chile. United Nations publication, Sales No. E.10.II.G.4.

___(2008), "Offshore corporate services in Latin America and Caribbean", paper presented at the seminar on Offshore Corporate Services in Latin America and the Caribbean.

Farell, Diana and Jaana Remes (2007), "Latin America's Potential in Services", *The McKinsey Quarterly*, New York.

fdimarkets (2010), Foreign Direct Investment (FDI) database [online] http://www.fdimarkets.com/.

Friedman, L. Thomas (2004), "Doing our homework", *New York Times*, 24 June.

Gartner (2009), "Picking the Right Country Destination for Offshore Services", Partha Iyengar, Gartner Outsourcing & Vendor Management, Summit, 4-6 May.

Gereffi G., M. Castillo and K. Fernandez-Stark (2009), *The Offshore Services Industry: A New Opportunity for Latin America*, Center on Globalization, Governance & Competitiveness, Duke University.

Lewin, A.Y. and V. Couto (2006), *Next Generation Outsourcing, Offshoring Research Network*, Duke University School of Business.

McKinsey's Global Institute (2005), "The Emerging Global Labor Market, Part I – The Demand for Offshore Talent in Services", June.

Ministry of Economic Affairs of Chile (2010), "Memoria 2008-2010", Santiago.

National Academy of Public Administration (2006), "Offshoring, an Elusive Phenomenon", Panel Report, Washington, D.C.

OCO Global & fDi Markets (2009), "FDI opportunities for Chile in the BPO sector".

OECD (Organization for Economic Cooperation and Development), "Chile, Science, Technology and Industry Outlook, Country Notes", Paris.

___(2006), *Science, Technology and Industry Outlook*, Paris.

UNCTAD (United Nations Conference on Trade and Development) (2008), *World Investment Report 2008*, Geneva.

United Nations (2009), World Population Division Database, Department of Economic and Social Affairs [online] http://www.un.org/esa/population/.

Wilson, Michael (2007), "Good Morning Vietnam", IT21, Olathe, Kansas.

Chapter IV

Business models for trans-Latins: Latin American investments in Asia [1]

Andrés López

Daniela Ramos

Iván Torre

Introduction

In recent years Latin America has exhibited strong economic growth, supported by a favourable international context including high prices for its main export commodities and cautious macroeconomic management, particularly on the fiscal front. Also helping to drive growth, an economic policy formulated to keep exchange rates high has boosted export performance.

However, the outlook for the global economy is highly uncertain. Although the worst effects of the 2008-2009 crisis have seemingly been avoided, the next few years' global growth rates are likely to fall short of pre-crisis levels, with developing countries growing faster than developed economies. The possibility of the developed world relapsing into recession cannot be ruled out. This means that international conditions will favour Latin America's growth far less than in 2003-2008 (ECLAC, 2010).

[1] The comments of German King, Joaquin Piña and Jaesung Kwak on a previous version of this report are gratefully acknowledged. The authors would also like to thank Sofía Fernández Guerrico for her valuable assistance.

Although developing countries are expected to keep growing even in this less favourable scenario, slacker growth of the international economy will act as a drag on international trade as developed countries' demand for imports falls and developing countries' export opportunities consequently shrink. Moreover, competition for exports and investments will be tougher than before, underlining the need for many developing countries to rethink their specialization patterns and network of trade and investment relations in order to adapt to the new scenario (ECLAC, 2010).

In this regard, it is important to recall that concerns about the sustainability of growth in Latin America existed even during the recent high-growth period. At the time, many analysts warned that the fair-weather period should be used as an opportunity to make the structural transformations needed to put the region on a growth path that would be sustainable over time.

How to integrate the region into the world economy was one of the main points on this agenda of structural change. This issue, in turn, needed to be addressed in the context of a global scenario characterized by growing integration among national economies —through trade, investment, finance, and so forth— and the increasing internationalization of global value chains. Although the crisis has hurt trade and investment, trends towards production internationalization will not be reversed (although they may be slowed for a time). Accordingly, the question of how to integrate Latin America into global value chains remains highly relevant.

This issue has many angles. First, it involves questions related to foreign trade flows, that is, the geographical and sectoral patterns of exports and imports in the region. Second, it touches upon investment —both FDI inflows (in relation to the objectives, strategies and impacts of foreign transnational corporations investing in Latin America) and FDI outflows (investments by the homegrown multinationals that have come to be known as trans-Latins). Third, both trade and investment issues need to be analysed in the context of the creation of global value chains, which are deployed not only in manufacturing but also in services (López, Ramos and Torre, 2009).

East Asian countries are, on the one hand, a potential threat for Latin American countries because they compete for foreign markets and for investment and are a growing source of imports for many Latin American countries (which means that some domestic industries in the latter could suffer). On the other hand, Asia has been a key driver of world economic growth in recent years and its role will be even more important in the coming years. This means that Asian countries are also attractive markets for Latin American firms wishing to export and invest abroad and that they offer opportunities for partnerships in many areas where complementarities between both regions exist.

All forecasts indicate that Asia's weight in the world economy will keep growing. GDP in East Asia and the Pacific expanded at more than 8% yearly in 2010 and 2011, vis-à-vis 2.7% and 3.2% for the world as a whole (World Bank, 2010). After falling in 2009, FDI from Asia jumped 35% in 2010 to levels above those recorded in 2008 (IIF, 2010).

The share of South and East Asia (excluding Japan) in total FDI inflows grew from 8.4% in the 1970s to 9.5% in the 1980s, 16.6% in the 1990s and 15.1% in the 2000s. The region absorbs more than half of all FDI flowing into developing countries (UNCTAD). The Asian region presents market opportunities and attracts efficiency-seeking investments. South and East Asian countries are well integrated into global value chains. Each one offers distinctive advantages and capabilities, from low labour costs to huge domestic markets and a store of technological expertise. Moreover, many countries are upgrading their integration into global value chains; China, for instance, is now hosting research-and-development oriented investments.

But Asia is also a destination for FDI. The share of South and East Asia in terms of global FDI outflows grew from 0.2% in the 1970s to 4% in the 1980s and 8% in the 1990s and 2000s (based on UNCTAD data).

The emerging role of Asia, and in particular of China and India, poses challenges and opportunities for the world; Latin America is not an exception. This report will focus on opportunities for Latin American firms to invest in Asia. These firms need to rethink their business models in order to adapt to the new global scenario. Although FDI sourced in Latin American countries is nothing new, the region as a whole is not a major player in the world of emerging transnational corporations —with the partial exception of Brazilian companies in recent years. Because developed countries may be entering a phase of lower growth and fewer investment opportunities, investing in Asia may be an attractive option for many Latin American firms seeking to internationalize their business strategies.

The aim of this paper is to examine the experiences of a few manufacturing companies that have invested in Asia, not only through distribution channels but also by setting up manufacturing facilities. The prime focus will be on successful trans-Latin investments in Asia, especially their strategies, objectives, perceived opportunities for further investments and the challenges of and requirements for investing in the region. The results of this study will facilitate the design of strategies aimed at fostering such investments, which could help counterbalance the current economic relationship between the two regions. That relationship is based mostly on exports of natural resources from Latin America and imports of manufactured goods from Asia, with low bilateral FDI flows between them.

A. Latin America in global value chains: foreign direct investment

South and East Asia (excluding Japan) account for a growing share of total foreign direct investment (FDI) inflows, climbing from 8.4% in the 1970s to 9.5% in the 1980s, 16.6% in the 1990s and 15.1% in the 2000s. This region now absorbs more than half of total FDI inflows going to developing countries (UNCTAD). It receives both market-seeking and efficiency-seeking investments. South and East Asian countries are well integrated into global value chains, with each country offering distinctive advantages and capabilities that range from low labour costs to huge domestic markets and a store of technological expertise. Moreover, many countries are upgrading their integration into global value chains; China, for instance, is now hosting research-and-development oriented investments.

But Asia is also a source of FDI. South and East Asia's share of global FDI outflows grew from 0.2% in the 1970s to 4% in the 1980s and 8% in the 1990s and 2000s (based on UNCTAD data).

The emerging role of Asia, and in particular of countries such as China and India, poses a number of challenges and opportunities for the world as a whole. Latin America firms are no exception, and they are rethinking their business models in order to adapt to the new global scenario.

1. Inward FDI

Figure IV.1 shows FDI inflows into Latin America in recent years. These inflows have mostly followed the global trend, although with a higher degree of volatility. After a sustained fall during the early 2000s, FDI started to recover —slightly at first and more strongly in the past few years.

The main investors in Latin America are developed countries. According to ECLAC data, in 2004-2008 around 30% of inward FDI came from the United States, 15% from the Netherlands, 10% from Spain and 5% from Canada. Investment from within the region accounted for only 6% of total inward FDI.

Asian investment in Latin America has been very limited, accounting for only 1.7% of total FDI to Argentina in 2008. In the case of Brazil, Asian countries were the source of 4.6% of total inward FDI in 2008; 4.4% came from Japan alone. In many Latin American countries, Asian investment is so small that it is included in the "other countries" category of official statistics, making it impossible to identify the exact amount.

Figure IV.1
WORLD AND LATIN AMERICA: INWARD FDI FLOWS
(Billions of dollars)

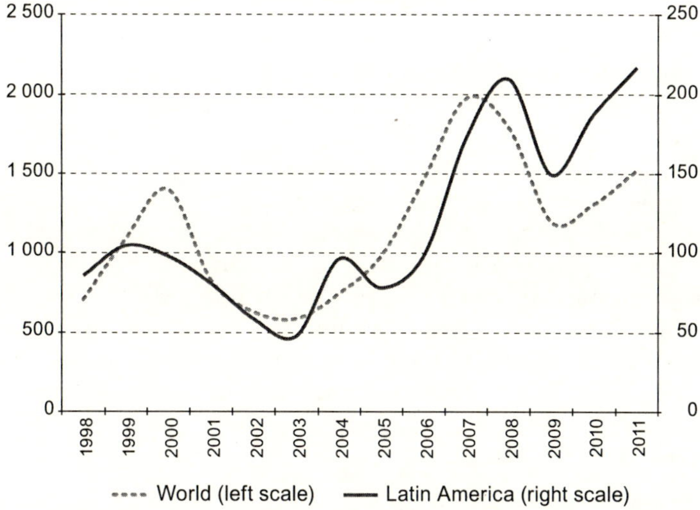

Source: United Nations Conference on Trade and Development (UNCTAD), 2011.

The bulk of FDI coming into Latin America has been going to the services sector —mainly telecommunications, finance and public utilities— although natural resources have been attracting a larger share in the past few years. While in 2000 about 60% of total inward FDI went to the services sector and 10% to natural resource exploitation, by 2008 these percentages had shifted to 50% and 25%, respectively. Manufacturing retained a stable 20% share throughout the period (ECLAC, 2009).

There is a strong relationship between trade patterns and the type of FDI received by subregions of Latin America and the Caribbean. In South American countries, exploitation of natural resources and access to national or regional markets (resource- and market-seeking strategies) seem to be the determining factors behind FDI location decisions, and they centre primarily on natural resource sectors, some manufacturing activities (mainly the automobile, chemical and food industries) and services (such as public utilities, banks and commerce). On the other hand, Mexico, Central America and the Caribbean, by and large, receive efficiency-seeking investments in the industrial sector (including automobiles, textiles, garments and electronics) drawn above all by low labour costs. Geographical proximity to the main consumption markets can act as another driver of investment decisions. These investments mainly target labour-intensive stages of the transnational corporations' production networks and, as explained earlier, tend to operate as enclaves with low levels of integration into the domestic (host) economy.[2]

The different degrees and forms of Latin America's insertion into global value chains through transnational corporations do not seem to generate notable differential FDI impacts in the region. In the case of MERCOSUR, research (see Chudnovsky and López, 2006) shows that the macroeconomic impacts of FDI have not been significant, with no effect on GDP growth or investment. But the microeconomic impacts of FDI seem to have been stronger, albeit uneven. While subsidiaries of transnational corporations are more integrated from a foreign trade viewpoint than domestic companies are, this does not generate spillover to local firms (that is, it does not help them become exporters). The exception is Brazil, where such spillover seems to have existed and has generally benefitted local firms with the highest productivity and hurt those with the lowest.

In terms of productivity, the presence of transnational corporations seems to have given rise to positive spillover to the local companies that supply them. However, horizontal spillover —that is, among companies that compete in the same market— is infrequent and seems to depend on the particularities of the local companies and the markets in which they operate[3] (Chudnovsky and López, 2006). Similar findings are reported for Colombia, where there is no evidence of horizontal spillover but there are cases of vertical spillover (Kugler, 2006).

In Mexico, FDI impacts, although positive in terms of exports, employment and wages (at least in certain regions of the country), have been weak in terms of production chains,[4] human resource training and technological development on a local level (Capdevielle, 2005;

---

[2] Mexico also received substantial market-seeking FDI flows, both in industrial and in service sectors.

[3] In Argentina, the companies with the most absorption capacity benefitted from the presence of transnational corporations; in Brazil, those that gained the most were national companies with the widest productivity gap vis-à-vis the transnationals. The hypothesis behind the finding in Argentina is based on the fact that the greater the absorption capacity, the easier it is to transfer knowledge from transnational company subsidiaries to local firms. In Brazil's case, the finding might be due to the effect of massive inflows of market-seeking FDI into a country, displacing local firms that compete directly with foreign subsidiaries in the same markets (Chudnovsky and López, 2006).

[4] The percentage of local input in the total intermediate consumption of Mexico's manufacturing activity has been in the region of 10%; in temporary import-for-export programmes the respective figures double. Nevertheless, only 30% of such inputs are industrial, the rest being services that are difficult to replace with imports because of physical barriers (Capdevielle, 2005).

ECLAC, 2005; Dussel Peters, 2003). Weak local innovation dynamics limit the learning process; weak local linkages obviously curtail potential spillover. In more general terms, maquila industries and similar ones did see product and process upgrading, and even greater organizational complexity and subsidiary autonomy, but this has not been accompanied accordingly by functional upgrading nor has it prevented labour from being the most important local added value in such operations (Capdevielle, 2005). FDI in this region does not seem to have generated externalities for local companies by means of human capital mobility either. Additionally, in many countries a dual export —and industrial— structure has emerged, since national companies specialize in primary and traditional goods and, even where they produce the same goods, serve different markets (Ciarli and Giuliani, 2005; Bair and Dussel Peters, 2006).

In this general scenario, Brazil is the best-positioned country in terms of FDI impacts. Fleury and Leme Fleury (2006) report that in the face of China's emergence as a global competitor in the textile industry, transnational corporation subsidiaries located in Brazil have focused on specialized, high value-added products, which shows their interest in remaining in that market (as well as the fact that production is not primarily based on low labour costs). Brazil is also the location chosen by transnational corporations for research and development operations and for investing in high-tech sectors (not with maquila schemes).

2. Outward FDI

The share of world FDI outflows going to developing countries rose from 1.2% to 24.9% between the 1970s and 2010-2011 (see table IV.1). Latin America influences this trend less than the Asian economies. While the weight of the latter went from 19% of total FDI from developing countries between 1970 and 1979, to 65% between 2000 and 2010-2011, Latin America's participation dropped from 42% to 28% (and nearly half of it comes from major financial centres in the Caribbean).

According to UNCTAD statistics, outward FDI from Latin America[5] in 2010 amounted to US$ 61.4 billion —the second highest figure in the region's history, topped only by the US$ 49 billion reported in 2006 (see figure IV.2). The same data show that Mexico was, in 2010, the region's leading foreign investor, accounting for 23% of the total (after suffering the impacts of the global financial crisis in 2008), followed by Brazil (19% of Latin American outward FDI in 2010) and Chile (14%).

---

[5] Includes South and Central America and Mexico.

Table IV.1
SELECTED DEVELOPING COUNTRIES AND REGIONS: SHARE IN GLOBAL AND DEVELOPING COUNTRY FDI OUTFLOWS, 1970-2011
(Percentages)

	1970-1979		1980-1989		1990-1999		2000-2009		2010-2011	
	Of world total	Of DC[a] total	Of world total	Of DC[a] total	Of world total	Of DC[a] total	Of world total	Of DC[a] total	Of world total	Of DC[a] total
Developing countries	1.2	100	6.4	100	10.7	100	14.8	100	24.9	100
South, East and South-East Asia	0.2	19.0	3.9	61.8	7.9	73.3	9.0	60.7	16.3	65.3
Latin America and the Caribbean	0.5	41.2	1.2	18.7	2.4	22.0	4.3	29.3	7.0	28.0
Argentina	-0.0	-2.0	-0.0	-0.1	0.3	3.1	0.1	0.5	0.1	0.3
Brazil	0.3	24.9	0.2	3.8	0.2	2.1	0.5	3.5	0.3	1.3
Chile	0.0	0.6	0.0	0.2	0.2	2.1	0.3	2.1	0.7	2.7
Colombia	0.0	3.4	0.0	0.7	0.1	0.6	0.1	0.8	0.5	1.9
Costa Rica	0.0	0.0	0.0	0.1	0.0	0.0	0.0	0.0	0.0	0.0
Mexico	0.0	0.1	0.1	1.4	0.1	1.4	0.3	2.3	0.7	2.9
Peru	0.0	0.0	0.0	0.1	0.0	0.1	0.0	0.1	0.0	0.0
Uruguay	0.0	0.0	0.0	0.0	0.0	0.0	0.0	0.0	-0.0	-0.0
Venezuela (Bolivarian Republic of)	0.0	0.0	0.1	1.5	0.1	1.1	0.1	0.5	0.1	0.4

Source: UNCTAD.
[a] Developing countries.

FIGURE IV.2
WORLD AND LATIN AMERICA: OUTWARD FDI FLOWS
(Billions of dollars)

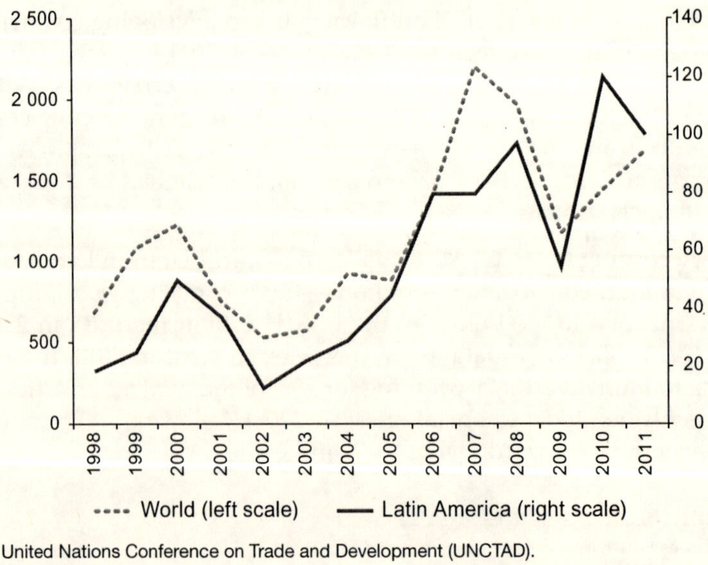

Source: United Nations Conference on Trade and Development (UNCTAD).

Given Latin America's low share of global FDI outflows, it is not surprising that among the top 100 transnational corporations from developing countries in 2008, only nine are from Latin America (four from Mexico, three from Brazil, one from Argentina and one from the Bolivarian Republic of Venezuela). In addition to eight South African and Russian companies, three from Kuwait and one each from Egypt, United Arab Emirates, Qatar and Turkey, the remaining 68 are from South and East Asia (UNCTAD, 2010). Another ranking (which excludes transnational corporations from the more advanced Asian economies) shows that among the top 100 firms from emerging countries, China leads with 41 firms, followed by India with 20. Brazil is third and Mexico fourth (with 13 and 7 companies, respectively). As for the rest of Latin America, only Argentina and Chile are in this ranking, with one company each (see figure IV.3).

FIGURE IV.3
DEVELOPING AND TRANSITION COUNTRIES: NUMBER OF FIRMS IN THE TOP 100 GLOBAL FIRMS FROM EMERGING ECONOMIES, 2011

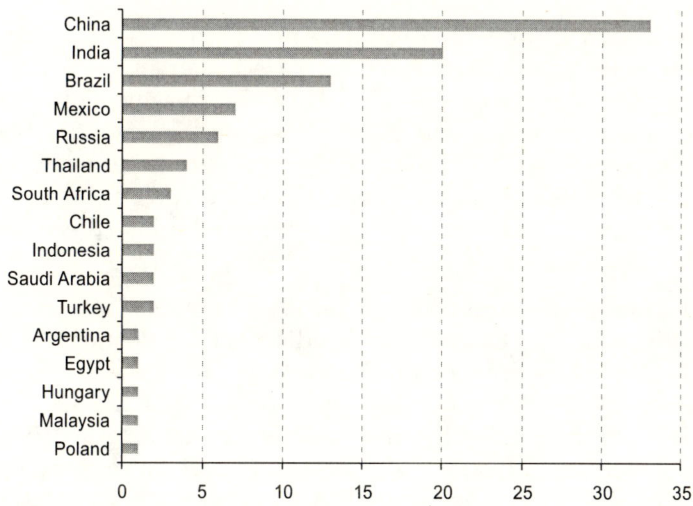

Source: Boston Consulting Group (2011).

The relative contribution by individual Latin American countries to FDI outflows from the region has changed over time. Argentina, whose companies were already FDI pioneers in the twentieth century and were a significant source of FDI in the 1960s, 1970s and 1990s, has seen its share slip in the past few years —basically due to the sale of a large part of its major companies to foreign transnational corporations. Nowadays, as said before, Brazil, Mexico and Chile have become leading sources of FDI outflows from the region.

FDI from the trans-Latins tends to be concentrated in basic industries (such as hydrocarbons, extractive mining and the steel and cement industries), food and beverages and some services (mostly, engineering and telecommunications). On the other hand, FDI from Asian companies tends to target high-tech sectors.[6] Asian transnational corporations increasingly base their activities on efficiency- or strategic-asset-seeking strategies; in the case of the trans-Latins the search for natural resources and markets prevails and may reduce potential positive externalities that might result from emerging economies.

However, there are cases of Latin American companies reaching world-class excellence levels in their respective industries (for example, Techint in Argentina, CEMEX in Mexico and Petrobras in Brazil). Some even compete in sectors that are subject to rapid technological change or in which competition on the basis of design and innovation is key. Examples include Embraer (Brazil) in the aeronautical sector (see Goldstein, 2002), Telmex and América Móvil (Mexico) in telecommunications and IMPSA (Argentina) in equipment.

Although most FDI in Latin America has been intraregional, in recent years trans-Latins have increased their investments outside the region. Brazilian firms such as Vale, Gerdau and Petrobras are a good example of this trend (see Niembro, Ramos and Simkievich, 2009). There are also examples in Mexico (Alfa Group and CEMEX) and Argentina (Techint, IMPSA). As seen below, although Asia is still not a major destination for most trans-Latins, there are some interesting cases.

The available information on destinations for outward FDI from Latin America (ECLAC, 2009) indicates that most of it is directed towards the American continent:in 2008 the main geographical destination of Brazilian outward investment was the United States (with 28% of the total), the financial centres of the Caribbean (25% of total Brazilian outward FDI) and the rest of Latin America (12%). Asia's share of Brazil's outward FDI stock barely surpassed 0.1% in 2008 and was concentrated in China and Japan (according to figures from Brazil's central bank). Chile's figures show that 72% of its outward FDI went to South America; Colombia's foreign investments were mostly concentrated in the United States (57% of the total). Between 1994 and 2009 outward Colombian FDI going to Asia was close to zero (Colombia's Banco de la República). There are no statistics available for the rest of the countries.

[6] Twenty-four of Asia's 76 major transnationals operate in IT, electronics and telecommunication sectors; only two trans-Latins do (UNCTAD, 2009).

Notwithstanding the lack of data, Asia is quite marginal as a target for Latin American foreign investment. But even if on a relatively small scale, Latin American companies do invest in Asia (this may be understated in official statistics due to registration issues).[7] The Vale Columbia Center (2007, 2009) has issued a series of reports with valuable information on the activities of trans-Latins, including their investments in Asia.

Argentina's leading multinationals have only a limited presence outside the Western Hemisphere, where 88% of their foreign subsidiaries are found. Europe accounts for 8% and the rest of the world for 4%. Argentina's top four multinationals have a presence in Asia; in order of size they are Techint (metals), Arcor (food), IMPSA (oil and energy) and Bagó (pharmaceutical). Among the Asian countries, China has received the most investments from Argentina, although on a small scale involving less than US$ 30 million per year according to López and Ramos (2009). These investments targeted the metal, food and energy sectors of the Chinese economy. Worthy of special note is the soybean crushing industry: in recent years Argentine soybean exporters have set up several processing plants in China, which is Argentina's largest soybean export market (López, Ramos and Simkievich, 2008).

The case of Mexican multinationals is similar: most of their presence outside the Western Hemisphere is concentrated in Europe, and their investments in Asia are limited. The main exception is the major Mexican cement producer CEMEX, which has investments in China, Philippines, Bangladesh, Malaysia and Thailand, among other countries. Other Mexican companies that have subsidiaries in Asia include ALFA and Grupo Carso (both are conglomerates), Gruma and Bimbo (food and beverages). Televisa (entertainment) and Grupo Modelo (food and beverages) have a joint venture with a Chinese company and sales offices in Tokyo, respectively.

The Latin American companies with the highest degree of involvement in the Asian economy are multinationals headquartered in Brazil, although, as mentioned earlier, the amounts of money invested are low in absolute terms. The top Brazilian mining corporation Vale do Rio Doce has large investments in China and other East and Middle Asian countries, as do Votorantim (a diversified group), WEG (metals) and Marcopolo (transport equipment), among other companies. However, according to Saslavsky and Rozemberg (2009) Brazil's highest-profile investment in Asia may have been airplane manufacturing company

[7] While a relevant share of outward FDI from Latin American firms goes to tax havens, the final destination of some of those flows may be Asia.

Embraer's US$ 50 million investment in China in the early 2000s to produce (in joint venture with a Chinese company) a Chinese version of its successful ERJ 145 regional jet.

Table 7 provides a non-exhaustive list of Latin American companies with investments in Asia. The list includes firms with production facilities and those with trade and technical assistance activities or sales offices. These two types of investment do not have the same implications in terms of value added or global value chain logic, but both have been included in the list because they constitute an important step in the corporate internationalization process. Some of the projects are wholly-owned by the trans-Latins while others are joint ventures with Asian partners. Brazil is the country with more firms investing in Asia, although a number of Mexican, Chilean and Argentinean firms also have a presence there. As would be expected, China is the main investment destination country. Another Asian giant, India, is also an important host country for Latin American firms. Other East Asian countries at the receiving end of investments from Latin America include Singapore, Indonesia, Japan, Malaysia, Hong Kong, the Republic of Korea and the Philippines.

Although the pattern is somewhat diversified, the food and beverage industry clearly stands out as the largest recipient sector. Other major recipient sectors are engineering and construction, steel and metallurgy, auto parts and transport vehicles and oil and mining. A number of Brazilian and Chilean banks have opened branches in some Asian countries.

In almost all of these cases, investments in Asia are very recent, that is, they have emerged in the secondary stages of the trans-Latins' internationalization process. This clearly suggests that Asia is not high on the agenda for the average Latin American company, which is more focused on expanding within the region and, eventually, in developed countries such as the United States or those that are part of the European Union. However, as Asia's role in the global economy grows it is likely to attract more investments from Latin American firms.

Table IV.2
LATIN AMERICAN FIRMS WITH INVESTMENTS IN ASIA

Home country	Company	Industry	Host countries with	
			Production facilities	Trade and technical assistance activities or sales offices
Argentina	Techint	Steel; engineering and construction	China, Japan, Indonesia, Saudi Arabia, India, Republic of Korea, Qatar, Kazakhstan, United Arab Emirates	Singapore
	IMPSA	Metallurgy	China, Malaysia, Philippines, Viet Nam	India, Hong Kong (Special Administrative Region of China), Indonesia
	Bagó	Drugs	Pakistan	
	Arcor	Food and beverages		China
	Chemo	Drugs	China	
Brazil	Vale (CVRD)	Mining	China, Indonesia, Japan, Republic of Korea, Oman, Kazakhstan, Philippines, Malaysia, Mongolia, Hong Kong	Singapore
	Petrobras	Oil	China, India, Japan	Iran, Singapore
	Votorantim	Mining and metallurgy	China	
	Embraer	Aircrafts	China	Singapore
	Odebrecht	Engineering and construction	United Arab Emirates	China
	Sadia	Food and beverages		United Arab Emirates, China, Japan
	Perdigão	Food and beverages		United Arab Emirates
	Vicunha	Textiles	China	
	Marfrig	Food and beverages	China, Korea, Thailand, Malaysia	
	Gerdau	Steel	India	
	Weg	Electric equipment	China, India	Korea, United Arab Emirates, Japan, Singapore, Thailand
	Banco do Brasil	Banking		China, Japan, Hong Kong (Special Administrative Region of China), Republic of Korea, United Arab Emirates
	Bradesco	Banking		Japan

Table IV.2 (concluded)

Home country	Company	Industry	Host countries with: Production facilities	Host countries with: Trade and technical assistance activities or sales offices
	Itau	Banking		China, Hong Kong (Special Administrative Region of China), Japan, United Arab Emirates
Brazil	Sabó	Auto parts	China, Japan	
	Marcopolo	Transport vehicles	India, China	
	Randon	Trucks and auto parts	China	United Arab Emirates
	Caixa Econômica Federal	Banking		Japan
	Iochpe	Auto parts and railway equipment	China	
	Andrade Gutierrez	Engineering and telecommunications	United Arab Emirates, Saudi Arabia, Qatar, Iran, China	
Chile	Sociedad Química y Minera de Chile	Chemicals and mining	China, India, Thailand	Japan
	Molymet	Chemicals		China
	Banco de Chile	Banking		China
	BCI	Banking		Hong Kong (Special Administrative Region of China)
	ENAP	Oil	Iran, Kuwait	
	Antofagasta	Mining	Pakistan	
	Viña Montes	Restaurant		Japan[a]
	Luksic	Wine	China	
Mexico	CEMEX	Cement	Philippines, China, Bangladesh, United Arab Emirates, Israel, Malaysia, Thailand	
	Televisa Group	Entertainment		China
	Bimbo Group	Food and beverages	China	
	Gruma	Food and beverages	China, Malaysia	
	Alfa	Auto parts	China	
	Grupo Modelo	Food and beverages		Japan
	Grupo Carso	Auto parts, electric equipment		China

Source: Prepared by the authors, on the basis of the companies' websites.
[a] Franchise.

B. Case studies of Latin American firms internationalizing in Asia

This section takes a closer look at the Asian strategies of some Latin American companies chosen as case studies. Techint and IMPSA are business groups with companies that operate in diverse fields; Bimbo and Embraer operate in their own specific sector. The internationalization strategy followed by each firm is examined separately.

1. Tenaris (Techint Group)

The Techint Group was created in 1945 in Italy as Compagnia Tecnica Internazionale. Its operations were transferred to Argentina the following year to pursue the opportunities the company's founder (Agostino Rocca) saw in providing the State-owned oil company YPF with seamless tubes for its rapidly increasing network of pipelines in southern Argentina.

Later on, Techint started diversifying its operations. In the 1960s, it began to provide engineering and construction services to the Argentine government, which made large investments in infrastructure —principally power plants. This experience helped Techint enter the international construction business, focusing on building pipelines and major infrastructure projects in developing countries (Castro, 2008).

Dalmine-Siderca, a Techint company related to steel production, began to internationalize in 1980 with its first exports to China and what was then the Soviet Union, countries out of the reach of seamless tube traders.

By the end of the 1990s, Techint had become Argentina's largest industrial group and was Argentina's leading multinational corporation. The 2000s saw a deepening of Techint Group's international strategy. In 2000, Siderca took control of the seamless tube business of NKK Corporation, one of Japan's leading steelmakers. In 2001 Siderca (which had been operating as DST, Dalmine-Siderca-TAMSA) was renamed Tenaris, its present name. The firm started construction of a local manufacturing facility in Qingdao, China, expected to produce about 50,000 tons of premium connections and couplings. In 2009,when the government of the Bolivarian Republic of Venezuela renationalized TAVSA (and Sidor), Tenaris expanded its operations to South East Asia by acquiring SPIJ, an Indonesian pipe producing company. Tenaris has a joint venture with Maharastra Seamless Ltd. in India, and four research and development labs, located in Argentina, Italy, Japan and Mexico.

Tenaris has deployed a strategy of complementary industrial plants that are specialized both in terms of products and in terms of regional markets. This has gone hand-in-hand with the creation of a complex commercial network that provides not only goods but also associated services and can meet the needs of different customers and demand segments. The internationalization process also included implementing a sophisticated financial strategy.

Techint Group is now a multinational corporation that employs over 57,000 people worldwide and had revenues of US$ 24 billion in 2011. Apart from Tenaris, Ternium and Techint Engineering & Construction, the group owns Tenova (previously called Techint Technologies), a firm that provides technology for the metal and mining industries, and Humanitas, which provides medical services, both headquartered in Italy.

Siderca (now part of Tenaris) first entered the Asian market by selling seamless tubes to Chinese state companies in the early 1980s. These transactions were carried out without establishing a sales office in the importing country. In the early 1990s, the company opened an office in Beijing and another in Singapore. The first focused on the Chinese market (at that time, State-owned clients only). The second targeted the Indonesian and Malaysian markets —two oil-producing countries with a big demand for seamless tubes. In Indonesia the customers were mainly foreign companies; in Malaysia, local and State-owned firms were the big buyers. Siderca's global growth strategy later led it to enter the Japanese market by signing a joint-venture agreement with JFE Corporation and creating NKKTubes, taking over the seamless tube division of NKK Corporation (Japan's leading steel producer) in 1999. The new company was capitalized at 3.2 billion yen, with Siderca holding 51% and NKK the remaining 49%. In order to enhance its Asian presence, Tenaris later invested in the construction of a manufacturing plant in Qingdao that started operations in 2008. The plant carries out the last stages of tube production for the Chinese market.

Tenaris now has 10% to 15% of its total production capacity in Asia. Its Asian operations are a net exporter for the entire corporation, accounting for about 6% of Tenaris' total revenues of US$ 9.9 billion in 2011. The main market in the region is China, with about 70% of Tenaris' regional revenues. The company's presence in the region consists of four manufacturing centres: two in Indonesia (one of which belonged to SPIJ, acquired in 2009 after the global financial crisis provided the opportunity to acquire a major company for a low price), one in Japan (NKKTubes) and one in China (the Qingdao plant). Tenaris also has a joint venture with Maharashtra Seamless Limited in India and sales offices in Kuala Lumpur, Singapore, Beijing, Seoul and Saudi Arabia. Tenaris employs 1,500 people in the region —about 6% of the total 26,980 employees the firm has around the globe. Just 28% of its employees are in Argentina. Table IV.3 shows Tenaris' capital investment allocation in Asia as well as its share in the joint venture.

Table IV.3
TENARIS' CAPITAL INVESTMENT ALLOCATION IN ASIA, 2008-2009

Tenaris' capital investment in Asia	Capitalization	Venture capital (2011)	Annual processing capacity (2011)	Employees	Products
SPIJ Seamless Pipe Indonesia Jaya	US$ 72.5 million	77%	120,000 tons	745 (2011)	Local Oil Country Tubular Goods (OCTG) processing with heat treatment and premium connection threading facilities
NKK Tubes Japan	¥3.2 billion yen	51%	260,000 tons	614 (2011)	Carbon steel seamless tubes
Qingdao Plant China	US$ 35 million	100%	40,000 tons	150 (2008)	OCTG pipes and premium connections

Source: "Company information", August 2012 [online] http://www.tenaris.com/default.aspx.

The main driver of Tenaris' investments in Asia was —and still is— the company's goal of being a world leader in the seamless tube market. To achieve this, the firm's strategy has always been to expand; Asia is one of the last stages. As seen in the historical background, Tenaris' business focus is not currently in Asia but in Europe and the United States.

Tenaris' deployment in Asia proceeded at a slow pace —in fact, it took almost 30 years for the company to go from remote exporting to its first greenfield project. Although the company had been producing in Asia since at least 1999, it was doing so in plants that were already up and running: namely, NKK plants in Japan. Company officials stressed that doing business in Asia is time-consuming, not because of red tape (except for India, where bureaucracy appears to be an issue according to the interviewees) but because of a different business culture.

Any company investing in a foreign country needs to adapt to a different business culture, so it is natural for internationalization not to be a speedy process because it takes time to learn the different practices, rules, languages and other particularities of the host country. But in this case there is also another dimension: the Asian business culture itself. In our interviews, officials pointed out that business relationships in Asia depend on strong interpersonal relationships —a feature not common to business relationships in most Western countries. It takes time to build links of trust and loyalty between people, so operating successfully in Asia will take a longer time than usual for Western companies. This adds to the already lengthy process of adaptation mentioned above. Interviewees have indicated that, in order to make a deal with an Asian counterpart, Western businesspeople have to engage in extensive talks and non-business activities, such as playing golf, that usually take a long time. This happens not only to Westerners (it is a general attitude towards all strangers), but foreigners are usually met with more diffidence.

To deal with these issues, Tenaris opts for a strategy that consists of training senior staff extensively before sending them to Asian subsidiaries and stationing them there longer than is the case for staff in Western countries. This allows company officials to establish their own interpersonal relationships in Asia. As a result, there is little turnover in senior positions in Tenaris' Asian subsidiaries. Another strategy the company used initially to narrow the culture gap and thus speed up its deployment in the region was to assign bicultural staff (for instance, a Chinese-Canadian director was assigned to the Chinese affiliate) who more easily adapted to the new environment and to doing business activities with local counterparts. The general feeling was that the company valued interpersonal relationships far more than formal contractual arrangements, which were nevertheless necessary.

The company's strong interest in building a stable and trusting relationship with local agents was also related to its intentions in entering the Asian market —that is, not using its Asian plants just as a base for exporting to other regions. The Qingdao plant opened in 2008 seeks to exclusively serve the premium portion of the Chinese tube market. To this end, the firm had already established strong relationships with its local customers, almost all of them State-owned companies. In the case of Japan, greenfield investments appeared to be unfeasible in light of the prevailing market conditions: foreign investment in Japan is severely restricted. The only possible way to access the market proved to be through a joint venture with a local company. Japan, per se, was not a very interesting market for Tenaris since it was already saturated. But the presence of a large and technologically updated steel industry made it the prime candidate for a regional base; in fact, having access to the Japanese industry enabled the company to later expand its product range to include new, high-tech products not being made at Tenaris' other plants. The Qingdao plant is now supplied by both the Argentine and the Japanese subsidiaries of Tenaris. So, it may well be that a company that is not seeking to enter the regional market but rather to use it as an export base to other regions might not (for reasons discussed later) have to follow a long deployment strategy such as the one Tenaris used. "Rooting" the company in the host country might not be so necessary.

Summing up, according to company officials Tenaris was successful in entering the Asian market because of its gradual, lengthy deployment strategy. But doing so requires a strong financial position because sunk costs are very high. In words of one of the interviewees, "to be successful in Asia you have to be successful back home". Asia cannot be an investment destination in the first stages of the international expansion of a Latin American company, but rather in the final stages. In order to overcome lack of brand recognition, a Latin American multinational should enter the Asian market not as a Latin company but as a multinational company.

An examination of Tenaris' Asian strategy shows that some aspects are different across countries in the region. Concerning the issue of human resources, regulations in some countries (Indonesia, for instance) prohibit the appointment of foreigners to certain important positions at subsidiaries of foreign companies. In China, such restrictions are informal; in Japan there are no restrictions at all. Ownership regulations also vary widely; in Malaysia foreigners may not own more than 49% of a company's shares. Differences in government policies across countries may also shape different deployment strategies. In Indonesia, for instance, the use of nationally-sourced inputs in the local oil industry is viewed positively, whilst in China the government subsidizes exports and not sales to local clients.

That said, Tenaris' strategy does not mesh perfectly with the incentives Asian governments provide. Far from being an exporter, the company's Chinese affiliate is focused on the growing local market even though this may preclude the company from receiving short-term benefits.

Diagram IV.1 shows the current set-up of Tenaris' operations in East Asia.

Diagram IV.1
TENARIS' OPERATIONS IN EAST ASIA

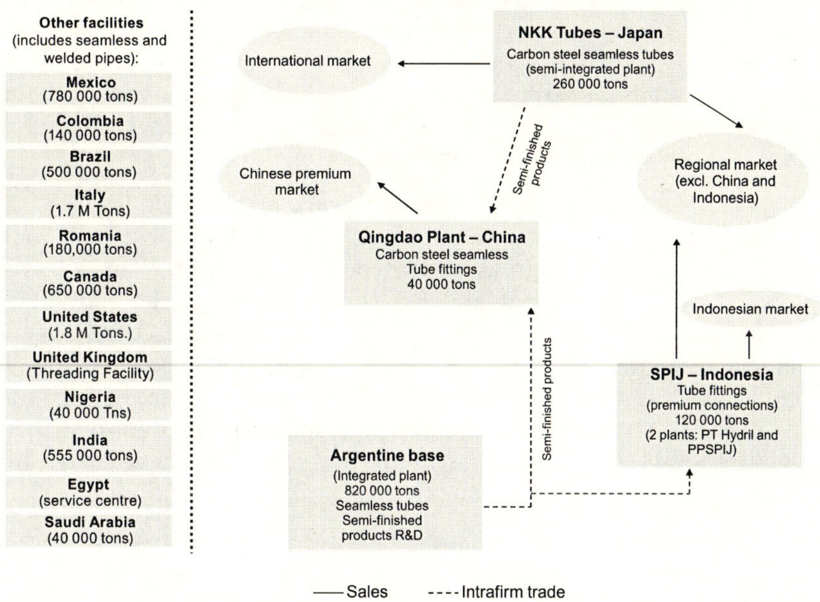

Source: Prepared by the authors.

A relevant difference the company observed across Asian countries was government attitude towards foreign investment, with Japan's appearing to be the most reluctant and China's quite the opposite, at least in the case of Tenaris. The Chinese State offered the firm a number of potential sites for its plant. Representatives from different regions made their offers in terms of tax exemptions and infrastructure, and Tenaris made the final decision. Income tax reduction was later granted. The company officials were positively impressed by the long-term investment in infrastructure the Chinese State carried out, a situation not found in other Asian countries. In India, for instance, investment in infrastructure is severely restricted by the activism of local residents, who are very aware of the potential negative impacts of large-scale public works on their communities. As Tenaris officials indicated, the Indian environment is often hardly receptive to any kind of large investment, even by local companies. They also pointed out that government attitude in the case of Thailand and Korea is more akin to that of China, i.e. more welcoming to foreign investment.

Concerning human resource management in Asia, there are two relevant dimensions. One of them concerns the quality of the available human resources. The second one is related to their cost. As for the quality dimension, Tenaris officials underlined the personal drive found in individuals all across East Asia. This makes the Asian workforce very dynamic; it is quite usual for senior staff to receive suggestions from plant workers about possible productive improvements. This ambition also makes individuals more sensitive to differences in pay between companies and leads to large turnover in junior and plant staff, although all are fully committed to the company during their tenure.

Workforce education qualifications vary across Asia; Japanese and Koreans workers are far more educated than their Chinese and South-East Asian counterparts. In all of the countries except for Japan there is a great deal of educational and job competition between individuals. This, coupled with strong personal drive among young Asians, results in a very dynamic job market. There are other differences that in some circumstances can be very important. For instance, Japan, as a country with a long industrial tradition, has a workforce that is used to stringent industrial security procedures. This is not so much the case in China because most of the workers come from a rural background.

Concerning the cost of human resources[8] in East Asia, company officials mentioned that wages across the region are converging with international levels and that cost-competitiveness is no longer a leading driver of investment in the region, at least not in the countries where

8 Workforce cost is not a major component of the overall costs of capital-intensive industries like this one, so it is a secondary issue in terms of business strategy.

Tenaris is present. India is an exception, but the regulatory environment there has limited the amount of investment the company has in India. In general, although wages are rising, productivity is, too, and these trends tend to offset each other. Tenaris now views cost-competitiveness in East Asia as similar to levels found in Latin America, at least in the area of human resources.

To conclude, what emerges from the Tenaris case study is that investment in Asia should be a long-term decision and that establishing a low-cost base in most countries of that region is an increasingly difficult proposition, at least for capital-intensive industries. Adaptation is difficult, and cost-competitiveness may not be as strong as expected. Only well established and globally renowned companies are well-positioned to engage in strategic investments in Asia. Once a company manages to gain a firm foothold in the region, expansion will accelerate because local markets are growing rapidly and many premium market segments are not well served by existing competitors. Tenaris, in fact, focuses its Asian sales on high-end products although its industrial presence in the region covers all stages of seamless tube production.

2. IMPSA

IMPSA, the flagship of the Pescarmona Group, traces its origins back to 1907, when Enrique M. Pescarmona opened a metalworking shop in Mendoza, Argentina, to provide the province's growing wine industry with machinery and spare parts. The company rapidly became successful and rose to the rank of industry leader in a few years.

In 1946, the Pescarmona family created Construcciones Metálicas Pescarmona (CMP) to design and build metal structures. In 1965, all the family's assets and liabilities where merged into Industrias Metalúrgicas Pescarmona S.A. (IMPSA). The new company's business focus became the supply of electrical turbines to hydroelectric power plants; its operations grew as the Argentine State built large hydropower plants in the late 1960s and early 1970s.

In 2002 IMPSA began to expand its international operations, driven in part by Pescarmona Groups' decision to reconvert and Argentina's economic crisis of 2001-2002. IMPSA Hydro (the division in charge of the hydroelectric machinery business) won several bids for the supply of equipment in the Bolivarian Republic of Venezuela, Ecuador, Colombia, Viet Nam, the Philippines and Malaysia. In Maylasia, IMPSA established a factory in Lumut, where it now builds port cranes and other hydromechanical equipment. Another related business into which IMPSA has expanded is the wind power industry. The Pescarmona holding presently employs more than 5,000 workers; its assets are worth some US$ 700 million.

IMPSA's internationalization process was based first and foremost on the engineering skills of its human resources. Second came the development of business models for delivering services associated with the sale of capital goods. Third came the company's accumulated technology and innovation capabilities, especially as a supplier of nuclear stations and in partnership with leading foreign firms (Kosacoff, 1999; Barbero, 2010).

The Pescarmona Group first ventured into Asia as the corporation expanded abroad during the 1980s. As indicated above, the group's investments in foreign countries were part of its diversification strategy. IMPSA's first operations in Asia involved delivery of port cranes and the execution of hydroelectric projects in China around 1986. The opening of a regional headquarters in Malaysia resulted in a market expansion of operations in the 1990s, culminating in the establishment of a joint-venture company with Malaysian investors and the installation of a manufacturing plant in the city of Lumut. The plant produces cranes and hydro components and is now the main production centre of the firm's Asian operations. In addition to its businesses in Malaysia, the company has completed several hydroelectric projects in Indonesia, Thailand, India, China, the Philippines and Taiwan Province of China. Its port division has delivered more than 100 cranes along with related services such as operation and maintenance, retrofits and upgrades.

The relevance of Asia to IMPSA's global operations grew steadily. By 2004, Asia accounted for about 30% of the company's revenues. The following years saw, nevertheless, a change in the firm's strategy in Asia. The company's intention to position itself as a world-class player in the renewable energy business lead IMPSA to restructure, in 2008, its port systems division (IPS), which operated mainly in South-East Asia and Latin America. That division was spun off from IMPSA and now operates as a different company under the name of South Asia Logistic Services Limited.

The change in the firm's strategy is clear when analyzing information from its balance sheets. In 2007, 32% of IMPSA's sales were from the Hydro division, 22% from port services and the rest from other operations. By 2008, the share from the hydroelectric business had gone up to 47% while port services had dropped to 6%. In 2009 sales from the Hydro division accounted for 42% of total sales, while a new division (Wind, devoted to the wind power business) had a 36% share. Combined, the renewable energy business was 78% of the firm's sales. The port services business accounted for only 4% of total sales.

According to company officials, the port and crane business was increasingly seen as unattractive, particularly because the products were becoming highly commoditized. Fierce competition from low-cost Chinese suppliers became an obstacle to adequate profitability. However, the Pescarmona group has not abandoned this business; the new company is now building around 17 cranes, almost all of them for Malaysia.

This restructuring resulted in a sharp drop in Asia's contribution to IMPSA global revenues because the new firm, IPS, absorbed most of the business in that region. In 2009, sales in Asia represented around 2% of the company's US$ 500 million in worldwide sales. This decline doesn't mean that the firm has abandoned the region —on the contrary, IMPSA is rebuilding its operations around the renewable energy business, in which it had already initiated operations in 2003 with investments in the Bakun hydroelectric dam project in Sarawak, Malaysia. In April 2010, IMPSA signed an agreement with PetroVietnam to manufacture wind turbines in Bin Thuang, Viet Nam for a value of around US$ 3 billion over a five-year period.

The key factors that drive the continued interest of IMPSA in the region include (i) the large size and promising growth prospects of many Asian economies; (ii) the abundance of natural resources in the mainland; (iii) attractive manufacturing costs; (iv) the existence of well-developed financial and other support services; and (v) a large and growing population. All these factors will drive energy and infrastructure needs up. Arrangements facilitating trade among the region's economies are another factor pushing IMPSA's investments in Asia.

IMPSA's structure in Asia includes the Lumut plant (where it has more than 500 employees and a network of over 300 subcontractors and vendors); the joint venture with PetroVietnam in Viet Nam; the Asian headquarters in Kuala Lumpur and offices in Jakarta, for commercial and operation activities; Hong Kong (Special Administrative Region of China), for financial and administration activities; Shanghai, for outsourcing and sales; Delhi, for the same activities as Shanghai; and Manila, for administrative operations.

The main geographic areas of strategic interest for the company (according to official documents) are South-East Asia (Malaysia, Thailand, Viet Nam, Indonesia, Myanmar, Philippines, Singapore, Cambodia, Laos and Brunei), South Asia (predominantly India, Sri Lanka and Bangladesh) and the Middle East. Far-East Asia (China, Republic of Korea, Taiwan Province of China and Japan) is not considered to be a strategic area because it is understood to be saturated and because there are well-established local companies that have some sort of protection in their home markets. In turn, North-West Asia (the former Soviet republics) is far from IMPSA's centre of operations in Malaysia, and competition from Russian and other European companies is tough.

The growth potential of the renewable energy business in South-East Asia is the main driver for the company's present investments in the region: almost all the power generated there comes from fossil fuels, and hydropower and wind power remain vastly underdeveloped. Hydropower installed capacity in South-East Asia, for instance, is expected to treble in the next ten years. IMPSA intends to gain an important share of that growing business.

IMPSA's prospects in the region will also depend on competition trends in the renewable energy market. In the case of hydropower, the main competitors are two types of companies. On the one hand, local companies in China and India, often with strong support from their home government, compete on the basis of low prices and are particularly active in large-scale projects. These companies benefit mostly from intergovernmental agreements and from subsidized funding. On the other hand are established European players with world-class reputations that have set up low-cost production plants in the region and concentrate their business on equipment supply and not on power plant development. These firms usually offer high-quality products at high but still-competitive prices. In the case of wind energy, there is still no clear legislation in place for developing this industry, so there are windows of opportunity for companies like IMPSA to take the lead in countries such as Viet Nam. However, the main markets, China and India, are dominated by local companies that compete on the basis of prices and have local preferences.

The advantage of IMPSA in this context lies in the combination of business know-how and technology. The firm has experience spanning the entire process of design, production and implementation of hydroelectric projects and wind farms. Furthermore, the company has been present in the region for more than 20 years and is capable of carrying out the manufacturing process locally, thanks to its production centre in Malaysia. The firm's broad footprint in the region has also opened the possibility for local-market funding —indeed, IMPSA is exploring the possibility of an Islamic bond issue in Malaysia.

The company's experience with human resource management in the region is quite positive, particularly in the case of Malaysia. Malaysia differs from other South-East Asian countries in that most university-educated individuals speak at least three languages, owing to the multiracial composition of Malay society. Malaysian universities —with whom the company has academic agreements— are well placed in the Asian context, and a large number of foreigners study there. This is a big advantage for the country and partly explains why IMPSA has its regional headquarters in its capital, Kuala Lumpur. Furthermore, the Malay legal environment for labour matters is, according to the company, possibly the best adapted to industrial development and well-suited for the dynamics of labour-intensive projects. Fixed-term contracts are renewable without establishing a permanent tie with the worker, therefore limiting severance payments.

Concerning the overall management of its subsidiaries in Asia, IMPSA has a policy of restricting the number of expatriate executives. The company's intention is to promote local managers to take on key positions in its subsidiaries. For instance, when the firm first established its subsidiary in Malaysia, the number of Argentine executives working there was 17. That number has gone down to four. This policy seeks to ensure the company's best possible adaptation to the local environment. For example, the decision-making process in Asia is very different from the Latin American one (which is certainly less concerned with interpersonal relationships —see the Techint case study). To narrow some of these business culture gaps, IMPSA trains its Asian executives in Argentina and in Brazil, its global headquarters.

What is clear is that IMPSA intends to become firmly rooted in its subsidiaries' countries. To do so, the company follows this management policy and builds academic and professional links with local universities —especially in Malaysia. Furthermore, the strategy of exporting to foreign markets from subsidiaries in Asia is seen by local governments as very positive, something that has strengthened the ties between the firm and host country authorities.

In short, IMPSA is a company whose main strategy for insertion in the Asian market has changed radically over the years. It started as a provider of port system goods and services and is now focused on the renewable energy business. How successful this business strategy change will be is still to be seen.

3. Bimbo

Grupo Bimbo, owned by the Servitje family, was established in Mexico in 1945 to produce bakery products. In only one generation, the company became one of the biggest Mexican multinationals. Currently, the firm operates in a multilevel environment, competes in domestic and global markets and exhibits leadership in brand positioning, sales and production volume. It is the largest bread baker in the world (BCG, 2011). Through its many subsidiaries, the company produces and distributes over 8,000 products (among them, loaf bread, pastries, cupcakes, and sweet and salted snacks) and has more than 100 brands (Bimbo, Lara, Marinela, Oroweat, Arnold, Entenmann's, Boboli, Ricolino, Colorado, Pullman, Plus Vita, among many others).

According to its 2011 annual report, the company has more than 127,000 employees and 156 facilities distributed in 19 countries throughout Latin America and Asia, plus the United States (see table IV.4). The bulk of its plants are in Mexico (42 plants). The group has developed a vast distribution network throughout the Americas, comprising 39,000 routes and more than 1,800,000 points of sale.

TABLE IV.4
BIMBO GROUP'S GLOBAL PRESENCE

Location	Manufacturing plants	Marketing companies	Brands
Mexico	42		14
United States	75	1	25
China	2		1
Central and South America	30	1	36

Source: Bimbo group, annual report.

From the point of view of its industrial organization, the company is highly product-diversified and vertically integrated —including transport, packaging, raw materials production and machinery manufacturing (see diagram IV.2). The vertical integration strategy deepened in the 1980s, as a consequence of (or as a defensive reaction to) the Mexican inflation crisis. As a result, the company brought the production of moulds and display equipment (Moldex), security for trucks and vehicles (Proarce) and legal paperwork (Exbim) into its core activities. At the same time, Bimbo imposed on itself a minimum outside purchase requirement of 25% to maintain good relationships with the Mexico's other agricultural and food companies (Moreno-Lázaro, 2010). As a consequence of this strategy, the company cut the strong dependency on United States technology that had exhibited until mid-1970s and began a period of in-house technology development that includes manufacturing ovens and equipment under its own patents (Moreno-Lázaro, 2010).

Diagram IV.2
BIMBO GROUP STRUCTURE, 1978

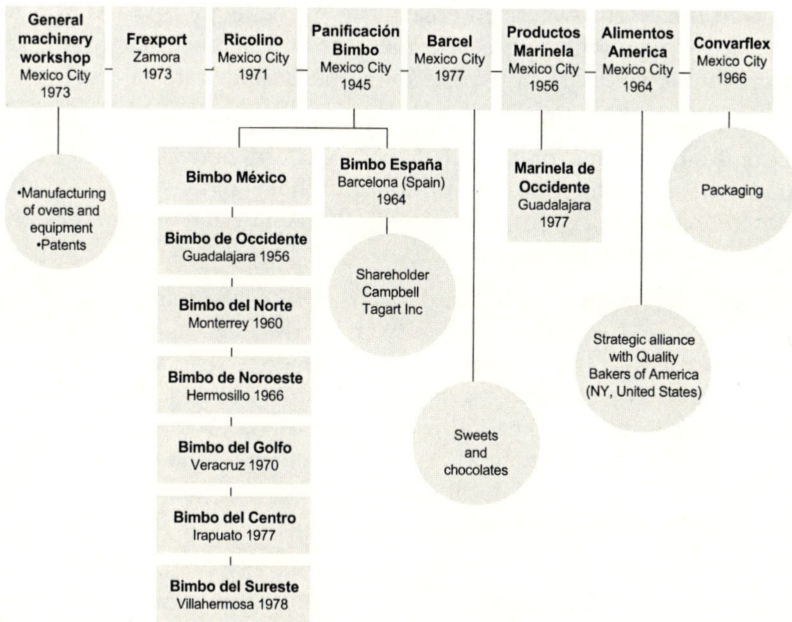

Source: Prepared by the authors on the basis of Moreno-Lázaro (2010).

The 1980s crisis gave Bimbo the opportunity to buy out some food companies that were facing difficulties. One of them was its main competitor, Wonder, which became part of the group in 1986 and allowed the company to definitively consolidate its monopoly position in the Mexican sliced bread market.

The internationalization of Bimbo appeared as a necessary step to cope with increasing competition from multinational food companies. It began in 1984[9] with the export of products to the nearest United States markets and continued with the creation, in 1989, of Bimbo Centroamérica. Nevertheless, the real international expansion of the group began in 1990 with the launch of an expansion plan aimed at gaining positions beyond Mexico's borders, following the steps of other Mexican companies such as

[9] Bimbo's first investment abroad was in 1964 in Barcelona as part of a personal strategy of one of the (Spanish) owners of Grupo Bimbo. None of the other shareholders of Panificadora Bimbo participated in this new company. Unfortunately, Bimbo ran into serious problems due to strong competition from a new bakery (Panrico). Some years later, the company received support from Grupo Bimbo, and its board of directors became more directly involved in the Spanish hub. In 1978 the subsidiary was taken over by an American company (Campbell Tagart Inc) that started using the Bimbo brand (Moreno-Lázaro 2010).

CEMEX, Alfa and Televisa (Moreno-Lázaro, 2010). As Franco-Navarrete (2010) points out, Bimbo is a first-class example of a Mexican company that perceived the North American Free Trade Agreement (NAFTA) as a good opportunity and, with aggressive mergers and acquisitions and a joint-venture strategy, successfully penetrated the United States market.

Investing in Asia is a strategy pursued by only a few companies; Grupo Bimbo is one of them. It succeeded in penetrating the Asian market through the US$ 18 million purchase of a subsidiary of its main competitor in Spain, Panrico. Bimbo Asia has 800 workers and a production plant in Beijing.

Before entering the Chinese market, the company had to adapt its processes and routines, especially in food safety matters. In regards to customer tastes, the company had to introduce several innovations in its know-how as well as in its range of products in order to satisfy local traditions. It developed a new line of wheat-based products and red bean paste. Today, the company markets 18 products in China through retailers (Carrefour, Walmart) and local supermarkets and plans to expand its operation beyond Beijing after consolidating its position in that city.

According to press releases, Grupo Bimbo has doubled its size in China since its establishment there, but its managers recognize that profit margins are very low due to fierce competition from local producers. According to its annual report, the company aims to acquire the Chinese firm Jin Hong Wei, which produces Chinese and Western-style baked goods.

Grupo Bimbo is one of the most interesting cases of internationalization of Latin American firms. The basis of this success might be found in some of the company's qualities. Among them, according to Franco-Navarrete (2010), is the firm's preference for financing expansion through reinvestment rather than credit. On the other hand, Moreno-Lázaro (2010) considers that the basis of successful expansion lies in organizing techniques, the policy of growth through vertical integration, the company's good relationship with trade unions, economies of scale and a smart and patient internationalization strategy. In the same sense, Vargas-Hernández and Reza (2010) mention as a successful strategy Grupo Bimbo's control of its logistics, physical distribution and supply chain throughout its history.

4. Embraer

Embraer (Empresa Brasileira de Aeronáutica) was created in 1969 as a State-owned enterprise resulting from an alliance between public-sector technologists and the military.

During the 1970s, Embraer concentrated on designing aircrafts, producing fuselages and assembling the final product, shying away from manufacturing high-value, high-technology components. Production started in cooperation with foreign partners, under co-production and licensing arrangements designed to achieve rapid market penetration without excessive technological dependence (Goldstein, 2002). Since the beginning, Embraer followed a long-term strategy of knowledge accumulation in aircraft design and manufacture; a strong focus on the export market was set as a priority. By the end of the 1970s, Embraer owned two best-selling planes, the Bandeirante and the Tucano.

The Tucano was the first Embraer military project of commercial significance. After signing a development contract with the Brazilian air force in 1978, Embraer launched this aircraft in 1980; it was first exported in 1983. The other military project of significance was the AMX, developed jointly with the Italian firm Alenia. With the AMX, Embraer left its traditional market niche (commuter and light trainer aircraft) in an attempt not only to supply the Brazilian air force but also to compete with American, French and Russian combat aircrafts in export markets (Frischtak, 1992).

The second internationalization step Embraer embarked on was the unit based in Le Bourget, Paris, inaugurated in May 1983 and aiming to concentrate sales activities and provide technical support to Embraer's new customers in Europe, the Middle East, and Africa. Embraer's main product, the Brasilia (EMB 120), was presented in 1980. By the end 1990, Brazilian market share in the 20-45 seat aircraft category was 25% worldwide.

During the 1970s, funding came from the Government of Brazil in the form of commissions for the air force, along with sharp growth in export sales. However, growing development costs and intensifying global competition jeopardized Embraer's sustainability due to financial difficulties. The worsening economic situation led the government, in January 1992, to include Embraer in the list of State-owned enterprises to be sold.

In December 1994, a consortium bought a controlling 45% stake for US$ 89 million. The new controlling shareholder embarked on a sweeping business transformation: production methods and processes were improved, including substantial investment in IT systems; a new organizational chart was introduced; and services such as site maintenance, transportation, catering, security and machinery upkeep were outsourced. In subsequent years, by launching new products for the defense market and entering the executive aviation market, Embraer significantly increased its market share, resulting in growing revenues in diversified marketplaces. In 1999, Embraer entered into a 60%/40% joint venture with Liebherr International AG to develop and manufacture landing gear and high-precision hydraulic equipment and provide related services for Embraer and other clients around the world. In connection with this joint venture, the company formed a new subsidiary, ELEB, to which it transferred all of its landing gear manufacturing activities, the employees and some liabilities related to those activities. In 2008, Embraer acquired, for US$ 20.0 million, Liebherr Aerospace SAS's 40% interest in ELEB.

Embraer was Brazil's largest exporter from 1999 to 2001 and the second largest in 2002, 2003 and 2004. The company is the world's third-ranked maker of commercial aircraft, after the United States giant Boeing and its European rival Airbus. With headquarters in São José dos Campos, Brazil, and offices, subsidiaries and customer service bases in China, France, Portugal, Singapore and the United States (see diagram IV.3)., it currently employs more than 16,853 people (excluding its subsidiaries OGMA and HEAI); 94.7% of them are based in Brazil.

Diagram IV.3
EMBRAER'S GLOBAL OPERATION

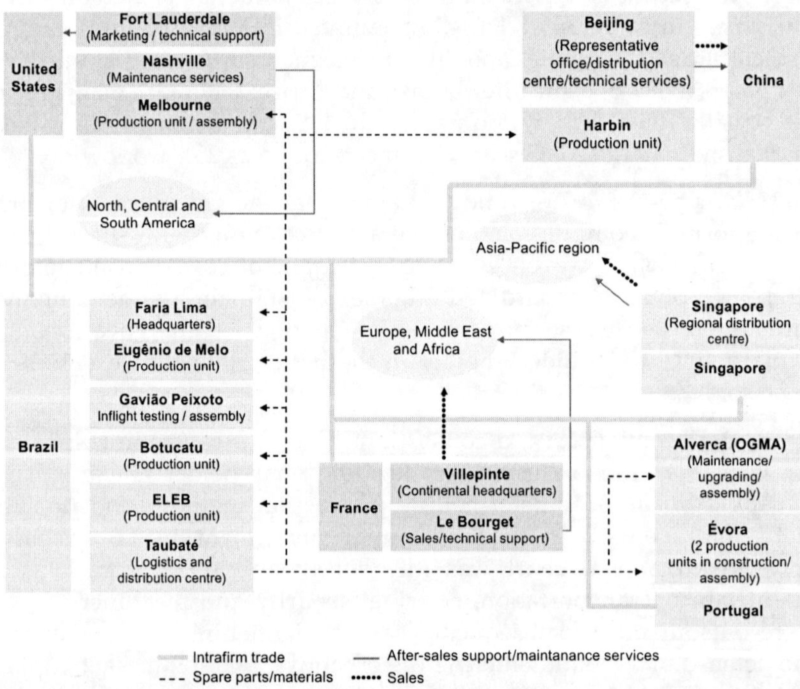

Source: Prepared by the authors, on the basis of information from Embraer.

Embraer has become one of the largest aircraft manufacturers in the world by focusing on specific market segments with high growth potential in commercial, defense and executive aviation. Since the early 2000s Embraer has expanded its global presence with several operating units around the world. With representative sales offices and distribution centres in China and Singapore, Embraer set foot in Asia.

In 2008, the opening of the Melbourne facility, Embraer's first industrial site in the United States, showed the company's broader strategy of bringing operations closer to customers and to its largest market. That same year, the deployment of two new plants in Portugal, both based in the city of Évora, south of Lisbon, was announced for 2010.

In May 2000, Embraer established its Beijing representative office, which handles sales and marketing, customer support and services, government relations and public relations for the Chinese-speaking world. Embraer also opened its Beijing distribution centre, which is jointly run with China Aviation Supplies Import and Export Corp. Embraer's distribution centre is a 750-square-meter facility that inventories more than 6,000 different aircraft spare parts and components. It is electronically connected to other storage centres in Brazil, Australia, England, France and the United States, enabling customers to place purchase orders in real time. Finally, in light of the steady growth of its customer base in China, Embraer created its wholly-owned subsidiary, Embraer China Aircraft Technical Services Co., Ltd., in July 2010. Its business scope covers logistics and spare parts sales, as well as consulting services regarding technical issues and flight operations.

Embraer's sales office in Singapore was established in December 2000 to serve the Asia-Pacific region. In 2007, the company opened a regional distribution centre for round-the-clock Embraer spare part operations and to provide maintenance, repair and inventory services to its commercial aircraft customers in the region. That same year, a world-class training centre for E-Jets was created and located at the Changi airport. In 2010, all logistical and part support for Embraer's commercial aircraft in the region, as well as for executive jets, went on to be managed by the regional distribution centre in Singapore.

In December 2002, Embraer signed an agreement to build a production unit in China through a joint venture with HAIG (Harbin Aircraft Industry Group Co. Ltd.) and HAI (Hafei Aviation Industry Co. Ltd.); both are subsidiaries of AVIC II (China Aviation Industry Corporation II). This joint venture, Embraer's first industrial initiative outside Brazil, was set up to cooperatively develop commercial regional jets and expand its presence in the flourishing Chinese market. The contract covered the manufacturing, assembly, sales and after-sales support of the ERJ 135/140/145 family of aircraft. Embraer contributed US$12 million in cash, tooling and inventory to the joint venture; its joint venture partners contributed land use rights in Harbin, capital of Heilongjiang province, and they contributed US$ 11 million in cash and facilities to the joint venture. Embraer owns 51% of the equity of the company, called Harbin Embraer Aircraft Industry Company Ltd., whose production facilities occupy an area of 24,000 square meters.

The roll-out of the first ERJ 145 manufactured by the joint venture occurred in December 2003. The joint venture entered into its first sales contract for six aircraft with China Southern Airlines in February 2004. In March 2005, Embraer entered into a second sales contract for five aircraft with China Eastern Airlines. As of March 31, 2009, Harbin Embraer Aircraft Industry Company Ltd. had secured contracts with five Chinese airlines for a total of 71 ERJ 145 aircraft. In October 2007, the thousandth jet of the ERJ 145 family was delivered at Harbin Embraer Aircraft Industry Co. Ltd. Embraer currently produces a 50-seat commercial jet in China with Aviation Industries of China and is waiting for a Chinese government permit to build a 120-seat model. The Asia Pacific Region represented 23% of the company's revenue in 2011 (see figure IV.4).

Figure IV.4
EMBRAER REVENUES BY REGION, 2011

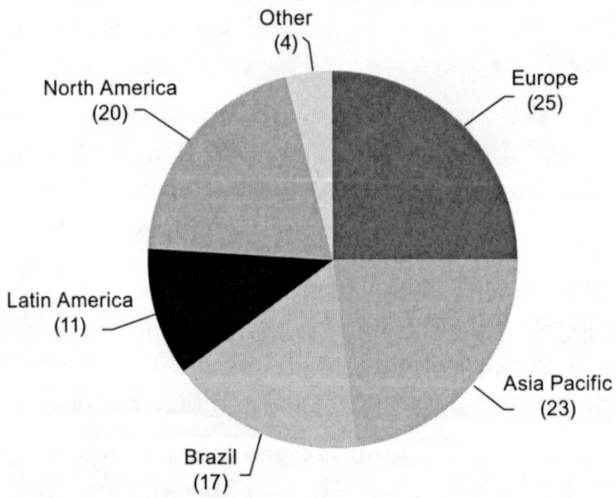

Source: Embraer.

Throughout its history, Embraer has been involved in the design, development, manufacturing, sales and after-sale support of aircraft in the commercial aviation, executive aviation, defence systems and agricultural aviation segments. It has produced more than 5,000 aircraft that operate in 92 countries on five continents, and it is the market leader for commercial jets with up to 120 seats. As a State-owned company, during the 1970s and 1980s, Embraer showed special interest in expanding its global presence. This tendency was reinforced after privatization in the 1990s. As a result, Embraer has continued to internationalize, not only in terms of sales offices and distribution centres, located worldwide, but also in terms of its industrial facilities strategically located in United States and China to bring operations closer its largest markets.

C. Concluding remarks

The experiences of Latin American companies that have been operating in Asia during the last twenty years are similar in a number of ways. These companies were leaders in their business sector back home. Investing in Asia for firms coming from a culturally and geographically distant region such as Latin America requires the expertise and financial backing that only a solid position in home markets can offer. In other words, investment in Asia appears not to be a strategy fit for new and inexperienced companies.

Furthermore, Asian markets cannot make up for a lack of success in regional markets. Investment in Asia comes only after the companies have successfully expanded in neighbouring countries. For instance, it was not until 2008 that Tenaris opened its first manufacturing plant in Asia, more than twenty years after the company's holding group (Techint) had set up its first plants outside Argentina. IMPSA opened its Lumut plant after it had well-established subsidiaries in Brazil. Investing in Brazil is an almost indispensable step for a firm seeking to expand its operations outside its borders. Brazilian companies have the advantage of being the incumbents in such a large market.

In none of the cases was deployment in Asia a rapid process. On the contrary, it was rather lengthy. Both Tenaris and IMPSA started their first commercial operations in Asia in the 1980s, but it was not until the 1990s they went beyond that stage, and manufacturing plants were only built in the last decade. However, there are some differences between the approach taken by the two companies. Tenaris first bought local companies and then carried out greenfield investments. IMPSA followed the opposite strategy, first building its own structure and then enlarging it by investing in other firms. Adaptation to the local environment is crucial.

The cases of Tenaris and IMPSA prove that, in order to successfully adapt to the Asian market, it is not so much the deployment strategy in itself but how the firms adapt to micro business practices. All of the interviewees mentioned that strong interpersonal relationships are vital for a successful blending into Asian markets. The presence of local executives in top managerial positions at foreign subsidiaries is virtually indispensable for any kind of operation in Asia. In some countries, such as Indonesia, there are legal restrictions concerning appointing foreigners to managerial positions; in others (such as Malaysia and China) there are no legal limits but having local people in key positions is positively viewed by both local governments and business partners. Moreover, even when there are no restrictions, local authorities particularly welcome export-oriented investments and those that seek the development of linkages with domestic suppliers. Latin American companies need to understand the importance of these informal practices that are so different from Western-style business practices, and adapt to them.

Host governments actively promote foreign investment; incentives range from subsidies and tax exemptions to infrastructure building. Both IMPSA and Tenaris have benefited from positive synergies with local governments in their deployment strategies. Any newcomer to the Asian market should consider establishing a good relationship with local authorities.

Concerning human resources management, cost differences with Latin America are not as big as might be expected. All of our interviewees underscored that the idea of Asia as a low labour cost base is vanishing quickly in many countries. Wages are rising fast, and skills are improving, thus reducing the pool of cheap unskilled labour. The positive side of this is that labour productivity is also on the rise; Asian workers are described as being very willing to learn and to improve how they perform their daily tasks. The quality of labour is heterogeneous: some countries such as Malaysia and some regions of China fare better in terms of overall skills and education than other less developed countries of East and South-East Asia.

Although most Asian countries have excellent growth prospects and hence attractive investment opportunities, they differ in many significant ways (such as legal environment, prevalent business practices, the availability of skilled human resources, existing business opportunities and the level and strength of competition from installed investors). All firms seeking to invest in the region must take these factors into account if they are to design an adequate business strategy.

The big picture that emerges from the Tenaris and IMPSA case studies is that investment in Asia cannot be handled in a simple and conventional manner. Adapting to the local business environment is a key factor. In general, Asia is not a region were local bureaucracies are an impediment to investment —on the contrary, local governments are very keen to attract foreign investors. The difficulties lie mainly in establishing successful links with local agents (like suppliers, workers and universities). To overcome them, companies should support their operations with policies oriented to building solid ties with the local environment both inside the firm (by hiring local executives and involving them in key decision-making), and outside the firm (by investing time and resources in cultivating interpersonal relationships). It is clear that companies that enjoy a good position in their home market are best suited to carry out investments in Asia, not only because they may have more expertise in their business but also because the deployment strategy may take several years, something that requires a continuous flow of resources towards a project that will take several years to provide healthy profits.

Bibliography

Bair, J. and E. Dussel Peters (2006), "Global commodity chains and endogenous growth: Export dynamism and development in Honduras and Mexico", *World Development*, vol. 34, No. 2.

Barbero, M. I. (2010), "Los grupos económicos en la Argentina en una perspectiva de largo plazo (siglos XIX y XX)", Buenos Aires, unpublished.

BCG (Boston Consulting Group) (2011), "Companies on the move. Rising stars from rapidly developing economies are reshaping global industries", January.

___(2008), *New Global Challengers from Emerging Economies.*

Bimbo Annual Report (2010) [online] www.grupobimbo.com.mx.

Capdevielle, M. (2005), "Globalización, especialización y heterogeneidad estructural en México", *Heterogeneidad estructural, asimetrías tecnológicas y crecimiento en América Latina* (LC/W.35), Mario Cimoli (ed.), Santiago de Chile, Economic Commission for Latin America and the Caribbean (ECLAC)/Inter-American Development Bank (IDB).

Castro, C. (2008), "Paradigma tecnológico, empresa y transformaciones cualitativas. Techint y el desarrollo energético en la Argentina de posguerra", Universidad de San Andrés.

Chudnovsky, D. and A. López (2006), "Inversión extranjera directa y desarrollo: la experiencia del Mercosur", *15 años de Mercosur. Comercio, macroeconomía e inversiones extranjeras,* J. Berlinski, F. Pires de Souza, D., Chudnovsky and A. López (coords.), Montevideo, Red Mercosur.

Ciarli, T. and E. Giuliani (2005), "Inversión extranjera directa y eslabonamientos productivos en Costa Rica" *Heterogeneidad estructural, asimetrías tecnológicas y crecimiento en América Latina* (LC/W.35), Mario Cimoli (ed.), Santiago de Chile, Economic Commission for Latin America and the Caribbean (ECLAC)/Inter-American Development Bank (IDB).

Dussel Peters, E. (2003), "Ser maquila o no ser maquila, ¿es esa la pregunta?", *Comercio Exterior*, vol. 53, No. 4.

ECLAC (Economic Commission for Latin America and the Caribbean) (2005), *Foreign Investment in Latin America and the Caribbean. 2004 Report,* Santiago, Chile.

___(2009), *Foreign Direct Investment in Latin America and the Caribbean, 2008, Santiago, Chile.*

___*(2010), Preliminary Overview of the Economies of Latin America and the Caribbean (LC/G.2480-P), Santiago, Chile.*

EMBRAER [online] www.embraer.com.

Fleury, A. and M. T. Leme Fleury (2006), "China and Brazil in the Global Economy", *IDS Bulletin*, vol. 37 No. 1, January.

Franco-Navarrete, A. (2010), "Outward foreign direct investment: the case of Mexico", National Auotonomous University of Mexico.

Frischtak, C. (1992), "Learning, technical progress and competitiveness in the commuter aircraft industry: An analysis of Embraer", *Industry Paper series*, No. 58, Washington, D.C., World Bank, Industry and Energy Department (IEN).

Goldstein, A. (2002), "EMBRAER: From national champion to global player", *CEPAL Review*, No. 77 (LC/G.2180-P/I), Santiago, Chile, Economic Commission for Latin America and the Caribbean (ECLAC).

IIF (Institute of International Finance) (2010), "Capital flows to emerging market economies", *IIF Research Note*.

Kosacoff, B. (1999), "El caso argentino", Las multinacionales latinoamericanas. Sus estrategias en un mundo globalizado, D. Chudnovsky, B. Kosacoff and A. López, Buenos Aires, Fondo de Cultura Económica.

Kugler, M. (2006), "Spillovers from foreign direct investment: Within or between industries?", *Journal of Development Economics*, vol. 80.

López, A. and D. Ramos (2009), "The Argentine case", *China and Latin America: Economic Relations in the Twenty-First Century*, Studies, No. 49, R. Jenkins and E. Dussel Peters (eds.), Bonn, Deutsches Institut für Entwicklungspolitik/German Development Institute.

López, A, D. Ramos and C. Simkievich (2008), "A study of the impact of China's global expansion on Argentina. Soybean value chain analysis", *The Impact of China's Global Economic Expansion in Latin America*, Working Paper, No. 2, World Economy and Finance Research Programme, University of East Anglia, December.

López, A., D. Ramos and I. Torre (2009), "Las exportaciones de servicios de América Latina y su integración en las cadenas globales de valor", *Project document* (LC/W.240; LC/BUE/W.37), Buenos Aires, Economic Commission for Latin America and the Caribbean (ECLAC).

Moreno-Lázaro, J. (2010), "Spanish emigration and the setting-up of a great company in Mexico: *Bimbo*, 1903-2008", University of Valladolid.

Niembro, A., D. Ramos and C. Simkievich (2009), "El papel del MERCOSUR en la llegada de IED a Brasil y en la internacionalización de empresas brasileñas", Buenos Aires, Research Centre for Industrial Transformation (CENIT).

Saslavsky, D. and R. Rozemberg (2008), "A study of the impact of China's global expansion on Brazil", *The Impact of China's Global Economic Expansion in Latin America*, Working Paper, No. 8, World Economy and Finance Research Programme, University of East Anglia, December.

Tenaris [online] http://www.tenaris.com/default.aspx.

UNCTAD (United Nations Conference on Trade and Development), "FDI Statistics" [online] http://unctadstat.unctad.org/.

___(2005), *World Investment Report 2005. Transnational Corporations and the Internationalization of R&D*, New York.

___(2009), *World Investment Report. Transnational Corporations, Agricultural Production and Development*, New York.

___(2010), *World Investment Report 2010. Investing in a Low Carbon Economy*, New York.

Vale Columbia Center, "Emerging Market Global Players" Reports on Multinationals of Argentina (2009), Brazil (2007 and 2009) and Mexico (2009) [online] http://www.vcc.columbia.edu/content/emerging-market-global-players.

Vargas-Hernández, J. and M. Reza Noruzi (2010), "An exploration of the status of emerging multinational enterprises in Mexico", *International Business and Management*, vol. 1, No. 1 [online] www.cscanada.net

World Bank (2010), *Global Economic Prospects: Crisis, Finance and Growth*, Washington DC.

NACIONES UNIDAS
UNITED NATIONS

CEPAL
ECLAC

Publicaciones de la CEPAL
ECLAC publications

Comisión Económica para América Latina y el Caribe
Economic Commission for Latin America and the Caribbean
Casilla 179-D, Santiago de Chile. E-mail: publications@cepal.org
Véalas en: www.cepal.org/publicaciones
Publications may be accessed at: www.eclac.org

Revista CEPAL / *CEPAL Review*

La Revista se inició en 1976 como parte del Programa de Publicaciones de la Comisión Económica para América Latina y el Caribe, con el propósito de contribuir al examen de los problemas del desarrollo socioeconómico de la región. Las opiniones expresadas en los artículos firmados, incluidas las colaboraciones de los funcionarios de la Secretaría, son las de los autores y, por lo tanto, no reflejan necesariamente los puntos de vista de la Organización.

La *Revista CEPAL* se publica en español e inglés tres veces por año.

Los precios de suscripción anual vigentes son de US$ 30 para la versión en español y US$ 35 para la versión en inglés. El precio por ejemplar suelto es de US$ 15 para ambas versiones. Los precios de suscripción por dos años son de US$ 50 para la versión en español y US$ 60 para la versión en inglés.

CEPAL Review first appeared in 1976 as part of the Publications Programme of the Economic Commission for Latin America and the Caribbean, its aim being to make a contribution to the study of the economic and social development problems of the region. The views expressed in signed articles, including those by Secretariat staff members, are those of the authors and therefore do not necessarily reflect the point of view of the Organization.

CEPAL Review is published in Spanish and English versions three times a year.

Annual subscription costs are US$ 30 for the Spanish version and US$ 35 for the English version. The price of single issues is US$ 15 for both versions. The cost of a two-year subscription is US$ 50 for the Spanish version and US$ 60 for the English version.

Informes periódicos institucionales / *Annual reports*

Todos disponibles para años anteriores / *Issues for previous years also available*

- *Informe Macroeconómico de América Latina y el Caribe, junio de 2012*, 86 p.
- ***Macroeconomic Report on Latin America and the Caribbean - June 2012*, 80 p.**
- *Balance Preliminar de las Economías de América Latina y el Caribe 2012*, 102 p.

***Preliminary Overview of the Economies of Latin America and the Caribbean 2012*, 98 p.**

- *Estudio Económico de América Latina y el Caribe 2012*, 162 p.
  ***Economic Survey of Latin America and the Caribbean 2012*, 154 p.**
- *Panorama de la Inserción Internacional de América Latina y el Caribe 2011-2012*, 126 p.
  ***Latin America and the Caribbean in the World Economy 2011-2012*, 116 p.**
- *Panorama Social de América Latina, 2012*. 252 p.
  ***Social Panorama of Latin America, 2012. Briefing paper* 60 p.**
- *La Inversión Extranjera Directa en América Latina y el Caribe 2011*, 198 p.
  ***Foreign direct Investment in Latin America and the Caribbean 2011*, 184 p.**
- *Anuario Estadístico de América Latina y el Caribe /* ***Statistical Yearbook for Latin America and the Caribbean***, 2012, 224 p.

Libros de la CEPAL

115 *The changing nature of Asian-Latin American economic relations*, German King, José Carlos Mattos, Nanno Mulder and Osvaldo Rosales (eds.), 2013, 196 p.

114 *China y América Latina y el Caribe. Hacia una relación económica y comercial estratégica*, Osvaldo Rosales y Mikio Kuwayama, 2012, 258 p

114 China *and Latin America and the Caribbean Building a strategic economic and trade relationship*, Osvaldo Rosales y Mikio Kuwayama, 2012, 244 p.

113 *Competitividad, sostenibilidad e inclusión social en la agricultura: Nuevas direcciones en el diseño de políticas en América Latina y el Caribe*, Octavio Sotomayor, Adrián Rodríguez y Mônica Rodrigues, 2012, 352 p.

112 *El desarrollo inclusivo en América Latina y el Caribe.* Ensayos sobre políticas de convergencia productiva para la igualdad, Ricardo Infante (ed.), 2011, 384 p.

111 *Protección social inclusiva en América Latina. Una mirada integral, un enfoque de derechos*, Simone Cecchini y Rodrigo Martínez, 2011, 284 p.

110 *Envejecimiento en América Latina. Sistema de pensiones y protección social integral*, Antonio Prado y Ana Sojo (eds.), 2010, 304 p.

109 *Modeling Public Policies in Latin America and the Caribbean*, Carlos de Miguel, José Durán Lima, Paolo Giordiano, Julio Guzmán, Andrés Schuschny and Masazaku Watanuki (eds.), 2011, 322 p.

108 *Alianzas público-privadas. Para una nueva visión estratégica del desarrollo*, Robert Devlin y Graciela Moguillansky, 2010, 196 p.

107 *Políticas de apoyo a las pymes en América Latina. Entre avances innovadores y desafíos institucionales*, Carlos Ferraro y Giovanni Stumpo, 2010, 392 p.

106 *Temas controversiales en negociaciones comerciales Norte-Sur*, Osvaldo Rosales V. y Sebastián Sáez C. (compiladores), 2011, 322 p.

105 *Regulation, Worker Protection and Active Labour-Market Policies in Latin America*, Jürgen Weller (ed.), 2009, 236 p.

104 *La República Dominicana en 2030: hacia una sociedad cohesionada*, Víctor Godínez y Jorge Máttar (coords.), 2009, 582 p.

103 *L'Amérique latine et les Caraïbes au seuil du troisième millénaire*, 2009, 138 p.

102 *Migración interna y desarrollo en América Latina entre 1980 y 2005*, Jorge Rodríguez y Gustavo Busso, 2009, 272 p.

101 *Claves de la innovación social en América Latina y el Caribe*, Adolfo Rodríguez Herrera y Hernán Alvarado Ugarte, 2009, 236 p.

Copublicaciones recientes / *Recent co-publications*

***Decentralization and reform in Latin America. Improving Intergovernmental Relations,* Giorgio Brosio and Juan Pablo Jiménez (eds.), ECLAC / Edward Elgar Publishing, United Kingdom, 2012.**

Sentido de pertenencia en sociedades fragmentadas. América Latina desde una perspectiva global, Martín Hopenhayn y Ana Sojo (comps.), CEPAL / Siglo Veintiuno, Argentina, 2011.

Las clases medias en América Latina. Retrospectiva y nuevas tendencias, Rolando Franco, Martín Hopenhayn y Arturo León (eds.), CEPAL / Siglo XXI, México, 2010.

***Innovation and Economic Development. The Impact of Information and Communication Technologies in Latin America,* Mario Cimoli, André Hofman and Nanno Mulder, ECLAC / Edward Elgar Publishing, United Kingdom, 2010.**

Las clases medias en América Latina. Retrospectiva y nuevas tendencias, Rolando Franco, Martín Hopenhayn y Arturo León (eds.), CEPAL / Siglo Veintiuno, México, 2010.

Sesenta años de la CEPAL. Textos seleccionados del decenio 1998-2008, Ricardo Bielschowsky (comp.), CEPAL / Siglo Veintiuno, Argentina, 2010.

El nuevo escenario laboral latinoamericano. Regulación, protección y políticas activas en los mercados de trabajo, Jürgen Weller (ed.), CEPAL / Siglo Veintiuno, Argentina, 2010.

Internacionalización y expansión de las empresas eléctricas españolas en América Latina, Patricio Rozas Balbontín, CEPAL / Lom, Chile, 2009.

Gobernanza corporativa y desarrollo de mercados de capitales en América Latina, Georgina Núñez, Andrés Oneto y Germano M. de Paula (coords.), CEPAL / Mayol, Colombia, 2009.

Coediciones recientes / *Recent co-editions*

Perspectivas económicas de América Latina 2013. Políticas de Pymes para el Cambio Estructural, OCDE / CEPAL, Chile, 2012.

***Latin American Economic Outlook 2013. SME Policies For Structural Change,* OECD / ECLAC, Chile, 2012.**

Perspectivas de la agricultura y del desarrollo rural en las Américas: una mirada hacia América Latina y el Caribe 2013, CEPAL / FAO / IICA, Chile, Octubre, 2012.

Reforma fiscal en América Latina. ¿Qué fiscalidad para qué desarrollo?, Alicia Bárcena y Narcís Serra (editores), CEPAL/SEGIB / CIDOB, Chile, 2012.

La sostenibilidad del desarrollo a 20 años de la Cumbre para la Tierra. Avances, brechas y lineamientos estratégicos para América Latina y el Caribe, CEPAL / Naciones Unidas, 2012.

***Sustainable development 20 years on from the Earth Summit. Progress, gaps and strategic guidelines for Latin America and the Caribbean,* ECLAC / United Nations, 2012.**

Perspectivas económicas de América Latina 2012.Transformación del Estado para el desarrollo, CEPAL / OCDE, 2011.

***Latin America Outlook 2012. Transforming the State for Development,* ECLAC/OECD, 2011.**

***Perspectives économiques de l'Amérique latine 2012. Transformation de l'État et Développement,* CEPALC / OCDE, 2012.**

***Breeding Latin American Tigers. Operational principles for rehabilitating industrial policies,* Robert Devlin and Graciela Moguillansky, ECLAC / World Bank, 2011.**

Espacios iberoamericanos: Hacia una nueva arquitectura del Estado para el desarrollo, CEPAL / SEGIB, 2011.

***Espaços ibero-americanos: A uma nova arquitetura do Estado para o desenvolvimento.* CEPAL / SEGIB, 2011.**

Cuadernos de la CEPAL

100 *Construyendo autonomía. Compromiso e indicadores de género*, Karina Batthyáni Dighiero, 2012, 338 p.

99 *Si no se cuenta, no cuenta*, Diane Alméras y Coral Calderón Magaña (coordinadoras), 2012, 394 p.

98 ***Macroeconomic cooperation for uncertain times: The REDIMA experience*, Rodrigo Cárcamo-Díaz, 2012,164 p.**

97 *El financiamiento de la infraestructura: Propuestas para el desarrollo sostenible de una política sectorial*, Patricio Rozas Balbontín, José Luis Bonifaz y Gustavo Guerra-García, 2012, 414 p.

96 *Una mirada a la crisis desde los márgenes*, Sonia Montaño (coordinadora), 2011, 102 p.

95 *Programas de transferencias condicionadas. Balance de la experiencia reciente en América Latina y el Caribe*, Simone Cecchini y Aldo Madariaga, 2011, 226 p.

95 *Conditional cash transfer programmes. The recent experience in Latin America and the Caribbean*, Simone Cecchini and Aldo Madariaga, 2011, 220 p.

94 *El cuidado en acción. Entre el derecho y el trabajo*, Sonia Montaño Virreira y Coral Calderón Magaña (coords.), 2010, 236 p.

93 *Privilegiadas y discriminadas. Las trabajadoras del sector financiero*, Flavia Marco Navarro y María Nieves Rico Ibáñez (eds.), 2009, 300 p.

Cuadernos estadísticos de la CEPAL

40 *América Latina y el Caribe: Índices de precios al consumidor. Serie enero de 1995 a junio de 2012.* Solo disponible en CD, 2012.

39 *América Latina y el Caribe: indicadores macroeconómicos del turismo.* Solo disponible en CD, 2010.

38 *Indicadores ambientales de América Latina y el Caribe, 2009.* Solo disponible en CD, 2010.

37 *América Latina y el Caribe: Series históricas de estadísticas económicas 1950-2008.* Solo disponible en CD, 2009.

Observatorio demográfico / *Demographic Observatory*

Edición bilingüe (español e inglés) que proporciona información estadística actualizada, referente a estimaciones y proyecciones de población de los países de América Latina y el Caribe. Incluye también indicadores demográficos de interés, tales como tasas de natalidad, mortalidad, esperanza de vida al nacer, distribución de la población, etc.

Desde 2013 el Observatorio aparece una vez al año. Valor por ejemplar: US$ 15.

Bilingual publication (Spanish and English) proving up-to-date estimates and projections of the populations of the Latin American and Caribbean countries. Also includes various demographic indicators of interest such as fertility and mortality rates, life expectancy, measures of population distribution, etc.

Since 2013, the Observatory appears once a year. Per issue: US$ 15.

Notas de población

Revista especializada que publica artículos e informes acerca de las investigaciones más recientes sobre la dinámica demográfica en la región, en español, con resúmenes en español e inglés. También incluye información sobre actividades científicas y profesionales en el campo de población.

La revista se publica desde 1973 y aparece dos veces al año, en junio y diciembre.
Suscripción anual: US$ 20. Valor por cada ejemplar: US$ 12.

Specialized journal which publishes articles and reports on recent studies of demographic dynamics in the region, in Spanish with abstracts in Spanish and English. Also includes information on scientific and professional activities in the field of population.

Published since 1973, the journal appears twice a year in June and December.
Annual subscription: US$ 20. Per issue: US$ 12.

Series de la CEPAL

Comercio Internacional / Desarrollo Productivo / Desarrollo Territorial / Estudios Estadísticos y Prospectivos / Estudios y Perspectivas (Bogotá, Brasilia, Buenos Aires, México, Montevideo) / ***Studies and Perspectives*** (The Caribbean, Washington) / *Financiamiento del Desarrollo / Gestión Pública / Informes y Estudios Especiales / Macroeconomía del Desarrollo / Manuales / Medio Ambiente y Desarrollo / Asuntos de Género (ex Mujer y Desarrollo) / Población y Desarrollo / Políticas Fiscales / Políticas Sociales / Recursos Naturales e Infraestructura / Reformas Económicas / Seminarios y Conferencias.*
Véase el listado completo en: www.cepal.org/publicaciones /
A complete listing is available at: www.eclac.org/publications

كيفيـة الحصـول على منشـورات الأمـم المتحـدة

يمكـن الحصول على منشـورات الأمم المتحـدة من المكتبات ودور التوزيع في جميع أنحـاء العالـم . استعلـم عنها من المكتبة التي تتعامـل معها أو اكتـب إلى : الأمـم المتحـدة ، قسـم البيـع في نيويـورك أو في جنيـف .

如何购取联合国出版物

联合国出版物在全世界各地的书店和经售处均有发售。请向书店询问或写信到纽约或日内瓦的联合国销售组。

HOW TO OBTAIN UNITED NATIONS PUBLICATIONS

United Nations publications may be obtained from bookstores and distributors throughout the world. Consult your bookstore or write to: United Nations, Sales Section, New York or Geneva.

COMMENT SE PROCURER LES PUBLICATIONS DES NATIONS UNIES

Les publications des Nations Unies sont en vente dans les librairies et les agences dépositaires du monde entier. Informez-vous auprès de votre libraire ou adressez-vous à : Nations Unies, Section des ventes, New York ou Genève.

КАК ПОЛУЧИТЬ ИЗДАНИЯ ОРГАНИЗАЦИИ ОБЪЕДИНЕННЫХ НАЦИЙ

Издания Организации Объединенных Наций можно купить в книжных магазинах и агентствах во всех районах мира. Наводите справки об изданиях в вашем книжном магазине или пишите по адресу: Организация Объединенных Наций, Секция по продаже изданий, Нью-Йорк или Женева.

COMO CONSEGUIR PUBLICACIONES DE LAS NACIONES UNIDAS

Las publicaciones de las Naciones Unidas están en venta en librerías y casas distribuidoras en todas partes del mundo. Consulte a su librero o diríjase a: Naciones Unidas, Sección de Ventas, Nueva York o Ginebra.

Las publicaciones de la Comisión Económica para América Latina y el Caribe (CEPAL) y las del Instituto Latinoamericano y del Caribe de Planificación Económica y Social (ILPES) se pueden adquirir a los distribuidores locales o directamente a través de:

Publicaciones de las Naciones Unidas
2 United Nations Plaza, Room DC2-853
Nueva York, NY, 10017
Estados Unidos
Tel. (1 800)253-9646 Fax (1 212)963-3489
E-mail: publications@un.org

Publicaciones de las Naciones Unidas
Sección de Ventas
Palais des Nations
1211 Ginebra 10
Suiza
Tel. (41 22)917-2613 Fax (41 22)917-0027

Unidad de Distribución
Comisión Económica para América Latina y el Caribe (CEPAL)
Av. Dag Hammarskjöld 3477, Vitacura
7630412 Santiago
Chile
Tel. (56 2)210-2056 Fax (56 2)210-2069
E-mail: publications@cepal.org

Publications of the Economic Commission for Latin America and the Caribbean (ECLAC) and those of the Latin American and the Caribbean Institute for Economic and Social Planning (ILPES) can be ordered from your local distributor or directly through:

United Nations Publications
2 United Nations Plaza, Room DC2-853
New York, NY, 10017
USA
Tel. (1 800)253-9646 Fax (1 212)963-3489
E-mail: publications@un.org

United Nations Publications
Sales Sections
Palais des Nations
1211 Geneva 10
Switzerland
Tel. (41 22)917-2613 Fax (41 22)917-0027

Distribution Unit
Economic Commission for Latin America and the Caribbean (ECLAC)
Av. Dag Hammarskjöld 3477, Vitacura
7630412 Santiago
Chile
Tel. (56 2)210-2056 Fax (56 2)210-2069
E-mail: publications@eclac.org